The Cavalier Presidency

The Cavalier Presidency

Executive Power and Prerogative in Times of Crisis

Justin P. DePlato

LEXINGTON BOOKS
Lanham • Boulder • New York • Toronto • Plymouth, UK

Published by Lexington Books
A wholly owned subsidiary of Rowman & Littlefield
4501 Forbes Boulevard, Suite 200, Lanham, Maryland 20706
www.rowman.com

10 Thornbury Road, Plymouth PL6 7PP, United Kingdom

British Library Cataloguing in Publication Information Available

Library of Congress Cataloging-in-Publication Data

Library of Congress Cataloging-in-Publication Data Available
ISBN 978-0-7391-8884-2 (cloth : alk. paper)
ISBN 978-0-7391-8885-9 (electronic)

♾™ The paper used in this publication meets the minimum requirements of American National Standard for Information Sciences Permanence of Paper for Printed Library Materials, ANSI/NISO Z39.48-1992.

Printed in the United States of America

I dedicate this work to my family, especially my wife. Without her steadfast support, critique, encouragement, and confidence, I doubt I ever could have completed this arduous task.

I also dedicate this work to the noble, humble, and paramount journey of research, scientific inquiry, and the pursuit of knowledge. As a scholar, I am forever humbled that what I knew yesterday is less than what I know today.

Contents

Figures

Tables

Acknowledgments

I would be remiss not to acknowledge the steadfast commitment of my wife throughout this journey, as well as with the critical, steadfast, dedicated, and intellectual eye of my mentor, Dr. Stephen Halpern. I am forever grateful for his insight, his commitment to me and my project, and his commitment to the pursuit of knowledge, all of which has made me a much better scholar than I was before I began this journey. I thank the anonymous reviewers, whose thoughtful critique aided in fruitful revisions. I acknowledge all other editorial contributions to this work and am grateful.

Introduction

The highest law in the nation is the safety of the People.

—Cicero

Constitutional democracies are designed to protect liberty. In order to preserve liberty, constitutional democracies have mechanisms inherent to as well as explicitly stated in their constitutions to guarantee free elections and legitimate institutions, all of which are derived from the will of the people. To ensure that individual liberties are not trampled, constitutional states are designed to diffuse power away from the central government, thus preventing tyranny.

In the United States a system of separation of powers and checks and balances on each branch's power diffuses the central government's power. The founders envisioned a system of government that would never tend more favorably toward one agent of government over another but instead would always tend toward popular sovereignty. Therefore, in the United States the concentration of power toward the federal government is generally perceived negatively, whereas decentralizing power is seen as an advantage. Furthermore, in the American political system adhering to the rule of law is of paramount concern for the governed, and the governing.

During periods of crisis, however, power needs to be strengthened and centralized in order to respond to the problem effectively. At these times in the United States governmental power tends to reverse itself from the normal trajectory and instead moves to centralize around Washington. These periods, which would be critical for any republic, pose a noteworthy danger for the U.S. system of governance. In addition to the risk that the actual emergency presents, during crisis in the United States the system of separated powers and checks and balances is also under assault, as power necessarily centralizes in order to address the crisis effectively. This means that the rule of law is likewise in danger. During a crisis those valued American principles of governance—the diffusion and decentralization of power as well as the maintenance of popular sovereignty—are under assault. Therefore, executive emergency power is a unique power in a constitutional democracy because it works against the fabric of this system of governance. Consequently, executive emergency power is a power of crisis.

American constitutionalism prides itself on the idea that the Constitution reigns supreme. In fact, here a person's claim that another's act is unconstitutional is not only significant; that act could also be viewed as treasonous behavior. It follows, then, that the law is paramount above all, and this includes the realm of the presidency. In general, in the United States the creation of a system of checks and balances, separation of powers and federalism, constrains the executive. Emergencies, however, change the scope and dynamic of the normal democratic process. Addressing a crisis may require quick and robust responses, some of which, although done to protect and preserve the nation, may not adhere to normal constitutional practices. This prompts us to examine to what extent an executive may act when responding to an emergency and whether his actions, if executed for the good of the nation, can ever be deemed unconstitutional.

Unequivocally, governments will face perils and challenges. Although some governments will find resolve and, as a result, reinforce their principles and ideals through the process of handling the emergency, others may fear it and, possibly, crumble under the duress of the weight and ramifications of the crisis. Likewise, some governments will build flexibility into their laws and institutions so as to be able to confront an emergency appropriately without sacrificing the ideals of the state; however, some governments snap in the aftershocks of the crisis, thereby leading the way for a tyrannical or despotic ruler to rise to power.

In recent history the United States faced an earth-shattering national crisis. The attacks of September 11, 2001, the worst terrorist attacks in U.S. history, shocked the nation, leaving an indelible mark on the American soul. Not since the attacks on Pearl Harbor in 1941 had the United States suffered such a horrific event. In sum, the nation lost approximately thirty-one hundred souls that day, with countless more lives irrevocably affected and even destroyed in the aftermath of violence, from the men and women deployed to Afghanistan and Iraq to those who have suffered terrible illnesses as a result of working to pick up the pieces left behind at the attack sites. But before the dust could even settle from the collapsed towers, the nation turned to the president to confront the crisis and bring those who had attacked us to justice.

President George W. Bush faced the difficult responsibility of taking action against the terrorists. Before he could do so, however, his administration needed to understand what authority he could wield to confront the crisis: how much power did he have to defeat the terrorists and bring justice to those affected by the violence on September 11, 2001? To answer this question, the Bush administration would need to construct and adopt a theory of executive emergency power, and this theory would, in turn, raise the question of whether President Bush used power as it was explicitly or inherently provided in the Constitution as well as whether he believed the law limited his power to combat the emergency or if he was authorized to act beyond the scope of U.S. law. Further, what is the American model of executive emergency power? Is executive emergency power an unfettered executive prerogative, thus determining how and when emergency power is exercised, and may or may not go beyond the scope of law? Or does the Constitution authorize executive emergency power, thereby determine how and when to exercise that power and also placing limitation on emergency power? Through thorough examination of the intellectual history of political theorists' conceptualizations of executive emergency power along with analysis of American presidential writings and rhetoric, this book will assess and determine what the American model is for exercising executive emergency power.

With crises come reasonable questions regarding how the state should respond. Before ever addressing the specifics of the crisis, the state must determine which institution, apparatus, or person will be responsible for confronting and handling the crisis. Historically, democratic states have entrusted this monumental power and responsibility with the executive—but why? Perhaps because theorists posited that emergency powers should be an executive function because the executive will use the power solely to preserve the state. Because of this, examining the intellectual history of the theory of executive emergency powers is crucial to understanding the assumptions and ideological structures that have undergirded U.S. presidential interpretations and applications of such power. Particularly in light of the George W. Bush administration's responses to the September 11, 2001, attacks, about which some scholars have suggested that Bush inappropriately and perhaps unconstitutionally used executive emergency powers,[1] we need to render the abstract concepts as tangible as possible—like the foundation of a building, but instead of an actual architectural structure, the end product is a written document outlining the reasons and schema for executive emergency powers. Just as we use bricks to construct a building, placing one at a time until it is completed, laying out the philosophical history shows us how our current system of executive emergency powers has developed.

In formulating my book, I use the most recent occurrence of executive emergency power as a departure point to examine not only the Bush administration's interpretation of these essential powers but also other presidents' interpretations, including those of the nation's founders, as well as political philosophers throughout history so as to help me clarify the dynamics of this exceptional authority structure. Through this examination of the intellectual history and analysis of executive emergency power, we are able to understand better the nature of this unique authority and, therefore, propose structures that, if put in place, could help safeguard a nation from the risks and uncertainties that executive emergency power raises while also maintaining the necessary centralized power needed to address a crisis appropriately.

INTENTIONS AND STRATEGY

In this book I set out to address the justifications and reasons why crisis leads to the centralization of power toward an executive and to determine what the American model is for exercising executive emergency power. Perhaps centralizing power is necessary to preserve the state, thus rendering it a benevolent rather than a malicious power during a crisis. Perhaps this kind of power is inherent within the Constitution, or perhaps it is completely unchecked and beyond the scope of the written law. Regardless of how a government shifts power structures and procedures during a crisis, an emergency nonetheless threatens the essence of a constitutional state. Because of this, understanding executive emergency power—its theoretical history as well its historical applications—is of great interest to scholars as well as citizens. Importantly, we should explore the effects of executive emergency power on the normal processes of government; the administration of power during the crisis; the limitations, if any, on the scope of power used to combat the crisis; the balance of power between the branches of government during the crisis; the effects on the law—is the law crippled during crisis; and the resetting of power back to normalcy following the crisis.

In order to ascertain whether emergency power is or should be unlimited, I review the intellectual history of the theory of executive emergency power, including classical, Renaissance, twentieth-century thinkers, and twenty-first-century thinkers as well as U.S. presidential interpretations of the power, ranging from early U.S. history to the crisis following the attacks of September 11, 2001. When looking at the intellectual history, I will study in particular the ideas on the need for and the justification and the legal limits of such power. I then use this philosophical breadth to draw connections among the theoretical and constitutional interpretations as well as actual applications of executive emergency powers throughout U.S. history.

Rather than exploring only the tangible actions of emergency power in history, I focus on the theoretical reasons granting an executive broad encompassing power to combat a national crisis. By doing so, I am better able to understand the nature of emergency power as well as the democratic government, including its institutions and respect for law. All of these factors help us to see why some governments rise above the crisis and remain free democratic societies whereas others succumb and fail to maintain themselves as democratic states. Therefore, the narrative lays bare how, on one hand, an emergency causes a great tragedy for some democratic states, and on the other, the resolve and will of the republic prevails over the emergency, leaving it with a resounding record of triumph in the annals of its national history.

Furthermore, I explore the theories of executive emergency power in order to understand why executives—versus, say, the legislative or judicial branches—are traditionally given such powers. I trace the intellectual history of executive emergency power as far back as the classical period, beginning with Plato and then continuing on with Renaissance, twentieth-century theories, and twenty-first-century theories. After examining all three periods, I then explore the similarities and differences among these classical, Renaissance, and twentieth- and twenty-first-century theorists' reasons, constitutional schemas, and conditions for executive emergency power, considering both the nature and definitions as well as any limitations or checks of these powers.

I also analyze the reasons and justifications for American model for exercising executive emergency powers. This is done by surveying the Federalist–Anti-Federalist debates during the founding of the nation in order to, first, determine the reasoning behind creating American executive emergency power, and, second, understand whether such power is stated in the Constitution explicitly or if it is an implied, inherent power. I also consider different approaches to instituting a structure of executive emergency power, particularly whether it should be an implied or an explicit schema of power within a constitution.

Consequently, I construct my analysis by methodically exploring executive emergency power through both theoretical propositions and historical and contemporary applications in four primary steps. First, I lay out a general philosophical trajectory of the development of political thought regarding the issue of emergency power ranging over almost two and a half millennia and thoroughly examine the intellectual history of the theory of executive emergency power so as to ascertain the justifications, reasons, and limitations of such power.

Second, I present the general political and philosophical context at work during the composition of the U.S. Constitution. I do this to demonstrate and delineate the complexity of thought, particularly as it related to classical and Renaissance theoretical contributions on the issue, with which the founders struggled when addressing the issue of exercising executive power, especially in the event of a national crisis.

Third, I present a series of historical examples of individual presidents' approaches and utilizations of executive power during emergencies, emphasizing their interpretations, indicated through their words and writings, determining avocation for an American model of executive emergency power.

The American model for exercising executive emergency power will include theoretical conceptualizations from both Locke and Hamilton, in which executive prerogative will determine how and when to exercise emergency power that is an inherent constitutional power lawfully granted to an executive under authority given to him in Article II of the Constitution.

Finally, returning to my original impetus for beginning this analysis, I investigate our most contemporary example of the exercise of executive emergency power, the Bush administration's actions following the attacks of September 11, 2001, with two aims. First, I do this to understand Bush's particular interpretation of his emergency authority: Did Bush's interpretation adhere to a constitutional schema in which executive prerogative determined how and when to exercise emergency power that is an inherent constitutional power lawfully granted to an executive under authority given to him in Article II of the Constitution, or did President Bush depart from the American model for exercising emergency power and set out on a new course? Further, is the determination and use of presidential emergency power a unilateral action, or, rather, is such action limited by congressional consultation and oversight or by some other means in the American political system? Second, I consider how the interplay between presidential historical precedent and a dramatically different nature of emergency—an enemy without nation or traditional structure functioning in a technologically advanced society—affects how emergency powers must be enacted, maintained, and controlled. In the conclusion I then review these four steps and, based on philosophical investigations, political theory, U.S. presidential history, analyzing executive orders, presidential signing statements, primary letters, papers from the constitutional convention, previously classified legal documents, and an assessment of current fluctuating political and social conditions.

Overall, I argue that executive emergency powers are part of a much larger philosophical trajectory of development rather than unnatural consequences of a government's reaction to crises; executive emergency powers are natural to the processes and health of the state. In the United States these powers are inherent to governance rather than fatal weaknesses of the modern state, designed to devolve the state into tyranny or dictatorships. But let me state this very important note of caution about presidents determining their power and use of such power to combat a crisis: the determination and use of presidential emergency power is consistently more unilateral and less overseen by any kind of regulatory force capable of maintaining its slide into a disregard for the rule of law. Such presidential prerogative to determine their own power and use of that power without congressional consultation or oversight is very dangerous and harms the basic precepts of American republicanism, which is defined by decentralized power, limited power, separation of powers, and checks and balances. When presidents, in times of crises, act completely unbound, unlimited, or unchecked when determining and exercising emergency power, they are increasingly more powerful, essentially cavalier, and often times dictatorial.

Finally, the very existence of this philosophical history elucidating schemas for exercising executive emergency powers indicates that such powers are not static or exclusive to one time but instead are integral, continual, and necessary to preserving and protecting a democratic state from grave injury or harm.

In this book I will explore this philosophical and intellectual history in chapter 1, outlining the theories regarding why executives have such powers, the justifications they have to use them, constitutional schemas for exercising that power, and the limitations, if any, on such powers. In this chapter I will also establish the framework for understanding U.S. presidential interpretations for exercising executive emergency powers. In chapter 2 I examine the U.S. founders' original debate regarding the intent and exercise of emergency power in order to determine whether such powers are granted within the Constitution or if they are implied. Chapters 3 through 6 look closely at different presidents' rhetoric indicating support for an American model for exercising emergency power so as to ascertain their interpretations of this power. Specifically, chapter 3 examines George Washington and Thomas Jefferson to see how our foundational first presidents set the first precedents for the American model for exercising executive emergency power; chapter 4 compares James Madison and Andrew Jackson to gain perspective on handling the schema and boundaries for applying this power, with one erring too cautiously and the other reaching too far; chapter 5 assesses what I see as the most critical exercise of emergency power in the United States: Lincoln during the Civil War; and finally, chapter 6 presents George W. Bush's interpretation and exercise of executive emergency power, using what has been shown in the previous five chapters to determine whether his exercise of emergency powers was congruent with the American model for exercising executive emergency power. The conclusion then reviews all of these elements and then summarizes with some final thoughts on the possible future of executive emergency power.

CRISIS

Aristotle once declared that the state is a creation of nature and that "humans are evidently political animals."[2] Following Aristotle's logic, one may construe that, as a byproduct of the state as natural and of humans as political, crises will likewise be a natural inevitability accompanying the existence of the state, as the fact of multiple states and multiple interests will undoubtedly bring about crisis, confrontation, and, thus, the necessity to deal with an emergency.

Before diving into this book, then, it is important to realize and define the nature of crisis, or emergency; after all, executive emergency powers are contingent on the existence of an emergency. Emergencies are nothing new to any political state, and an executive will often use the term *emergency* to describe the dire effects or consequences of a recent event. Nor is "emergency" limited to one party affiliation. For example, President George W. Bush, following al-Qaeda's attacks on September 11, 2001, declared that the country faced a great crisis and emergency. Likewise, during his presidential candidacy in 2007, Barack Obama declared that the financial collapse of major financial institutions was a great crisis facing our nation and a crucial economic crisis. After becoming president, Obama then confirmed and continued to use this language early in his first term as he pursued crisis-management legislation. U.S. history is awash with further examples of presidents dealing with emergencies or crises, but as is apparent from the examples mentioned here, the nature of the crisis can come in very different forms.

Scholars have suggested that there are three types of crises that modern nations confront: war, rebellion, and economic depression. In each case the crisis serves as a government's justification for broadening powers, also known as emergency powers. In the first instance, war is a crisis as it repels an attack and/or invasion. As a result, the state converts its peacetime social and political order into a robust fighting machine. Without this transition the likely outcome would be dire if the state did not confront the crisis swiftly, powerfully, and effectively; the nation could be conquered and reduced to great poverty, suffering, and, likely, enslavement of the people to the enemy.

In the second instance rebellion occurs when a large number of people (citizens) oppose or resist the government, engaging in violent insurrection against the state's laws and their subsequent enforcement in order to dissolve or overthrow the established government. In such an instance, the government must confront the rebellion in order to preserve the order of the state, and to do so, it would need to exercise broadened—or emergency—powers.

The final instance is economic depression or financial calamity, although anyone familiar with the theory of business cycles will advise that booms and busts are natural, and the ebb and flow of economics is common. What is not common, however, is a financial calamity of immense magnitude that threatens the stability of economic institutions, consumer confidence, and belief in the entire financial system. Thus, a financial calamity must be severe in order to justify significantly altering the political system and order so as to overcome it. For instance, during the Great Depression of the 1930s, following the collapse of the stock market in 1929, the United States was in the clutches of a seemingly unstoppable downward spiral in which normal aggregate economic data became nightmarish: the unemployment rate peaked at 25.6 percent, the nation's liquidity plummeted to historic lows, consumer spending came to a standstill, mortgage delinquencies reached historic highs, and monetary policy ventured into realms never before witnessed. This spiraling economic crisis resulted in the populace placing enormous pressures on the government to respond, intervene, and end the calamity. History reminds us of the difficult nature of correcting economic paths; the magnitude of the Great Depression has been referred to as a "lost" decade. Herbert Hoover's failed policies at the onset of the crisis resulted in Franklin Roosevelt needing to "re-invent" the economic "wheel" in order to preserve the Union. As a result, the Great Depression became Roosevelt's defining moment, as he did everything in his power to help the nation return to economic stability. Although this economic crisis was not a war or an insurrection, it was just as devastating to the populace.

I would also like to add to scholars' crisis classification to include events brought on by Mother Nature. Floods, fires, earthquakes, droughts, and so on can wreak havoc on a citizenry, causing great peril and bringing about pressure from the people for a governmental response. As with the three previously mentioned crises, governments must face natural disasters head on, though, generally speaking, these do not render the same magnitude of crisis as the others. However, a natural disaster and its aftereffects must be dealt with quickly, boldly, and responsibly; otherwise, it could ignite anger that could then develop into an even more pressing crisis, an insurrection.[3]

As scholar Clinton Rossiter once wrote, "wars are not won by debating societies, rebellions are not suppressed by judicial injunctions, and the reemployment of twelve million jobless citizens will not be effected through a scrupulous regard for the tenets of free enterprise, and hardships caused by the eruptions of nature cannot be mitigated by letting nature take its course."[4] Hence, weak executives, such as the administrations of James Buchanan, Chester Arthur, William Howard Taft, or Herbert Hoover, were unable to resolve the terrible crises, and as a result, their successors then had to deal with both the crisis and its effects thus far. Rossiter further suggested that responding to crisis and using emergency powers effectively and wisely is inherent to a great leader.[5]

Finally, possibly the greatest concern regarding the nature of emergency or crisis is correctly deciding when one is in fact occurring. Because a ruler could choose to use "an emergency" for his or her own benefit and political gains—although we would hope this does not happen—being able to judge as a populace what constitutes a "crisis" is imperative for maintaining the delicate balance of power the founders instituted. Former Secretary of the Treasury Henry Paulson once said that "being in Washington, is it's very, very difficult to get Congress to act on anything that's big and difficult and controversial if there's not an immediate crisis."[6] Paulson, an outsider before coming to Washington, was struck by the fact that the relevant need for change conditioned the nature of policy outcome or its process. In other words, the less the *perceived* need, the less likely policymakers will be able to achieve any kind of effective outcome. If this is in fact true, if presidents come to the same realization, then they could decide to mislead the nation regarding the veracity of an emergency so as to gain political power and affect their desired policy outcomes. After all, because the government determines the nature and severity of an emergency, so a Machiavellian leader could use the power of emergency to his or her benefit.

What exists to prevent such deceptions? Consequently, we as citizens need to be very wary of government officials' rhetorical use of "emergency" or "crisis." Although I will not delve deeply into the topic of the legitimacy of crisis, understanding what's at stake with the politics of crisis undergirds the scope and trajectory of my book's research and argument.

The main argument of this book is that governmental power centralizes and increases during times of crisis. Often the governmental powers are illegal, unconstitutional, and dictatorial. Cavalier presidents using their prerogative determine what executive emergency powers are and how to exercise them. Often cavalier presidents' determinations of executive emergency powers and how to exercise them are unconstitutional and illegal. Thereby, cavalier presidents are unconstitutional dictators.

The following chapters elucidate the theory of executive emergency power, evidencing two competing models for the determination and exercise of such power: Unfettered Prerogative or Constitutional Dictators. Further, the American study evidences that the founders envisioned an executive having an unfettered prerogative to determine what executive emergency powers are and how to exercise them. Presidents who have exercised an unfettered prerogative to determine emergency powers and the use of them are cavalier presidents.

NOTES

1. Garry Wills, *Bomb Power: The Modern Presidency and the National Security State* (New York: Penguin Press, 2010); Louis Fisher, *Presidential War Power*, 2nd ed. (Lawrence: University Press of Kansas, 1995).

2. Aristotle, *Politics*, Book I, in Michael Morgan, ed., *Classics of Moral and Political Theory* (Indianapolis, IN: Hackett Publishing, 1992), 386–87.

3. The recent tsunami in the Pacific Rim as well as the earthquake in Haiti are prime examples of Mother Nature causing great human suffering and peril. The swiftness of response in both instances was necessary, unilateral, and global. The emergency powers bestowed, however, during a natural disaster are those of humanitarian need, not necessarily powers in direct violation with a governing apparatus or constitution.

4. Clinton Rossiter, *Constitutional Dictatorship: Crisis Government in the Modern Democracies* (Princeton, NJ: Princeton University Press, 1948), 6.

5. Ibid.

6. *Meet the Press*, MSNBC, February 7, 2010.

Chapter One

The Theory of Executive Emergency Power

In this chapter I explore the main reasons why classical, Renaissance, and twentieth-century thinkers suggest that an executive should be armed with emergency power during a time of crisis. Generally speaking, liberal democracy is based on the idea of protecting civil liberty, and one way to do this is to diffuse power away from a centralized government and maintain the principle of popular sovereignty. However, the question arises: In a time of crisis, do the usual tenets of constitutional democracy reverse themselves, thereby creating a situation in which power is centralized toward a single person?

To answer this I explore the theory of executive emergency power so as to understand (1) why executives have emergency power, (2) if their executive emergency powers are limited, (3) if explicitly legal parameters stated in a constitution bind these powers, and, finally, (4) after the crisis, how these powers are relinquished.

In order to understand the theories of executive emergency powers I employ a large research agenda spanning ancient Roman/Greek, Renaissance, twentieth-century thinkers, and twenty-first-century thinkers in order to gather relevant data to flesh out the competing reasons and justifications for as well as legal limitations on executive emergency powers.

Before discussing at length the reason why an executive may have extraordinary emergency power to combat a crisis, I offer here a basic definition of executive emergency power. Executive emergency powers in their simplest, purest form are those powers the executive has, gains, or uses during a time of crisis to end the event and preserve the state.

The concept of executive emergency powers is present across a substantial expanse of history and has spurred considerable debate among political theorists. However, traversing this entire landscape to examine all the vicissitudes that may confront the state is an arduous task. Scholars pay significant attention to emergency powers used to resolve a crisis, because emergencies occur across all time periods. The state should allow an executive to expand his or her power during an emergency, thus creating a centralization of power, which will be (1) aimed at preserving the state, (2) swift with the appropriate amount of energy in response to the crisis, and (3) more easily held accountable if the response is singular to the crisis. These premises are deeply rooted in the teachings of democratic political theory that, in its traditional and contemporary expressions, has supported the notion that abandoning the processes of democratic government is the essential response to emergency conditions.

Historically, political theory is rife with concepts and ideas that explain the nature of political phenomena and their reasons for existing; the same is true for executive emergency power. The nature of executive emergency power is partly a creation of the state and partly a product of necessity. Once created, states would inevitably face emergencies, and when these occur, the collective will of the state would have to decide how to confront them. A democratic state would likely turn to its formal institutions, which have likewise formal legal powers, to determine which should act to combat the emergency. A state may choose to grant emergency powers to the ruler because the state has determined that that individual will be the best suited to combat the emergency, possibly because he is unitary or because he is able to respond to the crisis swiftly, unlike the legislature or the courts, which are too numerous in composition and are passive institutions in that they are incapable of acting quickly.

In this chapter I explore the theoretical contributions that explain why executive emergency powers transcend time and why they are a fundamental component of any state. I argue that the notion of executive emergency powers has been developing philosophically for over two millennia and is part of a greater paradigm regarding governmental structure. This suggests that they are necessary to the existence of the state and, in fact, are natural powers within this paradigm necessary for preserving any state; emergency powers are as natural to the executive as voting is to a citizen. The first question one must ask when embarking on this path of inquiry is why do executive emergency powers exist? The simple, obvious answer is that emergency powers exist because emergencies and crises exist. Therefore, the more challenging question arises: Why do emergency powers rest with the executive?

CLASSICAL POLITICAL THEORISTS ON THE NATURE
OF EXECUTIVE EMERGENCY POWERS

Before embarking fully on this path of political inquiry, exploring key classical contributions to political theories will help give us a more comprehensive
understanding of the nature of emergency powers. Plato, who is traditionally
seen as rebelling against the nature of the Athenian democracy, might seem
like an odd place to begin.[1] Although an attempt to draw parallels between
his classical contribution to political theory and the existence of executive
emergency powers in the contemporary world may appear peculiar, an astute
exploration of Plato's writings elucidates his philosophy as an essential foundation for modern political theory. After all, Plato established the very nature
and existence of executive emergency powers when he suggested that a
"guardian class" will exist in his city and produce its rulers. Thus, the best
place to start any inquiry into executive emergency powers is Platonic
thought.

In order to understand how Plato's notion of a guardian class is essential
to the concept and existence of executive emergency powers, let me begin by
describing the reasoning for the guardian class and how this reasoning
brought about our contemporary idea of executive emergency powers. For
Plato, the guardian class is the source of the ruling executive in the ancient
world. Ultimately, the best possible ruler, the philosopher king, will derive
from the guardian class. A close examination of the *Republic* regarding this
class reveals that these philosopher rulers will embody absolute powers and,
most importantly for our purposes, will have an abundance of power when
the state is in crisis. Plato stated, "it is the rulers who will exert their greatest
force when the State is attacked, or invasion ensues."[2] Furthermore, he
argued that "it is the rulers who alone will orchestrate and command the
army as they repel the invasion."[3]

In Plato's great treatise the guardian class and, by extension, the rulers are
stripped of all wealth and material objects. This requirement of material
poverty is critical for understanding why, in contemporary political practice,
the emergency powers rest with the executive. Forbidding the ruling class to
have wealth is not done to prevent a happy existence for the guardian class
but rather to ensure that they are loyal only to the health and protection of the
state and not material and temporal things. In addition, the lack of material,
temporal wealth among the rulers not only prevents disloyalty to the state but
also infighting among the ruling class. All is equal in this setting, or at least
in the ruling class.

Plato's creation of a ruling class free from temporal constraints is important in relation to executive emergency powers because this notion of distinct
loyalty and commitment to the health of the state is a paramount reason why
such powers can be entrusted with the executive. I argue that Plato's key

contribution to this modern practice is that in order to entrust an executive with broad latitudes of power during an emergency, he must be constrained by his dedication, loyalty, and devotion to the very state from which he derives his power rather than bound by legal limitations. Furthermore, following Plato's logic, rulers rule for the sake and love of ruling, not for that of wealth or material gains; therefore, it is safe to entrust abundant powers during a crisis to the rulers because they will not use such powers for self-gain or to advance their own agenda. Instead, Plato's teachings make clear that these rulers will use the powers bestowed upon them to defend, protect, and preserve the state.

Plato is widely noted for his claim that democracy will be closest to tyranny on the proverbial government scale. The reason for this claim rests on his understanding of the concentration of power in a democracy and the people's willingness to relinquish power to a despot in return for security and peace, especially during an emergency. Plato suggested that democracy will likely devolve into a tyranny primarily because democracy breeds "mob rule" and allows the masses to choose their rulers. He famously reminded us to ponder the question, "Why let a son rule a father?"[4] We may contend that in a democracy such an illogical occurrence may happen. Nonetheless, however, the broader Platonic point must be made, particularly as it relates to executive emergency powers.

The critical point is that Plato suggested that the masses could be easily manipulated to choose an unjust or bad ruler. Plato argued that, over time, in a democracy, the social divisions will grow between the rich and poor, resulting in a revolt by the poor to regain power and equitable distribution of resources. As a result, Plato claimed that the "drones" will choose a ruler, but he will really be unfit to rule. Because the unjust ruler is deceptive and not a lover of ruling but instead a "lover of powers," as a result of settling the emergency and providing security for the people, the ruler is given substantial, if not all, power.[5]

Therefore, Plato suggested that the people's relinquishment of power, in which security is promised in exchange for power, is the shared flaw in democracy because the end result is a despot. For Plato, the very chance that a government may dissolve into a tyranny was unacceptable; hence, democracy is a failed political arrangement. Important for our discussion, though, is that, due to the heightened risk of the populace being manipulated in a time of emergency, the nature and growth of executive power during this time must be a real concern in a democratic society. Using Plato's logic, the "drones" of society will be easily manipulated and most vulnerable to the ascent of a charismatic tyrant at times of great distress; therefore, regarding the nature of executive emergency powers, later thinkers will have to acknowledge the concern that the people in a democracy may willingly surrender to a despot in return for peace and security as well as account for ways to prevent despotic rule from rising from the ashes of a war-torn democratic state.[6]

Plato's contribution to our understanding of executive emergency powers creates a necessary condition upon which all other theorists draw when discussing a key requirement or reason for executives' emergency powers: that citizens can trust an executive will not abuse his powers. Plato argued that in his just city, citizens can be sure that an executive will not abuse his power and become despotic during a time of emergency because the ruler rules for the sake of the community, not his own selfish interests. In Plato's world, the establishment of a just society cultivates this trust between citizen and ruler. A just society creates just rulers, and just rulers do not abuse power.[7]

In later political theory writings,[8] similar thinking will likewise argue to entrust the powers of emergency only with the executive, for he alone rules, and he rules with the intent of ensuring the well-being of all, not just himself. This notion of communal interest is of paramount importance and the very essence of this philosophical foundation, which later writers will ponder and agree upon, thus enabling the existence of emergency powers to rest solely with the executive. Hence, the seed of executive emergency powers is itself a product of the state's maturation toward a just government; it is as fundamental to the state as the citizen—without either the state would perish. Plato first observed this kernel of logical truth: as a byproduct of the creation of any state, executives can be entrusted to have emergency power if and only if the state is just.

Plato's great student and the father of political science, Aristotle, is the logical next step in our pursuit toward understanding the nature and necessity of executive emergency powers. Aristotle's key general theoretical contribution is his appreciation for a ruling approach that favors moderation and the rise of centrist equilibrium governance to bring about stability. Appreciating Aristotle's favor for moderation as a key governing approach is critical in order to understand how he would define and apply executive emergency powers in ancient Greece.

Aristotle suggested that, even during periods of emergency, the polity would rely on centrist concepts and ideas already a part of the constitution to deal with the emergency. As such, although the ruler will have broadened powers, the centrist model of government embodied in the constitution will continue to control him.[9] The classic Aristotelian sentiment is that "the affordance of latitudes, during the emergency, is determined by the parameters set in the constitution."[10] According to Aristotle—ever the realist—what's in the constitution is a product of what the people want in a constitution, so it could not contain fatal defects or weaknesses.

Therefore, I argue that if we agree with Aristotle that a state is a creature of nature and that human beings are therefore political animals,[11] then it is an agreeable Aristotelian conclusion that emergency powers—as the need to preserve the state in times of peril—are a natural extension of the state and its constitution. The necessities of the state—that is, military institutions and powers broadly defined—are established with the intent to preserve that state, and therefore, emergency powers are a pure and logical necessity of the state.

In relation to the extent of executive emergency powers and the constraints placed on them, whether it is extralegal or intralegal, Aristotle made it very clear that only the latter is acceptable. Aristotle stated, "He who trusts any man with supreme power gives it to a wild beast, for such his appetite sometimes makes him: passion influences those in power, even the best of men, but law is reason without desire."[12] Therefore, Aristotle acknowledged the intent of placing such immense power in the hands of one during an emergency is to protect the state, but clearly advocated that the power must be explicitly stated in the law or the constitution.

In order to demonstrate Aristotelian principles at work in Ancient Greece, I offer a brief examination of the Athenian state, of which Aristotle was part. Aristotelian ideas were incorporated into the Athenian constitution during the perilous times of the Athenian democracy, which the ruling period of Solon, who was elected chief magistrate of Athens, makes evident. His rise to power was the consequence of enormous turmoil within the democracy. In particular, the Athenian state was facing a historic financial crisis. As a result, Solon was granted "special powers," which the Athenian constitution explicitly granted. According to the Athenian constitution, inspired in part by Aristotle's treatises on government, emergency powers could be granted to the chief magistrate only in response to the threat or existence of civil war.[13]

Oppression of the poor citizens of the state through the neglect of the rich was the main cause of the Athenian civil war. Under Athenian law, creditors could "tie to the land" their debtors and have significant portions of the debtors' produce taken away as a lien until their entire debt was paid off.[14] Even more drastic, the law gave the creditors, if faced with obstinate debtors, the right to sell the debtor into slavery. For these reasons, it is not surprising that the poorer classes during this time in Athenian history felt unhappy and that their democracy did not protect them. In order to relieve this social discord and end the civil war, the masses elected Solon.[15]

The reason for Solon's prominence is that, with his emergency powers, he ended and canceled all current debts. He freed the land and those tied to it, and he purchased the freedom of those who had been enslaved.[16] Also with his emergency powers he bypassed the Athenian legislature and passed new debt laws, which were equal for all Athenian citizens. According to Solon, "the laws I passed were alike for the low-born and for high-born; my aim was straightforward justice for each."[17] Solon's broad and sweeping changes in ancient Athens were the first recorded instance in the Western world of elected leaders using emergency powers, in this case established by the constitution, in order to ease and then end the crisis confronting the state. [18]

Furthermore, in the Roman model of government executive emergency powers are explicitly granted in the constitution, and this can be traced back directly to Aristotelian thinking. In agreement with other scholars, I argue that the basic contemporary model of emergency power can likely be attributed to the Roman constitutional form. [19] The Roman constitution, according to Polybius, was rooted in Aristotelian principles and ideas; hence, the language of the Roman constitution regarding executive emergency powers is critical to this discussion because it empirically illustrates political theory becoming applicable laws. Secondly, the Roman model is crucial to understanding later Renaissance thoughts regarding executive emergency powers; Machiavelli, who often cites the Roman constitution as a primary example of the justification for emergency powers, established the apparent empirical support for this model. [20] Machiavelli most likely learned about executive authority during emergencies in Rome from either Polybius or Livy, two important Roman historians. More so than Livy, Polybius provided a robust reconstruction of the Roman constitution during the Republican era. I derive the following discussion mostly from Polybius's reconstruction of the Roman constitution.

The Roman constitution was complex and contained several provisions to confine and balance the exercise of executive authority. [21] For all intents and purposes, the executive offices were collegial, meaning that the two consuls whom the Senate chose to lead shared the highest executive authority and had command over the armies. [22] The Roman Senate, which for the most part was as much an executive authority as a legislative one, could issue edicts and decrees; effectively, the Senate governed Rome when the consuls were away from the city. Seemingly, the Senate might be a proper house for dealing with crises and emergencies, which might be true if the Senate was not so large and often rife with internal divisions. As such, the Romans, just like later modern constitutional governments, would realize the necessity for placing emergency powers in the hands of a singular or bi-joined executive in order to deal with the magnitude of an emergency quickly and with appropriate energy. [23]

During emergencies the Roman Senate could direct consuls to appoint a dictator for a period of up to six months. Roman law authorized this dictator to (1) suspend rights, (2) suspend legal processes, and (3) marshal military and all other forces to deal with the threat of invasion or insurrection against the Republic. The means of force were authorized only for the appropriate end in mind, so the dictator must use the extralegal and military force to resolve the crisis and preserve the Republic. Roman law stipulated that once the crisis was resolved, the dictator was to surrender all power and step down, resetting all extralegal authorities to status quo ante. [24]

RENAISSANCE POLITICAL THEORISTS ON THE NATURE
OF EXECUTIVE EMERGENCY POWERS

I will now examine developments concerning the nature of executive emergency power during the Renaissance era. In the following paragraphs I evaluate Renaissance thinkers' significant contributions to the topic in order to understand the critical merits of executive emergency powers. I will analyze how Renaissance thinkers understood why these powers rest with the executive, if there are any boundaries to executive emergency powers, and how or when emergency powers should be relinquished.

Although widely known for his ruthless interpretation of power and authority,[25] Niccolò Machiavelli unexpectedly suggested limitations on executive emergency powers, even considering whether the notion of absolute power is ever reconcilable with democracy. He stated that "in a well ordered republic it should never be necessary to resort to extra-constitutional measures; for although they may for the time be beneficial, yet the precedent is pernicious, for if the practice is once established of disregarding the laws for the good objects, they will in a little while be disregarded under that pretext for evil purposes."[26] Because Machiavelli argued that states should never allow for "extra-constitutional" measures, even during an emergency, as they may cause great harm to the republic, he advocated that "no republic will ever be perfect if she has not by law provided for everything, thus having a remedy for every emergency and a fixed rule for applying it."[27] Thus, Machiavelli suggested that the perfect constitutional democracy must have mechanisms and practices in place—more formally, laws—to combat or respond to any emergency. He based this argument—that executive emergency powers should be written laws, adhering to a rule of law model even in times of crisis—on the Roman model.

As stated earlier, the Roman model derived from explicit provisions in the Roman constitution that provided for the creation of a dictator during times of crisis. Machiavelli in his *Discourses* outlined his appreciation for the Roman model: "And truly, among the other Roman institutions [the dictatorship], is one that merits to be considered and counted among those which were the cause of the greatness of so great an Empire: For without a similar institution, the Cities would have avoided such extraordinary hazards only with difficult [sic]." Machiavelli averred that the reason why the Roman cities would have struggled to survive without the constitutional dictator during crisis is that "the customary orders of the Republic move too slowly, that the assembling together of opinions takes so much time; and remedies are most dangerous when they have to apply some situation which cannot await time."[28]

Because of delay and broad inactivity in response to crisis, Machiavelli argued clearly that if a republic lacks a method to combat crisis strongly and effectively, then it is doomed to perish. He made the following warning to modern-day republics: "those Republics which in urgent perils do not have resort either to a Dictatorship or a similar authority, will always be ruined in grave incidents."[29]

Later, Thomas Hobbes, the classic conservative thinker who wrote during a time of civil strife and war, did not directly acknowledge the existence of executive emergency powers. He did, however, illustrate tacitly the necessity of a strong sovereign in times of emergency. Hobbes did this by arguing that the sovereign, chosen from the people, must be strong enough to withstand the vicissitudes of political strife. He stated that the sovereign must "discern between good and evil, that the use of his power must be in the hand of another man, or assembly of men, which are to govern by his right . . . and therefore all the danger that can be reached or be pretended, must arise from the contention of those [divisions of power], in order to suppress the emergency."[30] In addition, Hobbes averred that the sovereign has full latitude to control and sustain peace; therefore, during emergencies, the sovereign has "the right to do whatever he thinks necessary for the preserving of peace and security and prevention of discord, therefore the sovereign may judge what opinions and doctrines are averse; who shall be allowed to speak to multitudes; and who shall examine the doctrines of all books before they are published."[31]

Perhaps Hobbes never directly commented on executive emergency powers because he considered emergency power to be inherent within scope of executive power. Hobbes may have come to this conclusion because the executive must hold such broad powers because human nature is violent. After all, the main reason Hobbes argued for the creation of the state is because man, left to his own vices, would be in a perpetual state of war against all (*Bellum omnium contra omnes*). Therefore, it is reasonable to conclude that Hobbes would favor a strong executive during an emergency because the sovereign was put in power to protect the subjects and maintain peace and order.[32]

Shortly following Hobbes, John Locke's contribution to the discussion on executive emergency power is rooted in his concept of "prerogative power." Describing the architecture of civil government, Locke called on the English doctrine of "prerogative power" to cope with the problem of emergency. He suggested that in a time of war, crisis, or danger to the nation, the normal laws set down by the legislature might be inadequate for or even a fatal obstacle to the promptness of action necessary to avert catastrophe.[33] Therefore, Locke posited that in such instances the Crown should retain a prerogative "power to act according to discretion for the public good, without the prescription of the law and sometimes even against it."[34]

Locke asserted that the executive—and not the other institutions—must have emergency power because "in some governments the lawmaking power is not always in being, and is usually too numerous, and so too slow, for the dispatch requisite to execution."[35] Furthermore, he suggested that the executive is the only governmental branch able to be flexible enough to act with vigor against the crisis because "it is impossible to foresee, and so by laws to provide for, all accidents and necessities that may concern the public, or to make such laws as will do no harm, if they are executed with an inflexible rigour, on all occasions, and upon all persons that may come in their way; therefore there is a latitude left to the executive power, to do many things of choice which the laws do not prescribe."[36]

He further argued that the prerogative "can be nothing but the people's permitting their rulers to do several things of their own free choice where the law is silent, and sometimes too against the direct letter of the law." However, Locke did not claim that the executive's emergency powers are unrestrained or unconditional. On the contrary, he clearly stated that executive emergency power is to be used only for "the public good and only in [the executive] acquiescing in it when so done."[37] Furthermore, Locke did recognize a moral restraint on executive emergency power: even when the ruler acts only in the interest of public good, moral restraint might not suffice to avoid abuse of prerogative powers. For instance, Locke considered the realistic concern of a government utilizing the prerogative powers for the public good (a cloak for broader social agendas) but after the crisis possibly pursuing or wishing to retain the powers. Hence, a democratic state in the midst of an emergency is concerned with determining ways to prohibit the executive from retaining the powers afforded during that emergency.[38]

The question then arises, who shall judge the need for resorting to the prerogative, and how may its abuses be avoided? To answer this question, Locke seemingly conceded that "the people have no other remedy in this, as in all other cases where they have no judge on earth, but to appeal to Heaven."[39] It is fair to suggest that Locke, realizing the inherent flaws of human nature, saw that the executive is constrained only by his own motives, his own respect for the law, and by God.

Locke, therefore, reminds us of the nature of the larger good that exists in all social contract theories: communal interest. Plato and Aristotle likewise shared this foundation of communal interest when they harbored—albeit limited—quibbles or concerns about the executive possessing such abundant powers. For them, the noble executive would be shackled by his love of ruling justly and preserving the community, and hence, he would not abuse his authority. As such, Locke must have shared this idea when he acknowledged that above all, the sanctity of the state during an emergency rests with the executive's love of ruling justly, manifested by his action to protect the state, and thus would not abuse his powers or destroy the communal interest.

Locke presumably supported Plato's broader notion of communal interest, evinced in the main tenets of his theory of civil government, particularly his tenet regarding the communal devotion to natural rights and property. According to Locke, the state should not subvert a citizen's will due to, first, the natural right of individuality, and, second, man's right to property.[40] When taking these two main principles together, for Locke, the executive, even when confronted with crisis, should only preserve the two aforesaid principles and, therefore, should not abuse his authority.

I argue that Locke's reasoning for why an executive would not abuse his power is valid because if the executive overreaches his prescribed emergency powers by usurping and retaining them, he would violate the nature of individual liberty and property rights. Therefore, I claim that Locke envisioned a just ruler, not only constrained by the communal interest during a crisis, but also, and more appropriately, constrained once the crisis is over. According to Locke, a ruler is bound by the trust placed in him by the people.[41] Here we begin to see the reasons why a reset of powers in the democratic state following the crisis is not only necessary but also reasonable within this governmental paradigm; rulers must maintain their trust with the citizenry, so resetting emergency power after a crisis will accomplish just that.

The purpose for executive constraint while using emergency power is further elaborated in a critical tenet of Locke's theory of civil government: the adverse consequences of hoarding resources. Locke adamantly declared that "an individual can not hoard his property or possessions."[42] In so doing, the hoarder, according to Locke, would undermine the communal interest of the state and would ultimately harm the broader social contract of the government. Hoarding will create materialistic, individualist, greedy citizens in society who will not support the basic needs of the community, thus undermining the entire social structure.

How does the hoarding rationale apply to not only the citizen but also the ruler? A ruler's possessions are power. Thus, applying the same logic given to the citizen and his possessions, if a ruler hoards power, he too will undermine the communal interest and broader social contract of the state. If, through the proxy of hoarding power, a ruler favors himself, then he is favoring individual over communal interest, which, in Lockean terms, would not benefit the interests of the social contract. Therefore, executive emergency powers should not be displaced for a long period of time and must be relinquished following the emergency in order to prevent hoarding power. Not doing so would be insidiously unjust, unwise, and detrimental to the society.

James Harrington, Locke's contemporary, wrote on the necessity of emergency powers in his treatise regarding the commonwealth of Oceana, a fictionalized utopian republic that many saw as representing interregnum England. Like Locke, Harrington suggested that, as a consequence of great peril or emergency, enabling leaders to react faithfully so as to protect the state is necessary. Reliance on emergency power, Harrington claimed, rests on "requiring extraordinary speed or secrecy, either through unnatural haste or brevity" or else the permanent health of the state would be jeopardized.[43] Harrington did not specify the exact powers the ruler should have during an emergency, but he did suggest that the powers necessary to preserve the state are within the realm of emergency powers, stating, "the ruler may have the power to levy men and money, to make war and peace, and enact laws."[44]

Harrington stated that rulers may enact laws during a crisis in order to quell its effects. Harrington's claim that a ruler's law-*making* power should be enabled during a crisis contrasts starkly with the views of Locke, Aristotle, and, later, Rousseau and Hamilton regarding emergency powers. For example, Locke explicitly stated that during an emergency a ruler may "flex the laws" but cannot create new ones. By consensus, then, the scope of emergency power, therefore, remains solely within the boundaries of law and cannot be extended to create new laws. Only Harrington considered the need to preserve the state as so great as to justify endowing a ruler with unbounded authority to enact new laws, thus advocating extralegal parameters for a ruler in times of emergency. However, he did not suggest that an executive may create and yield laws haphazardly or against the interest of the commonwealth; instead, Harrington clarified that new laws created during an emergency may be used only "to the preservation of the Commonwealth."[45]

Harrington agreed with Locke that the scope and length of emergency authority afforded the rulers correspond only to the scope and length of the crisis and that defining the end of the crisis depends on the just nature of the ruler. Locke and Harrington avoided creating distinct parameters for the ruler's restraints, probably to ensure that the ruler does what is necessary to preserve the state. However, later writers enacted much more concrete guidelines for resetting authority and defining the end of a crisis.

Further, Harrington did not claim that, during an emergency, a ruler is unbounded or completely unrestricted; rather, all of the ruler's objectives during a crisis—the affordance of lawmaking, brevity, and resolve—must be aimed at preserving the state. According to Harrington, "the ruler shall have no power to do anything that tends not to his proper end and institution."[46] Clearly, during an emergency a ruler is bound by his own noble causes and the proper end of his pursuit, which must be the preservation of the state. Harrington's statement is ideal and noble, for it is not difficult to conceive a situation in which a ruler claims that he is using his extended powers to preserve the state, when in fact the truth of his motives may be less altruistic. Harrington likely envisioned rulers more Platonic in nature than the corrupt contemporaries of the twentieth century.

Jean-Jacques Rousseau, another enlightened social contract theorist, provided interesting insight into the reasons for, and limitations on, executive emergency powers. Rousseau's masterpiece, *The Social Contract*, outlines a very strong defense of the necessity of communal interest for the health of a state. According to Rousseau, people are willing to accept minor restraints on their liberty in return for protection, stability, and the ability to live relatively freely. In this sense, the primacy of the community enables individuals in that community to pursue and maintain their interests by freeing them from the continual threat of mob rule. Because Rousseau greatly emphasized the need for communal interest as well as the state's role in providing protection and stability for its people, that he favored broad executive emergency powers is not surprising.

Rousseau also supported the need for temporary suspension of normal democratic processes of government in times of emergency. He suggested that the suspension of normal democratic processes is the consequence of "the inflexibility of the laws, which prevents them from adapting themselves to circumstances." Thus, because the laws are not flexible enough to handle a sudden crisis, Rousseau proposed that "in certain cases, the normal democratic processes and laws may be rendered disastrous."[47] He went further still, stating that the emergency powers must rest with the executive because pursuing the normal democratic processes and law "may at a time of crisis, bring about the ruin of the State."[48]

As a consequence of this inflexibility of the laws and normal democratic processes, according to Rousseau, "it is wrong therefore to wish to make political institutions so strong as to render it impossible to suspend their operation."[49] By endowing the executive with expanded authority during an emergency, the state can overcome these inflexibilities. Therefore, Rousseau suggested that, when the crisis is so abnormal, unusual, and relentless, the only way to overcome the crisis "is to nominate a supreme ruler"[50] who "shall silence all the laws and suspend for a moment the sovereign authority."[51]

Although Rousseau argued for suspending normal democratic processes and the need for a supreme ruler in crisis, he nevertheless claimed that there needed to be boundaries on the executive's emergency powers. For him, the primary reason for suspending normal democratic processes is to ensure "the State will not perish."[52] He did not suggest that suspending the normal processes of the institutions is equivalent to abolishing them: "the suspension of the legislative authority is in no sense its abolition."[53] Even though the executive has more authority and has suspended the legislative process, this does not mean he rules supreme over it. In other words, just because he has "silenced the legislature does not mean he can make it speak," and just because he dominates it does not mean "he represents it." The executive can do whatever it takes to confront the emergency, but this does not mean he has the authority to make laws.[54] According to Rousseau, only the legislature can make laws, even during an emergency.

Rousseau did not fear that an executive would abuse an emergency dictatorship. Unlike Locke, he thought "indiscreet use" would cheapen the executive.[55] Therefore, if the executive abused his powers, over time this would de-legitimate the executive, and as a result, the state would regress back to normal processes. Recalling that Rousseau identified the greatest weakness in any state as any particular interests of individual citizens over the general will of the citizenry, I conjecture that if an executive were to go beyond the legitimate scope of power, this would constitute such particular interests. Based on Rousseau's logic, then, if a ruler usurps power, he would do so only for his own gain, which would counter the general will of the citizenry. Because the general will of the citizenry rather than an individual or particular interest is the true source of power, rulers bound by the general will would absolutely restrain themselves after the crisis. Rulers, who usurp power and, therefore, act indifferently toward the general will, invalidate the citizenry's obligation to abide by the larger social contract. Consequently, with this in mind, the citizenry should revolt against a ruler usurping power following a crisis. Finally, this ruler, if he abuses power, would be betraying the citizenry; therefore, if he is a just ruler, he should restrain himself.

More specifically, Rousseau theorized that prescribed duration should bind the executive, and this would likely avoid perpetuation of the dictatorship. He concluded by citing historical lessons learned from Ancient Rome. Therefore, and in corroboration with the earlier discussion of the Roman model regarding executive emergency powers, thinkers like Rousseau based their theories on Roman experience, recalling that although Rome had tyrannical rulers, these rulers were not permanent. In fact, Rousseau claimed, "Roman dictators held office for only six months; most of them abdicated before their time was up."[56] He further stated that the "dictator had only time to provide against the need that had caused him to be chosen; he had none to think of further projects."[57]

In summary, then, Rousseau suggested that (1) a dictator is necessary during an emergency; (2) suspending the normal institutions does not render the institutions servile to the dictator; (3) the dictator cannot create new laws; (4) the dictator's rule is to be fixed, and it will be held for a short period of time; and (5) the dictator will not abuse his new powers. Rousseau's claims regarding executive emergency powers, in comparison to Locke's, suggest one significant difference: Rousseau was unwilling to rely on an "appeal to Heaven" to restrain executive authority, whereas in Locke's conception only Heaven can control or deter the executive from forever ruling as a dictator.

Montesquieu delineated two types of existing governmental power: the sovereign and the administrative. The administrative powers are those with *legislative*, *executive*, and *judiciary* branches. He suggested that these institutions should be separate from and dependent on each other so that the influence of any one power could not exceed that of the other two, either singly or in combination. However, because an emergency would strain this balance of powers, Montesquieu suggested that in times of unparalleled strife, extraordinary measures may be necessary in order to confront the problem. He stated, "There is an exception to this rule, when the constitution is such as to have immediate need of a magistrate invested with extraordinary power."[58] This power would be extended only during a time of emergency, akin to ancient Roman dictatorships. As with other Renaissance thinkers, such as Rousseau and Machiavelli, Montesquieu drew much of his interpretation and defense of executive emergency powers from the Roman model.

Furthermore, Montesquieu asserted that the dictator would be limited to a short duration but would have unlimited powers. He wrote, "It was necessary that a magistracy of this kind should be exercised with lustre and pomp, the business being to intimidate, and not to punish, the multitude." Finally, he summarized, "it was also proper that the dictator should be created only for some particular affair, and for this only should have an unlimited authority, as he was always created upon some sudden emergency."[59]

In chapter 6 I will elaborate further to explain why Montesquieu's conception of the separation of powers is a paramount reason why the United States has never surrendered to a despotic tyrant during an emergency. The diffusion of power among branches of government prevents the total usurpation of power by any one branch, even in a crisis.

John Stuart Mill wrote that during a great emergency a temporary dictatorship may be necessary. Although Mill, often considered an ardent defender of representative democracy, is an unlikely theorist to support the notion of executive emergency powers—perhaps due to his pragmatic, realistic approach to theory—he did state, "I am far from condemning, in cases of extreme necessity, the assumption of absolute power in the form of a temporary dictatorship."[60] He acknowledged that the magnitude of emergency may be too great for the constitutional state to handle without enabling an absolute power source to resolve the crisis. Therefore, Mill explained, war may bring forth an absolute ruler and expose the inherent limitations and a fatal defect in a system of constitutional democracy. Further, he even seemed to indicate support for granting "absolute power" to a dictator during a time of emergency, but only because the democratic state is inherently flawed in that it is unable to resolve the emergency at hand without a supreme ruler.

TWENTIETH-CENTURY THINKERS

Frederick Watkins, while studying the Weimar experience and crisis government, suggested that emergency powers are constructed to preserve the established institutions from "the danger of permanent injury in a period of temporary emergency."[61] He stated that "the dictatorship serves to protect established institutions from the danger of permanent injury in a period of temporary emergency, and is followed by a prompt return to the previous forms of political life." He suggested, then, that "I can see no reason why absolutism should not be used as a means for the defense of liberal institutions."[62]

Furthermore, Watkins outlined two key elements of the problem of emergency governance: (1) increasing administrative powers of the executive while simultaneously (2) imposing limitations on that power. He rejected the idea that legislative checks on the exercise of executive emergency powers would be an effective method of imposing limitations because "it is clearly unrealistic to rely on the government controlled majority in the legislature to exercise effective supervision over that same government in its use of emergency powers."[63]

In addition, he suggested that the "delay inherent in judicial proceedings" would limit the court's ability to respond to a crisis appropriately. Therefore, Watkins argued, the dictatorship and broad use of emergency powers should rest with the executive. However, he did place conditions and limitations on this leader: (1) "the period of dictatorship must be relatively short," (2) "Dictatorship should always be strictly legitimate in character," and (3) "final authority to determine the need for dictatorship in any given case must never rest with the dictator himself."[64] In conclusion, Watkins thoroughly warned that the objective of an emergency executive—or as he termed it, constitutional dictator—should be "strict political conservatism,"[65] staying within the boundaries of the law as the constitution proscribed for creating an emergency dictator.

Carl Friedrich agreed with Watkins's main points for creating a constitutional dictatorship. He acknowledged that during a period of emergency the difficulty lies in being able to cope with the doctrine of separation of powers (which, although it creates balance in government, it also causes delays in governmental processes) while likewise understanding the necessity to deal with the emergency swiftly and appropriately. He suggested that the greatest challenge during the emergency is "to cope with the situations of unprecedented magnitude and gravity." He averred, "there must be a broad grant of powers, subject to equally strong limitations as to who shall exercise such powers, when, for how long, and to what end."[66]

To summarize Friedrich's main points supporting the creation of a constitutional dictator, he stated that "(1) the dictator must be derived from constitutional means and, therefore, legitimate; (2) he must not be able to determine his own emergency powers; (3) the emergency powers must be exercised under a strict time limitation; and (4) the objective of emergency action must be the defense of the constitutional order."[67]

Friedrich conceded that there are very few if any true institutional safeguards to prevent the constitutional democracy from completely degrading into a dictatorship following or during the emergency. Although it may seem that Friedrich feared a complete devolution of the constitutional state during an emergency, he did offer one solution to prevent out-of-control tyranny: the role of the courts during and after the crisis. Friedrich stated, "the courts, even though helpless in the face of a real emergency, may play to restrict the use of emergency powers to legitimate ends." He went on to state that the courts may "act as a sort of keeper of the President's and the people's conscience."[68]

Probably the most influential contribution on the matter of executive emergency power in modern democracies is Clinton Rossiter. In his classic *Constitutional Dictatorship*, he explored four distinct case studies, each a nation that faced major crises in the early to mid-twentieth century as a consequence of world wars. His study focuses on Great Britain, France, Germany, and the United States. In each he examined the causes in the political system or, rather, the weaknesses that brought forth a constitutional dictatorship. From this examination, he concluded that in modern Western democracies the inherent weakness or flaw in the system is government's structural inabilities to deal with crises without resorting to unusual consequences.

Rossiter offered eleven distinct claims associated to the conditions of success for a constitutional dictatorship. To begin, he argued that a government should not initiate a general regime or particular institution of constitutional dictatorship unless, of course, it is absolutely necessary. He conceded that the only reason for executive emergency powers is to preserve the state and its constitutional order. With this claim Rossiter appears to rely on the Lockean and Rousseauian concept of executive emergency power, which states emergency power ought to be used only in times of great and unprecedented emergency. Most important, he indicated that a constitutional dictator should never have the ability to expand his own authority during a time of emergency. Therefore, Rossiter suggested that the decision to institute the dictatorship should never be in the hands of the man or men who will constitute the dictatorship.[69]

With regard to the use of the emergency powers, Rossiter maintained that the powers and all adjustments in the organization of government should be directed in pursuit of constitutional or legal requirements. For Rossiter, the suspension of normal democratic practices, although he grants that this may become necessary, still must be carried out in a way that does not disregard the constitution. In addition, he asserted that no dictatorial institution should be adopted, "no right invaded, no regular procedure altered any more than is absolutely necessary for the conquest of the particular crisis."[70] Therefore, Rossiter argued that the only purpose for expanding executive emergency powers is to ward off the crisis that brought about the rise in executive authority in the first place. The rights of the citizenry should not be disregarded even during an emergency.

Furthermore, according to Rossiter, the term of the dictatorship should be limited: "the measures adopted in the prosecution of a constitutional dictatorship should never be permanent in character or effect."[71] In so doing, he averred that the decision to terminate the constitutional dictatorship, like the decision to institute it, should never be in the hands of the man or men "who constitute the dictator."[72] Unlike Rousseau, who argued that the expanded authority of the executive should be clearly defined and limited, or Locke, who considered the termination of the expanded executive authority to be up to the "heavens," Rossiter did not explore whether a standard amount of time would be allotted to the constitutional dictator.[73] It seems more likely that Rossiter would concede that the powers granted during the emergency would be terminated after the crisis had ended, as he stated that "no constitutional dictatorship should extend beyond the termination of the crisis for which it was instituted."[74] In so doing, the "termination of the crisis must be followed by as complete a return to as possible to the political and governmental conditions existing prior to the initiation of the constitutional dictatorship."[75]

Moreover, Rossiter also maintained that during a crisis the citizenry is not powerless; rather, they will have power because the dictatorship should be "carried on by person's representative of every part of the citizenry instead in the defense of the existing constitutional order."[76] Therefore, the will of the people is still explicit even during a period when there are enormous pressures against constitutionalism. In fact, Rossiter clearly stated that "ultimate responsibility should be maintained for every action taken under a constitutional dictatorship."[77] Thus, even though the executive may have unprecedented powers, this does not afford him the right to be irresponsible.

In a departure from Watkins's argument regarding the oversight of expanded executive emergency powers, Rossiter accorded to the legislature greater latitude in the oversight of the executive's exercise of emergency powers. According to him, the legislature should have the final responsibility for declaring when an emergency is over. However, this immediately prompts certain questions: What would happen if the legislature and the executive were of the same party? Would such an occurrence afford the executive more time and latitude during and after the emergency? Conversely, if the government was divided, would the crisis be terminated sooner or later? Rossiter did not address any of the aforementioned questions, though he did place great faith in the investigative legislative committees to maintain boundaries for executive power during an emergency.

Finally, Rossiter presented a lesser role for the judiciary during and after a crisis, arguing that because the court is a reactionary institution, its role in the political process will be delayed, rendering it an impotent overseer and interpreter of the war powers."[78] Therefore, the Court's ability to be a check on executive emergency power, at least during the crisis, would be restrained.

TWENTY-FIRST-CENTURY THINKERS

Further contemporary writing, such as David Gray Adler, Ackerman, Cronin, James Pfiffner, and Scott Matheson, argues that executive emergency power is acceptably needed in a liberal democracy in which presidents have a broad or extraordinary power, during crisis.[79] They do argue, however, that such power is not unbounded, unlimited, or unilateral; rather, these scholars generate a basic formula, extrapolated from early American writers, that presidents may use emergency power in extraordinary times with the understanding that while presidents are using their extraordinary power, they are constrained by the rule of law and they must maintain the following metrics:

- The use of power is in consultation with Congress.
- The power is exercised with restraint and prudence.
- The use of power is undertaken with the "explicit" understanding that such actions are extraordinary and subject to congressional and judicial oversight.

Contemporary thinking on the theory of executive emergency power is not confined to a discussion about whether an executive, rather than Congress, constitutionally can or morally and legally should have extraordinary power, but is instead focused on a debate over whether executives may use their extraordinary power without any congressional or judicial oversight. Thus, the main debate in contemporary writing on executive emergency power is whether an executive may act unilaterally while exercising his power, or whether he is constrained by other institutions that require consultation, or by legal restraints on his power? The remainder of this book will answer these questions by analyzing U.S. history so as to determine whether presidents exercise emergency power unilaterally or restraining their exercise of power by seeking consultation and oversight from other governmental institutions.

ANALYSIS OF THE THEORY OF
EXECUTIVE EMERGENCY POWER

To restate, I organize the theorists' thoughts on executive emergency power with the intent of organizing the theorists' conceptualizations of executive emergency power. I do this by categorizing them by constitutional schemas, which demonstrates the theorists' reasons, justifications, and limitations for executives exercising emergency power. The task and means of synthesizing, gathering, and reporting on a concise, coherent summary of intellectual thoughts spanning millennia is both intellectually and physically labor intensive. The theorists all agree that executive emergency power is an extraordinary power used solely to preserve and protect the state from grave injury or harm in the light of exceptional circumstances.

Further, the U.S. constitutional schema is a model for executive emergency power that generally favors an executive prerogative determining when to declare an emergency and how to exercise powers during an emergency. This model, however, will not acknowledge that a president may go beyond the scope of law, rather that the president's emergency power is an inherent constitutional power lawfully granted to him under the authority given to him in Article II of the Constitution. Theorists studied here in chapter 1, contributed to the conceptualization of the American model. However, the complete conceptualization of the model goes beyond the classical and Renaissance evidence presented here. The American model for exercising executive emergency power will be thoroughly evidenced in the remaining body of this book.

In the following summary I will review the theorists' major contributions around the following key points regarding executive emergency power: the constitutional schema authorizing executive emergency power, the resetting of executive emergency power after a crisis, and limitations on executive emergency power.

According to evidence presented here in chapter 1, the constitutional schema for executive emergency power could be one that explicitly authorizes executive emergency power with formal written provisions in the constitution (per Rossiter) or one that is potentially beyond the scope of law, with no written provisions in a constitution and relying solely on the executive's prerogative to act according to his own unfettered discretion, whereby the executive's prerogative determines whether to declare an emergency and determines how to exercise emergency power to combat that crisis (per Locke). Formally, we may think of the differences among the schemas, in light of crisis, as one of the following two approaches to exercising executive emergency power:

1. An unfettered, unlimited prerogative, whereby executive prerogative determines how an executive exercises emergency power, with no legal provision guiding his decisions to act (per Locke).
2. Explicitly written constitutional provisions, in which the executive's authorization to exercise emergency power is provided for through express rules for the use of that power and is not based on prerogative power (per Machiavelli and Rossiter).

Therefore, a major difference among the theorists concerns the formal constitutional schema that provides for the creation and limitation on executive emergency power.

THEORISTS SUPPORTING THE CONSTITUTIONAL MODEL TO EXECUTIVE EMERGENCY POWER

This model seeks to control or limit the executive prerogative by creating written rules authorizing how and when to exercise executive emergency powers. The theorists—Machiavelli, Aristotle, Rousseau, Friedrich, Rossiter, and Watkins—all agree that explicit provisions should exist in a constitution to authorize the expansion of executive power during a crisis, such as the creation of a constitutional dictator, or rather, a person who is constitutionally authorized to exercise emergency power. The theorists outline the following provisions as possible additions to a constitution, authorizing the creation of a constitutional dictator:

1. The legislature will appoint the dictator.
2. The legislature will declare the emergency.
3. The legislature will establish the dictator's powers to combat the crisis.
4. The legislature will establish how long the dictator will have to combat the crisis, thus placing a clear duration of time in which the emergency powers will be in effect.
5. The legislature will declare when the emergency is over. [80]

Thus, the theorists' previously mentioned provisions (not exact in language), in light of emergency, would authorize a constitutional dictatorship, which is an expansion of power to combat the crisis whereby the constitutional provisions also limit the power to the specific provisions enumerated.

THEORISTS SUPPORTING THE UNFETTERED EXECUTIVE PREROGATIVE MODEL

Locke, Plato, Harrington, Hobbes, and Mill suggest that no formal constitutional schema or provision should exist authorizing the exercise of executive power during crisis; instead, they argue that during crisis the executive should have full latitude to act according to his own prerogative, which may or may not be in accordance with the written law. These theorists never define precisely their meaning of the word prerogative—their lack to define prerogative leaves the courts today to determine whether or not prerogative power has any boundaries or limitations. Further, these theorists agree that the reasons an executive should exercise emergency power according to his own prerogative are because:

1. the law cannot foresee the magnitude of any crisis, thus the actions necessary to combat the crisis cannot be prescribed;
2. the legislature is too cumbersome, too delayed to act swiftly enough to determine how to combat the crisis;
3. the courts are passive institutions, therefore they cannot adjudicate until well after the events have happened; and
4. the executive will declare emergency and will do whatever is necessary to combat the crisis.[81]

Therefore, these previous claims support the theorists who urged an unfettered, or unlimited, executive prerogative that would not establish any formal constitutional provision(s) limiting the executive's authority to exercise emergency power during a crisis.

Finally, regarding the matter of whether to reset the executive emergency powers following an emergency, there is no variation among the theorists. They all agree that executives must relinquish emergency powers when the crisis is over.

In conclusion, the findings in this chapter confirm a general philosophical consistency throughout classical, Renaissance, and twentieth-century periods regarding executive emergency powers. That is, scholars agree that executives alone will have emergency power during a crisis to preserve and protect the state. The debate among the theorists is not whether to expand power during crisis or who will be authorized to use the power—they all agree on this—but rather focuses on the presence or lack thereof of checks or limitations, which would be specific, written, legal provisions on the executive emergency power. Therefore, when analyzing the theorists, one must determine which constitutional schema the theorists advocate for handling emergencies, the prerogative model or the constitutional dictator model. As stated previously, Locke, Harrington, Plato, and Mill argued for a prerogative model of executive emergency power, whereas Machiavelli, Aristotle, Rousseau, Watkins, Friedrich, and Rossiter asserted that even during a crisis the law is absolutely necessary, thereby favoring the creation of a constitutional dictator in whom constitutional provisions would authorize the exercise of emergency power while at the same time limiting his emergency power.

The rest of this book will delve deeper into determining what is the American model for the exercising of executive emergency power? To answer this question I will investigate the intellectual history of executive emergency power in early and modern America.

Finally, when glancing back at the theoretical contributions to the issue of executive emergency power, clearly the thinkers build on each other's theories on executive emergency powers to either (a) support earlier tenets, or (b) expand on the tenets already provided, particularly that regarding the creation of clearer checks on the expansion of executive emergency power (i.e., whether to create a constitutional dictator). The chronological evidence is not coincidental; it demonstrates a theoretical process that encouraged classical, Renaissance, and twentieth-century thinkers to reinforce and establish the natural necessities of executive emergency powers: the preservation and protection of the state.

In the following chapters I will explore in greater detail the American theory of executive emergency power. In order to assess and elaborate on the American model for exercising executive emergency power I will investigate both early and modern presidential rhetoric, all of which will evidence the rise of cavalier presidents.

NOTES

1. *The Republic* is a treatise written purposefully to refute democracy as a viable form of government. See especially books VI and VII of *The Republic*, in Michael Morgan, ed., *Classics of Moral and Political Theory* (Indianapolis, IN: Hackett Publishing Co., 1992), 543–600.

2. Plato, *The Republic*, 550–51.

3. Ibid., Book VI, sec. 433, 551.

4. Ibid., 550–660.

5. Ibid., Book VI, sec. 435, 550–66.

6. See Rousseau's *Social Contract* and Locke's *Treatise on Government* for further discussion of why democracies failed and devolved into tyrannies as well as why democracy may actually be a viable solution to governance in the future rather than feared, in the case of Plato.

7. Plato, *The Republic*, 601–3.

8. The writings of Rousseau, Locke, Hobbes, and Hamilton will be explored later in this chapter.

9. Aristotle, *Politics*, in Morgan, *Classics of Moral and Political Theory*, Book I, chs. 2–3, 743–45.

10. Ibid., Book I, ch. 3, 744–45.

11. Ibid., Book I, ch. 1, 722–23.

12. Aristotle, *Treatise on Government*, in Morgan, *Classics of Moral and Political Philosophy*, ch. 4, 743–45.

13. Herodotus, *Writings on Athenian Democracy*, in Morgan, *Classics of Moral and Political Philosophy*, 123–27.

14. Ibid., 124.

15. Ibid., 123–27.

16. Ibid., 125.

17. Ibid., 126–29.

18. Victor Ehrenberg, *From Solon to Socrates: Greek History and Civilization during the 6th and 5th Centuries B.C.* (London: Routledge, 1996), 101–3.

19. Herodotus, *Writings on Athenian Democracy*, 123–27.

20. Niccolò Machiavelli, *The Discourses*, in Morgan, *Classics of Moral and Political Philosophy*, Book 1, ch. 34, 1321–24.

21. In Ancient Rome the executive power rested in the hands of Senate Consuls, who were chosen by the Senate. An executive official always bore the "imperium," the power to conduct military operations outside of the city.

22. It is important to note that in Republican Rome, the sharing of power did at times work through alternation, coordination, and even by allowing a consul to rule a distinct region.

23. Polybius, *History of Rome*, in John Boardman, Jasper Griffin, and Oswyn Murray, eds., *The Oxford History of the Classical World* (Oxford, New York: Oxford University Press, 1986), 121–35.

24. Ibid.

25. As evidenced from his thoughts in *The Prince*.
26. Machiavelli, *The Discourses*, Book 1, ch. 34, 1321–24.
27. Ibid., Book 1, ch. 34, 1321.
28. Ibid., Book 1, ch. 34, 1321–24.
29. Ibid.
30. Thomas Hobbes, *The Leviathan*, in Morgan, *Classics of Moral and Political Theory*, part 2, ch. 18, 651–52, and ch. 19, part 2, 655–56.
31. Ibid.
32. Ibid.
33. John Locke, *Second Treatise on Civil Government*, in Morgan, *Classics of Moral and Political Theory*, Book II, ch. 14, 765–67.
34. Ibid., 765–66.
35. Ibid., 766.
36. Ibid., 765–67.
37. Ibid., 767.
38. Ibid., 765–67.
39. John Locke, *Of Civil Government*, in Morgan, *Classics of Moral and Political Theory*, Book II, ch. 14.
40. Locke, *Second Treatise on Government*, ch. 5, 697–701.
41. Ibid., 765–67
42. Ibid., 544–47.
    Ibid., ch. 14, 765–68.
43. James Harrington, *Commonwealth of Oceana*, in Morgan, *Classics of Moral and Political Philosophy*, 1234–41.
44. Ibid., 1236.
45. Ibid., 1234–41.
46. Ibid.
47. Jean-Jacques Rousseau, *The Social Contract*, in Morgan, *Classics of Moral and Political Philosophy*, 1153–54.
48. Ibid., 1155–56.
49. Ibid., 1153–54.
50. Ibid., 1155.
51. Ibid., 1157.
52. Ibid., 1153–54 and 1157.
53. Ibid., 1157.
54. Ibid., 1153–54.
55. Ibid., 1156.
56. Ibid., 1153–54.
57. Ibid., 1155.
58. Montesquieu, *Spirit of the Laws*, in Morgan, *Classics of Moral and Political Philosophy*, Book II, sec. 3, 834–36.
59. Ibid., Book II, sec. 3, 836.
60. John Mill, *Representative Government* (New York: Dutton, 1950), 274, 277–78.
61. Frederick Mundell Watkins, *The Failure of Constitutional Emergency Powers Under the German Republic* (Cambridge, MA: Harvard University Press, 1939), 12, 125–35.
62. Ibid., 124–25.
63. Ibid., 12, 125–35.
64. Ibid., 125.
65. Ibid., 126.
66. Carl Friedrich, "The Problem of Constitutional Dictatorship," in *Public Policy: A Yearbook of the Graduate School of Public Administration, Harvard University*, edited by C. J. Friedrich and Edward S. Mason, 338–58 (Cambridge, MA: Harvard University Press, 1940).
67. Ibid., 343–47.
68. Carl Friedrich, *Constitutional Government and Democracy: Theory and Practice in Europe and America* (Boston: Ginn & Co, 1950), 573–84.

69. Clinton Rossiter, *Constitutional Dictatorship: Crisis Government in the Modern Democracies* (Princeton, NJ: Princeton University Press, 1948), 554–65.

70. Ibid.

71. Ibid., 285–305.

72. Ibid., 285–90.

73. Ibid., 554–61.

74. Ibid., 78.

75. Ibid., 135.

76. Ibid., 136.

77. Ibid., 247.

78. Ibid., 301.

79. David Gray Adler, "Presidential Power and Foreign Affairs in the Bush Administration: The Use and Abuse of Alexander Hamilton," *Presidential Studies Quarterly* 40, no. 3. (September 2010): 531–44; Scott M. Matheson Jr., *Presidential Constitutionalism in Perilous Times* (Cambridge, MA: Harvard University Press, 2009); James P. Pfiffner, *Power Play: The Bush Presidency and the Constitution* (Washington, DC: Brookings Institution, 2008).

80. Rossiter, *Constitutional Dictatorship*, 75 and 300–305; Watkins, *The Failure of Constitutional Emergency Powers Under the German Republic*, 12, 125–35; Friedrich, "The Problem of Constitutional Dictatorship"; Machiavelli, *The Discourses*, 1321–24.

81. Locke, *Second Treatise on Civil Government*, 702–4; Mill, *Representative Government*, 274, 277–78; Hobbes, *The Leviathan*, 655–56.

Chapter Two

American Perspective on Executive Emergency Powers

Anti-Federalists versus Federalists

Historically, Americans have come to accept the claim that, during an emergency, their democratic government must transition to an authoritarian one. This is because they have become accustomed to an interpretation of the U.S. Constitution that suggests that in times of crisis the rigid restraints on governmental authority may not necessarily apply. As Americans have become complacent with this understanding, they have accordingly assigned to the Supreme Court the function of protecting the essentials of constitutionalism and democracy during periods of emergency and thereafter.

In this chapter I explore the American perspective on executive emergency power, particularly the debate between the Federalists and Anti-Federalists regarding these powers. I examine the following questions: What theories of executive emergency power did the Federalists and Anti-Federalists support, and how did their theories disagree with each other? Is it the sole domain of the executive, or do the other branches have latitude in the process of combating the emergency? Will executive emergency power be enumerated in the Constitution?

Drawing on their experiences during the tumultuous Revolutionary War and the inherent flaws and failures of the Articles of Confederation, the framers designed a constitution that would endow the federal government with sufficient authority to respond to any national emergency. In so doing, the framers were very aware of the possibility of insurrections, invasions, and catastrophes, all of which encouraged them to structure the federal government in a way so as to respond to such disruptions. They understood that in some cases—though not all—such emergencies could only be met with the use of force from the military, and this might even occur within the continental United States. However, the framers' failure to establish a federal government that could repel sudden attacks from either within or without the country was a significant deficiency of the Articles of Confederation. Prior to the Federal Convention, James Madison observed that the "want of Guaranty to the States of their Constitutions and Laws against internal violence" was the Articles' main difficulty. [1] Edmund Randolph argued accordingly, concerned that the previous government and the executive were unable to combat sudden attacks. Randolph stated at the convention on May 29, 1787, that "the confederation produced no security against foreign invasion; congress not being permitted to prevent a war nor to support it by their own authority . . . subsequently rendered the government ineffective and impotent against sudden attacks." [2]

The founders acknowledged the need to combat crises and, as they met at the Constitutional Convention, realized that they must address emergency power. As suggested by Madison's and Randolph's comments, a principal failure of the Articles of Confederation was the federal government's relative degree of weakness; because of this, when the founders arrived at the Constitutional Convention, they focused much of their debate around ways to strengthen the federal government. Particularly, in relation to emergency power the framers had to determine what branch of government will have such power and, hence, what branch of government will combat a crisis. Later, they also had to decide the scope of emergency power and establish a way to balance this emergency power with the rights afforded in the Bill of Rights. As the next section will show, resolving these objectives posed difficulty because the framers did not want to create a central government as weak as it was during the Articles of Confederation, but they also did not want to replace a king with another king.

THE FEDERALIST PERSPECTIVE ON
EXECUTIVE EMERGENCY POWER

To begin, I examine the Federalist perspective on executive emergency powers, giving particular attention to the writings of Alexander Hamilton because of his comprehensive explanation of the Federalists' approach to executive emergency powers. Here I will present Hamilton's argument, which suggests that, because the executive commands the army, he ought to have emergency powers and that these should be set in Article II of the Constitution. [3] I then investigate further why Hamilton thought emergency powers *necessarily* lie with the executive and why he argued for them to be inherent, as opposed to explicit, powers within the Constitution.

I draw the main points of Hamilton's argument regarding executive emergency powers from *The Federalist Papers*. He offered three main reasons why emergency powers must rest with the executive: (1) to respond to the crisis swiftly and energetically, (2) to preserve the state, and (3) to ensure accountability for the actions taken while responding to the crisis.

In part, Hamilton relied on history to explain why emergency power is critical to the health of the republic—because emergencies will happen and the republic must be able to deal with them. He recalled that rather than being unique to any nation, emergencies are an inevitable historical condition, and America invariably and unequivocally will experience such adversities: "Our own experience has corroborated the lessons taught by the examples of other nations; that emergencies of this sort will sometimes exist in all societies, however constituted; that seditions and insurrections are, unhappily maladies as inseparable from the body politic as tumors and eruptions from the natural body."[4] Thus, in the event of an insurrection or other such unhappy malady, according to Hamilton, governments must have the power and authority to use the military to defeat the attack.

Hamilton insisted that emergencies need responses, specifically a "swift" response, and this will require the executive to act and may call into question the "ordinary state of things."[5] Hamilton stated that "there are certain emergencies of nations in which expedients that in the ordinary state of things ought to be forborne become essential to the public weal."[6]

Furthermore, according to Hamilton, the boundaries or latitudes of executive action during times of emergency—the scope and duration of which cannot be predetermined, and, hence, enumerated in the Constitution—creates an un-enumerated constitutional power, having stated that "the government, from the possibility of such emergencies, ought ever to have the option of making use of them, because the circumstances which may affect the public safety are not reducible within certain determinate limits."[7] Again, Hamilton claimed that in times of great calamity, the government must do what is necessary to protect public safety, even if this means going beyond the scope of the law. His reasoning echoes Locke's claims that the executive, using his "prerogative," may have to act outside the "scope of the constitution."[8]

Hamilton also suggested that the executive must have the requisite energy to respond to a crisis, which the legislature and judiciary would not have in the time of peril. He explained that energy is simply the necessary powers for the government—in this instance, the executive—to act with appropriate ability to function, or, for this discussion, combat a crisis. Lack of energy, according to Hamilton, would equal feebleness; therefore, when measuring his concept of energy, one must consider that if a government's action is perceived feeble, then it lacked the necessary or appropriate energy. He stated, "Energy in the Executive is a leading character in the definition of good government." In order for there to be good government, Hamilton asserted that energy in government "is essential to the protection of the community against foreign attacks, it is not less essential to the steady administration of the laws, to the protection of property against irregular and high-handed combinations which sometimes interrupt the ordinary course of justice." He further stated that for good governance there must be "energy in the Executive [because it] is key to the security of liberty against the enterprise and assaults of ambitions, of faction, and even of anarchy."[9]

According to Hamilton, the executive's energy will consist of four key components: unity, duration, adequate provision for his support, and competent powers. He placed the most importance on unity, which, he argued, is indisputably "conducive to energy." He stated that, to yield the most beneficial outcome for the republic, unity is necessary if actions are to be taken during a time of peril. Hamilton stated, "A feeble Executive implies a feeble execution of the government. A feeble execution is but another phrase for a bad execution; and a government ill executed, whatever may be in theory, must be, in practice, a bad government."[10] Therefore, Hamilton argued that a government unable to act with appropriate power in light of an emergency would appear to the public as feeble. Because feeble execution makes apparent a feeble government, all governments, according to Hamilton, must be able to maintain their power and legitimacy during a crisis. In order to do so, the government must be able to act strongly enough so as to never appear feeble. Although limiting power, as would be the case in the American model of government, is good in theory, in application it could cripple the nation's response during a crisis, thereby creating feebleness. Consequently, the U.S. government, in order to avoid feebleness in the critical moment of a crisis, must be able to act with unlimited power.

Hamilton argued for a strong, unitary executive who is capable of combating the crisis swiftly, with enough political power to end the crisis, and is empowered with the political energy necessary at the time of the crisis to succeed. If the executive's ability to act is constrained in any way, then, according to Hamilton, the response to the crisis and execution of necessary actions will be feeble, which will endanger the very existence of the state.

During the state ratification conventions Hamilton's argument appealed to some. In particular, James Wilson of Pennsylvania agreed with Hamilton's proposal that executive power to deal with crises and perils as he sees fit should be assured and codified. Wilson stated, "we all know what numerous executives are. The Constitution has placed executive power in the hands of a single magistrate so as to bring strength, vigor, energy and responsibility to the execution of federal law."[11] Governor Randolph of Virginia also concurred with Hamilton and Wilson, saying, "All the enlightened part of mankind agree that the superior dispatch, secrecy, and energy with which one man can act, renders it more politic to vest the power of executing the laws in one man," especially during times of emergency.[12]

Hamilton asserted that in order to ensure accountability as well as a decisive response to an emergency, the presidency must be singular, not plural, for three distinct and significant reasons. The president must be unitary in order to lead effectively, execute laws, and command the army. If the president were a plural officer, then he would be hampered when making decisions, unable to respond swiftly, and lack the effective avenues of accountability. After all, how can you criticize effectively five different heads of one body? Which head is to blame most of all? Hamilton insisted that the president must have autonomy and full control over his domain, and this would likewise give the public a clear point of responsibility when they express either dissatisfaction or praise; hence, a transparent path toward accountability would be achieved through a singular executive officer.[13]

Hamilton, in describing the scope of executive emergency power, went as far as to suggest that the power may be unlimited because there can be "no limitation of that authority which is to provide for the defense and protection of the community in any matter essential to its efficacy." He asserted that the "competent powers" of the presidency will include the power to "combat emergencies" because an executive will be "responsible for the administration of government" when it falls "peculiarly within the province of the executive department."[14] He believed that the "province" of the executive department would include "the operations of war," especially in times of peril. Hamilton further suggested that the executive branch would be responsible for "the execution of the laws and the employment of the common strength, for the common defense," and this will be most critical during emergency because during an emergency, defending the nation is, of course, of utmost importance.[15] All of these excerpts of his argument thus suggest that Hamilton expected the executive to be responsible to combat crises and that the executive's response to a crisis should be based, at times, on his own discretion.

Comments Hamilton made regarding national security further demonstrate his support for executive emergency power. He asserted in Federalist No. 74 that an emergency will lead to a greater need to centralize power within the executive because one of the most important "concerns of government, the direction of war" must be the "exercise of power by a single hand."[16] Specifically, the executive must control command in war because "the direction of war implies the direction of common strength" and doing so is easier "if the army is commanded by a single chief." Furthermore, Hamilton makes clear that "the power of directing and employing the common strength forms a usual and essential part in the definition of executive authority"—especially during times of emergency—because "feeble execution, implies a feeble government."[17]

Scholars, such as Thomas Schelling, support Hamilton's arguments stating that "a nation state would want to have a communications system in good order, to have complete information, or to be in full command of one's owns actions or of one's own assets . . . hence the need for the Executive to have secrecy, energy and dispatch in times of emergency."[18] In addition, Edward Corwin observed the unique advantages that the executive will have during an emergency or in foreign affairs as a consequence of Hamilton's ideas: "the unity of office, its capacity for secrecy and dispatch, and its superior sources of information, to which should be added the fact that it is always on hand and ready for action, whereas the houses of Congress are in adjournment much of the time."[19]

Possibly the true genius of the Federalist argument for executive emergency powers is that it does not attempt to enumerate all of the powers afforded to the executive, both generally and during an emergency. By refraining from detailing the executive's powers, the Federalists provide the executive with the ability to respond to the protean nature of attacks and their frequency, thus enabling the executive to respond swiftly and with energy. Furthermore, this assumes that the Federalists saw the national government as possessing a broad authority to take action to meet any emergency. As Hamilton consistently observed, "the government is to possess an indefinite power of providing for emergencies as they might arise."[20] That "indefinite power" includes the authority to use force to protect the nation, as Hamilton stated that "it cannot be denied that there may happen cases in which the national government may be necessitated to resort to force."[21] Recall that he noted emergencies are not unique to any particular nation but rather are an inevitable historical condition, and as such, the United States will invariably and unequivocally experience such emergencies: "Our own experience has corroborated the lessons taught by the examples of other nations; that emergencies of this sort will sometimes exist in all societies, however constituted; that seditions and insurrections are, unhappily, maladies as inseparable from the body politic as tumors and eruptions from the natural body."[22] In the event of an insurrection or other such unhappy malady, Hamilton consistently concluded that governments must have the power and authority to use the military to eliminate the threat.

Though the Federalists agree with Locke's principle of implicit emergency powers—that is, the "prerogative"—the Federalists' manner of incorporating such power into the Constitution differs slightly from how Locke might have integrated them. Locke probably would have favored emergency powers to be completely "outside the boundaries of the Constitution,"[23] whereas Hamilton argued for such powers to be implicitly proscribed under Article II of the Constitution because emergency power will inherently be an executive function, as he commands the army.[24] The key difference between Locke and Hamilton is that Locke suggested that executive emergency power may be wholly unconstitutional, whereas Hamilton asserted that even though the power is not explicitly enumerated, it is still an inherent constitutional power.

In summary, the Federalist argument asserted that energy in the executive is "the leading characteristic of good government" and "essential to the protection of the community against foreign attacks . . . to the protection of property against those irregular and high handed combinations, which sometimes interrupt the ordinary course of justice, to the security of liberty against the enterprise and assaults of ambition, of faction and of anarchy." What's more, the main component to constitute energy is "unity." Further, the executive may have to be "secretive and swift" when responding to a crisis, though the Constitution and the "other magistrates" of government check the power of the executive. Finally, the executive's power during crisis is inherent in Article II of the Constitution. Though Hamilton himself never stated this, advocates of the Unitary Executive Theory make this case by combining two key provisions of Article II, the Vesting clause and the Commander-in-Chief clause.

Thus, the main points of the Federalist argument are

- the executive must have energy to respond to a crisis,
- the executive must be able to use the army to respond to the crisis,
- the executive will need to act swiftly and even secretly without initial congressional approval,
- the power is inherent within Article II of the Constitution, and
- the power is not unlimited but rather is checked by the other magistrates of government.

In conclusion, the previous Federalist claims, asserted by Hamilton, assert an American model for exercising emergency power, in which executive prerogative determines how and when to exercise emergency power and is an inherent constitutional power lawfully granted to an executive under authority given to him in Article II of the Constitution; thereby creating a cavalier president.

In chapter 6 I will examine specifically which clauses of Article II support Hamilton's ideas as I discuss the Unitary Executive Theory. Hamilton maintained that the formal powers of the presidency enable the president to act in times of emergency and follow his prerogative, thereby making the president's authority to act discretionary and constitutional in response to the crisis. His approach to emergency power may mean that a president has to act outside the boundaries of the explicit powers granted to the executive, but according to the Federalist philosophy, the power to act during an emergency would be constitutional. Thus, Hamilton and the Federalists advocated for a president who would be able to address any national crisis through his formal—and flexible—powers, stating, "The circumstances that endanger the safety of nations are infinite . . . and for this reason no constitutional shackles can wisely be imposed on the power to which the care of it is committed."[25] Therefore, in times of crisis the Federalists argued for implicit executive emergency powers, supporting Lockean notions of prerogative.

THE ANTI-FEDERALIST PERSPECTIVE ON EXECUTIVE EMERGENCY POWER

Conversely, the Anti-Federalists did not share or support this philosophy; they feared that if presidents wielded too much power during an emergency, this could lead to monarchy or despotism. To examine their position, in this section I outline the Anti-Federalist position concerning executive emergency powers, beginning with the main arguments of classical Anti-Federalists George Clinton, Richard Henry Lee, Patrick Henry, and Thomas Paine. Secondly, I review the main Aristotelian arguments for explicit emergency powers. Finally, I delineate the primary references supporting the Anti-Federalist position that emergency powers should be explicitly outlined in the Constitution.

The Federalists and Anti-Federalists clashed most over issues of presidential latitude and power as well as the general structure of the office—specifically, whether the office should be made up of one or multiple people. The Federalists insisted that the presidency is to be singular, so the executive is able to maintain national security and respond to emergency efficiently, but the Anti-Federalists disagreed.

The diffusion of presidential power was an important topic at the Constitutional Convention of 1787. Led by Edmund Randolph, the Anti-Federalists favored a committee-style presidency,[26] which would consist of several members from the Congress who would jointly constitute the executive branch. The committee that was responsible for hashing out the details of how the presidency should be structured would ultimately concede that the pluralistic theory of the executive would not only be useless and ineffective, but it would also not help unify the nation.

The Anti-Federalists, however, did come to recognize that the pluralist presidency would render a weaker president, and this would therefore attenuate the executive during an emergency. After all, until the Constitution was ratified, the ineffective Articles of Confederation had ill-fatedly served the American experiment, thereby rendering the executive impotent and useless. Thus, the debate over executive authority had already swung to support consolidating the presidency into a single, unitary executive.[27]

However, the numerical size or value of the American presidency was not the Anti-Federalists' only point of disagreement with the Federalists, prompting these questions: Why would the Anti-Federalists disagree with the Federalists on the notion of executive emergency powers? What did they fear most? In order to answer these questions, I examine the pertinent Anti-Federalist documents, including the Anti-Federalist papers, which indicate that they believed that executive emergency powers would lead to a tyrannical presidency.

The Anti-Federalists' primary concern over the Constitution and, importantly, over executive emergency power, was that it "smelled" of a "monarchy." In their writings the Anti-Federalists would often cite Montesquieu to remind the Federalists of the importance of separated powers. Richard Henry Lee expressed clearly the Anti-Federalist apprehension over an "unchecked" executive, stating, "It will destroy any Balance in the Government, and enable them to accomplish what Usurpations they please upon the Rights and Liberties of the People."[28]

George Clinton (writing as "Cato" in pseudonymous essays appearing in New York newspapers) reinforced Anti-Federalist concerns regarding the executive branch turning into a monarchy, asking, "Wherein does this president, invested with his powers and prerogatives, essentially differ from the King of Great Britain?" Other Anti-Federalists claimed that executive emergency power made the president "in reality to be a king as much a king as the King of Great Britain, and a King too of the worst kind; an elective King."[29]

Anti-Federalists harbored apprehension over the broad powers of the executive, especially during times of emergency, resting mainly in the Commander-in-Chief clause of Article II. The Anti-Federalists were concerned that the commander-in-chief power would entangle the president with a "standing army" and could thus cause havoc for the citizenry.[30]

"Brutus," a leading Anti-Federalist (likely Robert Tato) whose real identity is not definitively known, warned that "the evil to be feared from a standing army in time of peace may lead to military coups. . . . [An] equal, and perhaps greater danger, is to be apprehended from their overturning the constitutional powers of the government, and assuming the power to dictate any form they please." As noted above, the Anti-Federalists were primarily concerned with how much power an executive would have during emergency and whether the power would be unchecked or unlimited; the Anti-Federalists believed that under those circumstances, an executive could easily become a king or despot.[31]

"Tamony," another anonymous author whose identity has not been determined, echoed a similar Anti-Federalist worry that executive control of the army could lead to serious usurpations of powers, claiming, "the commander of the fleets and armies of America . . . though not dignified with the magic name of a King . . . will possess more supreme power, than Great Britain allows her hereditary monarchs." Furthermore, he stated, "the Executive's command of a standing army is unrestrained by law or limitation."[32]

In Anti-Federalist No. 69, Richard Henry Lee further elaborated their position regarding executive authority, in particular during emergencies and, more broadly, over time. Lee suggested that the greatest concern regarding the development of the executive branch should be to prevent "the perpetuation of any portion of power, great or small, in the same man or family."[33] The Anti-Federalists feared that an emergency might initiate a period of protracted executive rule, which may encourage an executive to go beyond the scope of the law.

Therefore, the Anti-Federalists favored limiting executive emergency powers, and they unequivocally expressed the need to enumerate explicitly such powers in the Constitution. Lee suggested placing a limit on how long a president may serve and on the extent of his powers: "the executive may not remain in power as to enable him to take any measures to establish himself."[34] He shared earlier political thinkers' general concern—thinkers such as Rousseau, who adamantly argued for an explicit duration of time in which the executive may have expanded emergency powers. This argument is also similar to Aristotle's, which was codified in the Roman model.[35]

Lee suggested certain provisions in order to prevent an undemocratic outcome during emergencies. For instance, he saw Congress and the Constitution as means to precluding prolonged or abusive presidents rising as a consequence of emergency. The Anti-Federalists did not dispute the inevitability of emergencies nor did they disagree that the state would need to act swiftly and with energy in response to an emergency; instead, they argued for a more diffused power that could provide a balanced response to the emergency and that this should be embodied explicitly in the Constitution. Lee stated, "There appears to me to be an intended provision [in the Constitution] for supplying the Office of the President, not only for the remaining portion of a term, but also in cases of emergency."[36] Lee argued that such provisions would fall under Article II of the Constitution, which, we may construe from Lee's statements, were to include emergency power.

I argue that Lee's statement demanding explicit enumeration of executive emergency powers constitutes the Anti-Federalists' distinct departure from the Federalists. Rather than favoring a "prerogative" power, the Anti-Federalists insisted on an unambiguous statement of executive power during emergencies because they, unlike the Federalists, feared that an executive with unlimited power during an emergency would place the republic in grave risk of degenerating into a tyranny. Therefore, an explicit constitutional check had to be placed on executive power—even during an emergency.

George Clinton further elaborated Lee's concerns regarding executive authority during emergencies in Anti-Federalist No. 67, discussing the imprudence of placing such power in the hands of one magistrate. He stated, "It is obvious to the least intelligent mind to account why great power in the hands of a magistrate may be dangerous to the liberties of a republic." According to Clinton, when too much power is in the hands of a single person, he will become "tempted to exercise his power unwisely, and to grow a train of dependents."[37]

For Clinton, the magnitude of ambition and pernicious behavior will exceed during times of emergency and thus lead the president to "unwisely lead the troops, control the army, navy, militia and enable an unrestrained power to pardon and to screen from punishment those instigating crimes."[38] Here, he appears to warn fervently of the consequences of martial law. Consider for a moment the rise of a martial state as a consequence of an unparalleled emergency: Would it be acceptable for the president to unilaterally control the army and subject the law to his own fancy?

The obvious answer is no. Accordingly, the Anti-Federalists were dubious of the idea of the noble leader who would not infringe upon civil liberties during a time of emergency. To animate this point, Lee robustly stated, "We may have, for the first president, and perhaps, one in a century or two afterwards, a great and good man, governed by superior motives, but generally this is not a likely outcome."[39]

Therefore, because the Anti-Federalists were deeply concerned about the true and sincere motives of the president, they saw emergencies as potential occasions to cause the greatest peril and opportunity for the president to manifest deceitful and insincere motives. Hence, the Anti-Federalists wanted to do everything they could to restrain executive power, even during times of emergency. This brings us to wonder how the Anti-Federalists would propose to restrain power while still ensuring that the republic could combat the crisis effectively. Their answer involved authority and autonomy of the legislature.

Clinton and the Anti-Federalists favored a robust legislature equipped with the ability to manage and defend the republic during any crisis, arguing that "though the president may recommend broad powers during an emergency, or at any point for that matter, the right of power must be construed only by the legislature." He went on to state that "of course the president is the generalissimo of the country, he may and will command the army, but he must not make war without the advice and approval of the legislature."[40]

Anti-Federalist papers No. 69 and 67 clearly indicate that the Anti-Federalists favored two distinct provisions that differed from the Federalists regarding executive emergency powers: executive emergency powers must be (1) clearly enumerated in the Constitution and (2) declared by Congress, akin to declaring war. If either of these provisions were not created, then the Anti-Federalists feared the worst outcome possible in a democracy—the rise of a tyrant. In fact, Clinton warned that constructing the republic poorly could in turn create a deceitful and irresponsible ruler, and this would lead to the republic's demise. He argued that if the founders were not careful in constructing the executive branch and, in particular, its emergency powers, then "an Angel of Darkness may resemble an Angel of Light."

Patrick Henry, one of the most ardent Anti-Federalists and a devout libertarian of his time, during the convention at Virginia in 1788, presented critical arguments against a robust president being afforded latitude during times of emergencies. He stated, "This Constitution is said to have beautiful features, but when I come to examine these features, Sir, they appear to be horridly frightful: Among other deformities, it has an awful squinting; it squints towards monarchy."[41] For Henry, the Federalists constitutional propositions point (squint) toward monarchy because of their recommended executive emergency powers and the president's relationship to the army.

Henry clearly connected the president's autonomy and his power over the military as key reasons for fearing a potential monarchical demise, stating, "Your president may easily become a king. . . . The army is in his hands, and if he be a man of address, it will be attached to him." He went on to state that coronating a king would be just as wise, for in so doing, "if we make him a king, we may prescribe the rules by which he shall rule his people and interpose such checks as shall prevent him from infringing them."[42] Therefore, Henry argued that executive emergency powers must be explicitly outlined in the Constitution because doing so would ensure strict application of the law and provide for limitations on such broad powers; for the appropriate structure granting executive emergency powers would have resembled the Roman model—favoring Aristotelian norms of explicit constitutional powers. As we know, however, the final U.S. Constitution contains no such provisions declaring boundaries on executive emergency powers.

Finally, Henry argued that during the crisis and thereafter, enabling a president to have implicit powers could jeopardize individual citizens' civil liberties, stating, "The President . . . at the head of his army, can prescribe the terms on which he shall reign master, so far that it will puzzle any American ever to get his neck from under the galling yoke." Again, he feared that the state may not be able to reset the powers of the presidency following an emergency. He said, "The yoke will forever endure leaving the burden and loss of liberty an eternal strife for Americans," and he went on to pose the following questions: "And what have you to oppose this force? What will then become of you and your rights? Will not absolute despotism ensue?"[43] The Federalists never answered these questions, yet one might consider them now in the twenty-first century and ponder, what may come of the Republic if executive emergency power is not restrained?

Henry continued to voice his concerns that an American president, in the mold of a Federalist, could, essentially, become a king. He stated, "The President may easily become King. . . . If your American chief be a man of ambition and abilities, how easy is it for him to render himself absolute!" He also declared, "at the head of the army the President can prescribe the terms on which he shall reign master and will violate the laws and beat down every opposition," especially in times of emergency.[44]

Thomas Paine, an ardent Anti-Federalist, in his main treatise, *Common Sense,* offered a final consideration regarding executive emergency powers. According to Paine, all Americans must be concerned about a monarchical ruler and must reject the very notion of having one. He questioned, "some may ask, where is the King in America?" Paine's answer provided two important reminders: The law is king and executive emergency powers are subject to the law. He elaborated that "the law reigns above, and doth not make havoc on mankind like the Royal Brute of Britain . . . let a crown be placed thereon, by which the world may know, that so far as we approve of monarchy, that in America the Law is King."[45] In robustly defending the very essence of the reign of law, Paine indicated that he would have supported explicitly outlining executive emergency powers within the Constitution. In other words, supporting tacit or implicit executive emergency powers would undermine Paine's call for a robust Constitution that would be a manifestation of the people's will. Therefore, I conclude—as did the Anti-Federalists—that the principal argument regarding executive emergency powers is that a sustainable power would need to be created explicitly within the Constitution, and this power must be reconcilable with the law and not include extralegal provisions that allow it to operate outside the boundaries of the U.S. Constitution.

However, the Constitution never even states the word *emergency*, yet we know presidents have used emergency powers. Chapters 3 through 6 will explore instances of presidents using emergency powers. But before I discuss presidential use of emergency powers, understanding where such powers rest in the Constitution is vital.

After having reviewed the Federalist–Anti-Federalist debate—which centered on whether to make executive emergency powers inherent in Article II of the Constitution as part of the executive's authority to command the army, as the Federalists suggest, or to exclude them in the Constitution altogether—I now examine Article II of the Constitution to demonstrate that executive emergency powers are both inherent and constitutional due to four particular clauses in the Constitution: the Oath, Take Care, Commander-in-Chief, and Vesting clauses. The Oath clause allows the president to defend from encroachments on executive prerogatives during a crisis as well as to protect the constitutional rights of individuals. The Take Care clause allows the president to interpret legislation so as to maximize his executive-branch preferences. The Vesting clause of Article II affords implicit powers within Article II of the Constitution, most importantly executive emergency powers. Finally, the Commander-in-Chief clause enables the president to command the army, and this is very critical during an emergency.

THE VESTING CLAUSE

In order to understand how the Vesting clause of Article II supports executive emergency powers, it is important to understand how it establishes implicit powers. It states, "The executive power shall be vested in a President of the United States of America." A cursory glance at this statement might suggest that it is relatively explicit; one can construe that a single person shall hold the office and shall have the power of the executive branch. However, in comparing the clause to its counterparts under the other Articles of the Constitution, scholars have noticed a particular difference, which warrants an investigation.

The difference lies in the Vesting clause of Article I, which states, "All legislative powers *herein* granted shall be vested in a Congress of the United States" (emphasis added). Unlike the Vesting clause of Article II, the Vesting clause of Article I includes the word "herein," which explicitly restrains the powers of Congress to only those powers that will be enumerated in the Article. For example, section 8 of Article I of the Constitution specifies many Congressional powers, such as levying taxes, declaring war, and raising an army, just to mention a few.[46] Because the Vesting clause asserts that Congress will only have powers "herein," we can construe that Congress is limited only to those enumerated powers.

Thus, an explicit word is included in the Vesting clause of Article I to limit the powers of the Congress only to the provisions in Article I that is not—nor is similar language—included in Article II. This indicates that the framers intended to grant the presidency more powers than they enumerate in the Constitution. The prima facie evidence would suggest that the Vesting clause of Article II of the Constitution does not limit presidential power to only those powers enumerated in the Article, therefore creating or allowing for an interpretation of presidential power to include inherent powers, of which emergency powers are included. Perhaps the framers wanted to enable the president to have inherent powers or discretionary powers not enumerated in the Constitution, such as that akin to "prerogative" power.

Locke's concept of prerogative power may help clarify the issue of inherent powers in Article II of the Constitution. In his *Second Treatise on Civil Government*, he suggested that, if the executive and legislative powers lie in "distinct hands," the executive may need the domain of prerogative powers. During an emergency or a crisis, Locke proffered, the executive may need unspecified powers to use at his discretion in order to maintain the public's security and safety. The laws that were inadequate to deal with the crisis might temporarily need to "give way to the executive power, viz., that as much as may be, all the members of society are to be preserved." Therefore, Locke proposed that a prerogative power of the executive is "the people's permitting their rulers to do several things of their own free choice, where the law was silent, or sometimes, too, against the direct letter of the law, for the public good, and their acquiescing in it when so done."[47]

Furthermore, Locke's notion of a prerogative power rests on five main principles: (1) it must exist when all other laws fail, (2) it must exist only when a law is not in place to deal with the situation, (3) events may dictate the necessities for a prerogative power, (4) it must be used only for the public good, and (5) the people always reign over the power and the executive. Thus, the president's authority rests on the notion that an emergency must create a void in the law—a crisis of constitutional merit—and due to their need for protection, security, and defense, the people must yield to the limitations of the president's authority. As Locke stated, "this power to act according to discretion, for the public good, without the prescription of the law, and sometimes even against it" is the very essence of the president's authority and establishes his prerogative power.[48] Consequently, Locke's definition and recommendation of a prerogative power grants the president enormous latitude of power and discretion as long as two conditions are present as he yields his prerogative power: (1) a crisis or emergency must exist, and (2) fear is present to mold public opinion in favor of the president's use of the prerogative power.

As the Federalist papers nos. 70 and 69 make clear, the Federalists supported Locke's notion of prerogative powers. In particular, Hamilton led this crusade, suggesting that a president must be able to repel sudden attacks, and Morris, the chief drafter for the committee of style at the Constitutional Convention (the committee in charge of "polishing" the language in the Constitution), supported a strong unitary executive.

Scholars have suggested that Morris intentionally worded the clause so as to differ from the language in the Vesting clause of Article I. Charles Thach suggested this was done to embolden the presidency: "Morris did his tinkering with full realization of the possibilities, that is, presidents could later claim that the different phrasing of the two branches' vesting clauses implies that there are executive powers beyond those 'herein granted.'" Thach went on to conclude that "whether intentional or not, the difference between the two vesting clauses admits an interpretation of executive power which would give the president a field of activity wider than that outlined by the enumerated powers."[49]

THE OATH CLAUSE

The Oath clause of the Constitution, found in Article II, Section I, clause 8, states that the president "will faithfully execute the Office of the President and will preserve, protect, and defend the Constitution of the United States."[50] I argue that this phrase authorizes the president to protect both the prerogatives of his office (faithfully execute) and the liberties of the individual. Of course, during a national emergency the prerogatives of the president become more crucial; hence, presidents should be more likely to invoke the Oath clause in order to support their behaviors at such times and should cite it as legal defense for their prerogative actions.

Steven Calabresi confirmed this point, declaring that "it is a duty of the President to preserve, protect and defend his office, which is, of course, a creation of the Constitution itself. The President takes an oath to uphold that Constitution and the public judges him, and ought to judge him, by his vigilance in fulfilling that oath."[51] Further, then, as a consequence of the president's responsibility to "uphold the Constitution," an emergency is the most crucial time; hence, this clause speaks directly to executive emergency powers.

In order to enforce the president's oath to protect the Constitution, the Department of Justice (DOJ) has carved out two primary caveats to the president's constitutional obligation to defend and enforce statutes: (1) the president is not to defend or enforce those statutes that are clearly "unconstitutional," and (2) the president is not to defend or enforce actions or legislation that encroaches upon the prerogatives of the executive branch.[52] These two caveats ensure the greatest latitude of presidential authority in relation to legislation or actions taken against the presidency and, most importantly, against the president's prerogatives.

This first caveat "accommodates the conflict between the constitutional mandate that the President execute the laws and his oath to support and to defend the Constitution," whereas the second "accommodates the occasional conflict between the roles of the President as the chief law enforcement officer of the United States and the role of the Attorney General as the advocate of the executive branch."[53] Thus, the most crucial component of the Oath clause, I argue, is that the president has the lateral authority to "uphold and defend the Constitution."

As such, the goal of the president's domains and powers constituted in Article II is to establish the executive as the "chief law enforcer"—that is, he is in charge of defending the Constitution (preserving the Union). Therefore, the Oath clause includes executive emergency powers. I will discuss in detail instances of individual presidents invoking the Oath clause as a legal right to use emergency power when investigating the presidencies of Abraham Lincoln and George W. Bush, chapters 5 and 6.

THE TAKE CARE CLAUSE

The Take Care clause is found in Article II, Section III of the U.S. Constitution, and it obligates the president to "take care that the laws are faithfully executed." Further, through this Article the president may solicit the opinions of the principal officers of the various executive branch agencies to help him ensure that the laws are faithfully executed. Scholars have argued that both components, when taken together, offer a "unified" interpretation of laws that the president then signs. For example, legal scholar Michael Herz wrote, "The *Take Care Clause* is backed up by the President's specific and unique oath to 'faithfully execute' his office. The use of the passive voice in the *Take Care Clause* indicates that the President will not necessarily be executing the laws directly, but only overseeing others to ensure their 'faithful' execution."[54]

In other words, according to Herz, the president is a unitary executive in charge of the complete supervision of the executive branch. This logic could suggest that presidential responsibilities are even greater during an emergency because of the president's duty to "faithfully execute" the law. In an emergency the law is of utmost concern; therefore, a president and his operatives, whom the president unitarily controls, are to exert his executive prerogatives, hopefully in conjunction with the law.

Additionally, as the Supreme Court has noted, "interpreting a law enacted by Congress to implement the legislative mandate is the very essence of execution of the law."[55] I argue that, at least from the Court's perspective, a president's duty is to "take care" of the laws—not only statutory law but also in relation to times of emergency, in which the full faith of the government must be directed toward ending the crisis. As Justice Douglas declared in *Home Building and Loan Association v. Blaisdell*, (290 U.S. 398, 1934), "There are two Constitutions, a peace time Constitution, and an emergency time Constitution. In the latter, it is the responsibility of government, mostly the executive, to faithfully execute the laws and to defend the Constitution, with the intent of preserving the Union."[56] Therefore, I suggest, emergencies call for "unitary" executives not only to take care of the law but also to extend any measure necessary to preserve the Constitution.

THE COMMANDER-IN-CHIEF CLAUSE

The most important clause in Article II regarding executive emergency powers is the Commander-in-Chief clause. Through this clause the president can seize power during an emergency in order to combat the crisis with the use of the armed services. Edwin Corwin called this clause of "uncertainty and of upmost importance."[57] Because Article II has inherent powers, the president is "left to interpret power," which is most crucial during a time of emergency. For Corwin, events "shape the nature of presidential power,"[58] and thus, during an emergency commanding the army and inherently controlling its powers is very crucial. The question then becomes, does the Constitution confirm that the president has unilateral control over the armed forces during an emergency?

The Commander-in-Chief clause reads, "The President shall be Commander in Chief of the Army and Navy of the United States, and of the Militia of the several states, when called into the actual service of the United States."[59] During the Constitutional Convention, the founders paid little attention to whom or what would control the army. In fact, because the Virginia Plan mentioned nothing concerning the control of the army, many of the delegates took for granted that the Congress would control the armed forces.[60] It was the Committee of Detail that actually inserted that the president, as an enumerated power, would command the army,[61] proposing that the president shall be "commander in chief."[62] However, the committee also recommended that Congress be empowered "to make war; to raise armies; to build and equip fleets; to call forth the aide of the militia, in order to execute the laws of the Union; enforce treaties, suppress insurrections, and repel invasions."[63]

With these two clauses in place, the delegates began to debate the merits of each clause. There was particular confusion regarding the clauses, as delegates were concerned about which branch of government could "make war" and which branch of government could "declare war." Clearly, Congress's power to "make" war included directing the actual conduct of the fighting, but so did the president's power as "commander in chief of the Army and the Navy."[64] Therefore, the delegates needed to determine which branch would actually order soldiers and sailors into action, which branch would tell the soldiers where to go and what to do once they arrived at the battlefield, and, finally, who would have the power and authority to combat and command responses to rebellions and insurrections.

Hamilton, as argued in Federalist No. 70, believed that the president should wield these powers, as did Pierce Butler from Delaware, who doubted that Congress would be able to act "quickly enough" on military matters if an urgent need should arise. He urged the convention to vest in the president the power to make war stating, "who will have all the requisite qualities, and will not make war but when the Nation will support it . . . it must be the executive."[65] Furthermore, James Madison and Randolph Gerry, two ardent Anti-Federalists joined Butler, confirming that the president must have the authority to combat insurrections. They noted that there may be times of emergency when Congress is not in session and, thus, prepared to declare war, yet a response to the action must take place; the president must be able to respond to crisis at any moment. Gerry stated, "The Executive should be able to repel and not commence war."[66] With the support of Madison and Gerry, the motion passed and the clause was adopted.

SUMMARY

Executive emergency power is an inherent power based on interpretations of the Vesting, Oath, Take Care, and Commander-in-Chief clauses of Article II of the Constitution. In chapters 5 and 6 I will examine how individual presidents have supported this interpretation of these clauses.

Table 2.1 summarizes the Federalist and Anti-Federalist arguments for executive emergency powers and the resulting outcome of their propositions. As indicated in table 2.1, the Federalists favored an implicit model for executive emergency power because they agreed with Lockean principles that because not all emergencies can be foreseen, laws cannot be written for all emergencies; thus, the legislature will be too slow to act swiftly and with energy. Consequently, the Federalists favored a centralization of power during a crisis.

The Anti-Federalists, however, opposed the Federalists' position; instead, the Anti-Federalists took a more Montesquieuean and Machiavellian approach to executive emergency power. Because they believed that the law should be paramount in all situations, including emergencies, they favored explicit laws that granted executive emergency power, thereby creating boundaries and limitations on emergency power. The Anti-Federalists wanted to reduce the risk of an executive becoming a tyrant as a result of gaining too much power; hence, they advocated that power should be decentralized, even during an emergency, so as to maintain a balanced system of separation of powers.

Based on the constitutional analysis above, executive emergency power appears to be inherent, or implied, in Article II of the Constitution; therefore, the Federalists prevailed. By interpreting the Vesting, Oath, Commander-in-

Table 2.1. Federalist versus Anti-Federalists interpretations for executive emergency power.

	Main points	Outcome
Federalists	• Favored strength, energy, and swiftness for the executive to respond to crises • Law cannot foresee all circumstances that could transpire to cause a crisis; therefore, executive emergency power must be implicit	Centralize power
Anti-Federalists	• Distrust for executive power • Diffuse emergency power among the branches • Maintain balanced system of power • Create explicit laws for executive emergency power	Decentralize power

Chief, and Take Care clauses of Article II of the Constitution, we see that executive emergency power is an inherent power. Not only have individual presidents, the action of whom I analyze later in this book, demonstrated in practice this interpretation of Article II, but the Supreme Court has also validated the inherent emergency power argument in its *Youngstown Sheet and Tube Co. v. Sawyer* (343 U.S. 579, 1952) ruling (also known as the Steel Seizure Case). In it, in Justice Robert H. Jackson's concurrent opinion, presidential emergency power may exist only under the following conditions:

1. When the president acts pursuant to an express or implied authorization of Congress, the president's authority is at its greatest.
2. When the president acts in the absence of either a congressional grant or denial of authority, he can only rely upon his own independent powers, but there is a zone in which he and Congress may have concurrent authority. When this is the case, the test depends on the imperatives of events and contemporary imponderables rather than on abstract theories of law.
3. When the president takes measures incompatible with the expressed or implied will of Congress, the authority of the president is at its lowest.

In the instance of the president seizing the steel mills, the Court found that Congress had explicated that the president may not, plus no clear emergency existed, hence the president had no authority to use emergency power, even if they may be implicit within Article II of the Constitution.

Let me pose this question: if the president has the sworn duty to uphold and defend the Constitution—thus, also, presumably the Union—as well as the authority to command the army and the obligation to execute the laws, and Article II does not limit him to powers herein, then should we agree that presidents have inherent emergency power? Or, to put it another way, if the founders believed that the president should have emergency power, then why not state such power explicitly? Establishing that the executive has emergency power would not limit his power, per se, but it would make clear that he at least does have such authority. Professors Richard Neustadt and Louis Fisher have both argued that because the power is not stated explicitly, it does not exist, and furthermore, before a president can command and use the military, the Congress must first declare war and then instruct a president to proceed.[67] They would suggest even in times of emergency Congress can act quickly enough to grant the president authority to respond to a crisis.[68] Over the next chapters I will explore and evidence presidential interpretation of emergency power and will show that presidents agree with the Federalist interpretation; the question becomes, why do they act without Congressional consent? Not all will act without congressional consent, but some will, and is the Republic safe in the hands of a president during times of emergency?

NOTES

1. James Madison, *The Papers of James Madison* (Chicago: University of Chicago Press), 345 and 350.

2. Edmund Randolph, "Second Day of Convention, Randolph's Notes and Speeches," in Max Farrand, *The Records of the Federal Convention of 1787*, 20–21 (New Haven, CT: Yale University Press, 1911), 20–21.

3. Alexander Hamilton, Federalist No. 70, in Alexander Hamilton, James Madison, and John Jay, *The Federalist Papers*, 354–61 (New York: Bantam Press, 1982).

4. Alexander Hamilton, Federalist No. 28, in Hamilton, Madison, and Jay, *The Federalist Papers*, 134–37.

5. Hamilton, Federalist No. 70, 354–61.

6. Alexander Hamilton, Federalist No. 36, in Hamilton, Madison, and Jay, *The Federalist Papers*, 169–75.

7. Alexander Hamilton, Federalist No. 39, in Hamilton, Madison, and Jay, *The Federalist Papers*, 189–94

8. John Locke, *Second Treatise on Civil Government*, in Michael Morgan, ed., *Classics of Moral and Political Theory*, 765–87 (Indianapolis, IN: Hackett Publishing Co., 1992), Book II, ch. 14.

9. Hamilton, Federalist No. 70, 354–61.

10. Ibid.

11. Randolph, "Second Day of Convention," ch. 1.

12. Ibid., 123–24.

13. Hamilton, Federalist No. 70, 354–61.

14. Alexander Hamilton, Federalist No. 23, in Hamilton, Madison, and Jay, *The Federalist Papers*, 111–15.

15. Hamilton, Federalist No. 70, 365–70.

16. Alexander Hamilton, Federalist No. 74, in Hamilton, Madison, and Jay, *The Federalist Papers*, 376–77.

17. Hamilton, Federalist No. 23, in Hamilton, Madison, and Jay, *The Federalist Papers*, 111–15.

18. Thomas Schelling, "Hamilton and Emergency Power," *Journal of Strategy and Conflict*, 18 (1960), 34–36.

19. Edward Samuel Corwin, Randall Walton Bland, Theodore T. Hindson, and J. W. Peltason, *The President: Office and Powers, 1787–1984: History and Analysis of Practice and Opinion* (New York: New York University Press, 1984), 201–3.

20. Alexander Hamilton, Federalist No. 34, in Hamilton, Madison, and Jay, *The Federalist Papers*, 159–64.

21. Hamilton, Federalist No. 28, in Hamilton, Madison, and Jay, *The Federalist Papers*, 134–37.

22. Ibid.

23. Locke, *Second Treatise on Civil Government*, ch. 14.

24. Hamilton, Federalist No. 70, in Hamilton, Madison, and Jay, *The Federalist Papers*, 356–62.

25. Ibid.

26. Other Anti-Federalists who supported Randolph's position included Patrick Henry, George Clinton, George Mason, and Eldridge Gerry. Farrand, *The Records of the Federal Convention of 1787*, 20–24.

27. Even Madison agreed with Hamilton that executive power should be consolidated into a single person. Farrand, *The Records of the Federal Convention of 1787*, 20–24.

28. Richard Henry Lee, Anti-Federalist No. 69, in Herbert J. Storing and Murray Dry, *The Complete Anti-Federalist*, 115–17 (Chicago: University of Chicago Press, 1981).

29. George Clinton, Anti-Federalist No. 67, in Storing and Dry, *The Complete Anti-Federalist*, 75–79.

30. Ibid.

31. Cato, Anti-Federalist Paper No. 10, in Storing and Dry, *The Complete Anti-Federalist*, 38–40.

32. Tamony, "Anti-Federalist Paper," in Storing and Dry, *The Complete Anti-Federalist*, 145–46.

33. Lee, Anti-Federalist No. 69, 115–17.

34. Ibid.

35. Recalling chapter 1, specifically when I discussed that Rousseau called for a specific duration of time for emergency power usage and that Aristotle's explicit model of emergency power is elaborated in the Roman model used during the Republic era.

36. Lee, Anti-Federalist No. 69, 115–17.

37. Clinton, Anti-Federalist No. 67, 75–79.

38. Ibid.

39. Lee, Anti-Federalist No. 69, 115–17.

40. Clinton, Anti-Federalist No. 67, 75–79.

41. Patrick Henry, at the Virginia Convention in 1788, in Ralph Louis Ketcham, ed., *The Anti-Federalist Papers; And, the Constitutional Convention Debates*, 213–14 (New York: New American Library, 1986).

42. Ibid.

43. Ibid.

44. Ibid.

45. Thomas Paine, *Common Sense* (Mineola, NY: Dover Thrift Editions, 1997), 31–32.

46. One could argue, based on an interpretation of the *Necessary and Proper* clause in conjunction with the enumerated powers of Article I, that Congress also has some inherent powers. For example, in *McCullough v. Maryland Marshall* the Supreme Court declared that Congress has the authority to create a national bank because it is a necessary and proper function of Congress's power to levy taxes. In other words, if Congress can levy taxes, then, inherently, it must have the power to put the money somewhere, that is, a bank.

47. Locke, *Second Treatise on Civil Government*, ch. 14, 765–67.

48. Ibid.

49. Charles Thach, *The Creation of the Presidency, 1775–1789: A Study in Constitutional History* (Baltimore, MD: Johns Hopkins University Press, 1922, 1969), 21–30.

50. U.S. Constitution, Article II, sec. I.

51. Steven Calabresi, "Advice to the Next Conservative President of the United States," *Harvard Journal of Law and Public Policy* 24, pt. 2 (Spring 2001): 369–80.

52. "Executive Discretion and the Congressional Defense of Statutes," *Yale Law Journal* 92, no. 6 (May 1983): 970–1000, 973.

53. Ibid., 973–74.

54. Michael Herz, "Imposing Unified Executive Branch Statutory Interpretation," *Cardozo Law Review* 15, no. 1–2 (October 1993): 219–20.

55. *Bowsher v. Synar*, 478 U.S. 714 (1986).

56. *Home Building and Loan Association v. Blaisdell*, 290 U.S. 398 (1934).

57. Corwin, *The President*, 201–4.

58. Ibid., 201–3.

59. U.S. Constitution, Article II.

60. Farrand, *The Records of the Federal Convention of 1787*, 65–70.

61. Corwin, *The President*, 201–4.

62. Ibid., 202.

63. Farrand, *The Records of the Federal Convention of 1787*, 65–70.

64. Ibid., 65–70.

65. Pierce Butler, "Papers from the Constitutional Convention 1787, Second Day of Convention," in Farrand, *The Records of the Federal Convention of 1787*, 22–25.

66. Randolph Gerry, "Papers from the Constitutional Convention 1787, Second Day of Convention," in Farrand, *The Records of the Federal Convention of 1787*, 20–21.

67. See Richard E. Neustadt, *Presidential Power and the Modern Presidents: The Politics of Leadership from Roosevelt to Reagan* (New York: Free Press, 1990); Louis Fisher, *Presidential War Power* (Lawrence: University Press of Kansas, 2004). Both scholars argue that emergency power is a shared power between Congress and the presidency.

68. Ibid., 92.

Chapter Three

George Washington's and Thomas Jefferson's Interpretations and Applications of Executive Emergency Power

In its infancy the United States faced an emergency; it was not spared from the disasters and misfortune that plagued previous civilizations. As such, in this chapter I examine two early and critical interpretations of executive emergency power at the founding of the nation: George Washington and Thomas Jefferson. Because executive emergency power is not explicitly stated in the Constitution, in order to understand it we must examine how early presidents who were contemporaries of the framers interpreted such power and, therefore, demonstrated the earliest applications of executive emergency power in the United States. In both cases I examine presidential rhetoric and declarations to show their interpretations of executive emergency power, and in so doing I draw connections back to Hamilton's argument for the implicit schema of executive emergency power.

GEORGE WASHINGTON'S CONCEPTION OF EXECUTIVE EMERGENCY POWER

In examining the presidency of Washington I focus on his support for Federalist/Hamiltonian ideas of emergency powers, his use of such powers in response to the Whiskey Rebellion, the Indian War in the Northwest Territory, and the public's reactions to his behavior. In 1794 militant opposition to a national excise tax on the production of whiskey arose in several parts of the country, particularly the western counties of Pennsylvania. The tax was a

product of Secretary of Treasury Alexander Hamilton's idea to collect reve-
nue for the federal government in the form of an excise tax.[1] According to
scholars, the initial public response to the tax was "unfriendly" and "discouraging" because Americans simply did not want to pay a tax on what was, for
some, a livelihood.[2] Further, as a major commodity in western Pennsylvania
at the time, whiskey was also used in place of money for purchasing and
trading goods. Pennsylvanians, however, had avoided paying the whiskey tax
ever since it was first levied in 1791 by avoiding and intimidating the collec-
tors to the point that they stopped coming to Pennsylvania.[3]

Nonetheless, in the summer of 1794 resistance to the tax turned into
defiance. In response, a federal marshal and excise inspector were forced to
flee western Pennsylvania in July, and for two weeks radical oratory, threats
to drive out all federal authority from Pittsburgh, and occasional acts of
violence agitated the region.[4] Dissenters refusing to pay the new excise tax
began to meet in Pittsburgh. In order to deal with these dissenters, President
Washington told Hamilton that "I have no hesitation in declaring, if the
evidence is clear and unequivocal, that I shall, however reluctantly I exercise
them [emergency powers], exert all the legal powers with which the executive is invested to check so daring and unwarrantable a spirit."[5]

With a rebellion burgeoning, the incumbent President Washington would
be hard pressed not to ignore the matter. In fact, the newly elected first
president would quickly have to breathe life into the presidential power to
"take Care that the Laws be faithfully executed."[6] Therefore, in response to
the Whiskey Rebellion, President Washington issued a stern proclamation on
August 7, 1794. However, Hamilton, not acting under the order of Washington, drafted the proclamation; in fact, according to Forrest McDonald and
Edward Corwin, not only did Washington never instruct Hamilton to draft
the proclamation, but Hamilton did so secretively and distributed the order
without the president's knowledge.[7]

Hamilton urged the president to proclaim concerns about the "irregular
proceedings of the rebels," who were holding antigovernment meetings in
Pittsburgh. In addition, Hamilton advised Washington to call for such meetings to be disbanded, thus "warning all persons to desist from similar proceedings and manifesting an intention to put the laws in force against such
offenders."[8] Washington did sign the proclamation on September 15 and
immediately sent it to Secretary of State Thomas Jefferson for his signature.
In the proclamation the president demanded that all the rebels "disperse and
retire peaceably to their respective bodies" and warned "all persons whom-
soever against aiding, abetting, or comforting the perpetuators of the treasonable acts."[9] Washington declared, "The Constitution and laws must strictly
govern," but, he observed, "the employing of the regular troops avoided if it
be possible to effect order without their aid; otherwise there would be a cry at

once [public]." Washington then concluded that, with this proclamation, "the cat is let out; we now see for what purpose an army was raised."[10]

Following the proclamation Washington called on the governors of Pennsylvania, New Jersey, Maryland, and Virginia to supply a militia army to put down the rebellion. In all, the Washington administration prepared an army of fifteen thousand troops to suppress the rebels.[11] He feared rumors circulating that Pennsylvania may secede from the Union or seek the aid of Great Britain;[12] newspapers in Philadelphia were growing sympathetic toward the rebels, as they feared the might of the federal government was "overbearing" and unchecked: "Shall Pennsylvania be converted into a human slaughter house because the dignity of the United States will not admit conciliatory measures? Shall torrents of blood be spilled to support an odious excise system?"[13] In response to such criticism, the Washington administration worried that the situation was getting out of control and that the only safe recourse was for the federal government to assert itself by enforcing the law.

The governors complied with Washington's request, and in September an army of thirteen thousand troops assembled in Harrisburg, Pennsylvania. It promptly marched into western Pennsylvania with Washington himself in command—the first and only time a sitting president has led American troops onto the literal battlefield. In the face of a Washington-led army, the rebellion dissolved. Although the rebellion ended quickly and with minimal combat, the president emphasized the importance of swift executive action in response to insurrections. He remarked to Congress on November 19, 1794, that "the prosperity and peace of the United States rests on the solid foundations, by furnishing an additional proof that the true principles of government and liberty must be designed and enforcing to protect and defend the Constitution."[14] Thus, he advocated Hamilton's theory of executive emergency power, in which executive prerogative determines when and how to exercise emergency power and in which power is inherent through the Constitution, lawfully granted to an executive under authority given to him in Article II. Further, during crisis it is necessary for government to assume more power so as to uphold and protect the state from grave harm or injury.

Later, scholars would note that Washington's actions, which were "vigorous" and "quick to reaction," established for future presidents the presidential interpretation to follow in response to an emergency.[15] Therefore, I argue that in the very first incidence of emergency in the United States, President Washington confirmed a pro-Hamiltonian, Lockean view of presidential emergency powers: that emergency power is an inherent power, used to dispel insurrections with the intent of preserving the Union and peace. Though, in this instance, Washington was simply enforcing the law, his interpretation still clearly demonstrates how the president, not Congress or the courts, uses emergency power.

A second instance of internal insurrection occurred during Washington's presidency, when he had to respond to and manage the Native Americans living in present-day Ohio. Upon taking office Washington considered the threat of the native tribes in the Northeast area as a major concern for the nation, partly because of skirmishes between these tribes and colonizing settlers along the Ohio Valley.[16] Even though in 1789 the United States did not have a standing army, Washington pursued military action against the natives, and according to David Currie, he would use the state of emergency as justification to push Congress to create a standing army.[17] As Currie stated, "While Washington did consider his powers to command the army to be limited, or narrow, this did not stop him from believing he had the right to command the army."[18] The way in which Washington handled the Whiskey Rebellion made evident his interpretation of emergency power—as an inherent power. He reinforced this interpretation when he used the natives' hostility in Ohio to support his claim of a national emergency, thus creating a crisis that then would require him to use emergency powers.

The native hostilities in Ohio gave President Washington the opportunity to push Congress for an army, and because he had both prestige and public support to combat the crisis, he was able to secure a victory: in late 1789 Congress approved the continued existence of a "small army."[19] It also gave the president power to "call on the state militias as he may judge necessary" and to "protect settlers against the hostile incursions of the Indians."[20] During the congressional debate over whether to grant such authorizations Representative Madison argued in support of the president's power to respond to national crises, stating, "by the Constitution, the President has the power of employing these troops in the protection of those parts, which he thinks requires them most."[21] Scholars have remarked that Madison's words echoed Washington's belief that the president should have "the power to deal with crises as he saw fit."[22]

With the approval of Congress to "command the army and militias," Washington pursued action against the native tribes. In October of 1789 President Washington ordered Arthur St. Clair, the governor of the Northwest Territory, to mobilize twelve hundred militiamen and to "launch punitive" attacks and operations against the natives living in Wabash and Illinois. Realizing that twelve hundred soldiers was insufficient to handle the Indian attacks and insurrections, a few months later Washington requested that the "standing army" increase to fifteen hundred and be maintained at that number indefinitely, that this should be the size of the U.S. standing army, in addition to militiamen "call ups."[23]

By the summer of 1790 Washington had decided that war was the only solution to the native presence in the Ohio valley. He ordered General Josiah Harmar and Governor St. Clair to organize a "punitive expedition into Indian territory to destroy bandits who were harassing settlements and apply pressure for a peace agreement."[24] According to military historian Richard Kohn, Washington would soon expand his aims to include "fielding an army of 2,000 troops, and to have the army attack major villages of the Ohio tribes, and to construct a permanent garrison to block any ties to Britain."[25] Kohn said that "the two-prong expedition fully committed the military, political, and moral prestige of the United States government, all without direct consent from Congress."[26] Although Washington did inform Congress about the general scope of the "Indian problems" in order to justify increasing the size of the army, scholars note that he never "sought authority from Congress for his plan" to drive deep into the Ohio territory.[27]

Even though the offensive was met with disaster, according to historians, Washington continued to work to defeat the Ohio tribes.[28] In order to secure victory, he formally sought more troops in a December 8, 1790, speech, in which he encouraged Congress to "provide more troops in order to protect the NW territory from the hostilities of the Ohio tribes."[29] There was minor dissent to the president's plans, according to Washington biographer John Bailey, but news of Indian massacres on the frontier would come to override any opposition.[30]

With the larger army, Washington ordered continued attacks on the Ohio tribes, who rigorously fought back.[31] John Slaughter wrote, "The Indians resilience is most noted by their surprise attack on November 4th, in which St. Clair's army was completely destroyed." The native attack, according to Slaughter, was the "most devastating" American military defeat to date, including those at Brandywine or Bunker Hill during the Revolution.[32]

The defeat in the fall of 1791 "echoed" around the nation's capital, harming Washington's administration. The news stunned Congress, which worried about the future of the American military and its leadership.[33] Congress feared that the presidential administration did not know how to manage the war, was forming poor strategy, and demonstrated blatantly "failed leadership."[34] However, the Washington administration, like future administrations, would not idly allow critics to assault their actions; instead, Washington instructed Secretary of War Henry Knox to draft a new war policy immediately.[35] Washington did not seek any authorization from Congress in the continued pursuit against the Indian tribes; rather, he "informed" Congress of his intentions and strategy to defeat the Indians.[36] His strategy included, yet again, increasing the size of the army, tripling military expenditures, and drafting a new offensive strategy, none of which obtained formal Congressional approval.[37]

Jeffersonian Democrats in Congress feared that the president's behavior was conforming to Hamiltonian ideas about the powers of the presidency and that Washington's actions could result in the United States adopting the "British military system," in which the Crown dictates completely the actions of the army without legislative approval.[38] Scholars Bailey and Corwin agreed that, at this time Hamiltonian "ideas were winning" in shaping the presidency, especially as it pertained to emergency powers.[39] Jefferson's argument resonated with many Americans, who were dissatisfied with the administration's "mishandling" of the war. Regardless, Congress did not impede the president's actions;[40] indeed, it did not limit any of Washington's actions during the crisis.

Consequently, armed with a larger force, Washington instructed General Anthony Wayne and Governor St. Clair to continue to pursue military action against the Ohio tribes, with Wayne leading the offensives. Wayne spent all of 1793 and early 1794 training his army for the upcoming combat.[41] Meanwhile, the Jeffersonian Democrats in Congress continued to criticize the administration's handling of the crisis and even "threatened to cut the size of the regular army in half"; however, no such action would ever take place. By August of 1794 Wayne began his offensives against the tribes. Unlike his predecessors, the general won decisive victories over the native forces, with his most famous at the Battle of Fallen Timbers, at which Wayne "permanently broke Indian military resistance."[42] Washington would finally achieve complete victory by the fall of 1794. Historians have remarked how these victories over the natives in Ohio "led to large scale settlement of the NW territory."[43]

Scholars have argued that Washington's actions set an example for future presidents faced with emergencies. Some scholars have claimed that the way Washington handled the Indian War, particularly with the increased standing army and the allocation of war funds, demonstrated his belief that the president needed to handle emergencies with "swiftness, assertiveness, and energy."[44] Scholars Christopher Yoo and Steven Calabresi agreed, stating that "Washington's use of power, and his initiative during the emergency exhibited a president willing to act swiftly and even unitarily in order to protect national security."[45] In all, Washington advocated and applied a Hamiltonian interpretation of executive emergency power, in which the president will act unilaterally, swiftly, and even at times without congressional approval or consent in order to combat an insurrection.

As mentioned earlier, not everyone agreed with Washington's handling of the Ohio tribes or the Whiskey Rebellion, however. Jeffersonian Democrats felt that, by acting alone, the president violated the Constitution. In hindsight, this criticism prompts the question of whether Jefferson maintained this position toward presidential authority or if, once he himself occupied the executive office, would behave similarly as Washington in response to crisis.

THOMAS JEFFERSON'S CONCEPTION OF EXECUTIVE EMERGENCY POWER

In the following analysis I examine the presidency of Thomas Jefferson, whom political scientists often cite—and mischaracterize—for his "limited presidential power." I will examine the purchase of the Louisiana Territory, which Jefferson considered to be of the utmost importance and national concern. I will evaluate why Jefferson bypassed Congress when purchasing the territory and how Jefferson's actions to purchase the land overtly favored Locke's concept of prerogative power.

Recent scholarship has suggested that Jefferson's presidency substantially contributed to our modern conception of what constitutes the American presidency by introducing the concept of Locke's prerogative power.[46] Scholars go on to suggest that Jefferson "advanced the theory" of Locke's prerogative—that the president "could act outside the Constitution" to protect the national interest of the country in moments of great peril or crisis.[47] Further, though he was a strict constructionist, Jefferson did not agree wholly with the Federalist notion that emergency power was consistent with the formal powers of the presidency, as prescribed in Article II of the Constitution.[48] Thus, although at times his actions conflicted with the Constitution, Jefferson nonetheless saw the proper understanding of executive emergency power to be derived explicitly from Locke's principle of prerogative, which afforded the president the power to protect the Constitution and preserve the Union.[49] As I will show shortly, Jefferson's pursuit and purchase of the Louisiana Territory aptly demonstrates his understanding of executive emergency powers. With the Louisiana Purchase, the president would (1) act outside the boundaries of the Constitution, (2) appeal to the public for their approval and support in exchange for his unconstitutional actions, and (3) test the legitimacy of his actions through national elections and, thus, strongly support the "will of the majority."[50]

Jefferson's attitude toward emergency as well as executive power was mostly the by-product of lessons learned while serving as the governor of Virginia during the Revolution. When British troops had American troops retreating, Jefferson formally constructed his ideas about executive power.[51] He would "appreciate matching the executive's powers to its responsibilities," the meaning of which became clear through discussions he had with colleagues regarding proposals for Virginia's new constitution after the Revolution, in which he argued that "executive power did not reach as far as the British Crown's prerogatives" but did at least include other powers not judicial or legislative in nature.[52] Although Jefferson did not elaborate on the extent of these powers, by analyzing his response to crisis we may be able to determine with greater certainty whether he thought executive emergency power was more limited in scope than his predecessor Washington believed—and whether it was limited in scope in comparison to Hamilton's theory of executive emergency power.

Furthermore, Jefferson urged his colleagues and friends to support and draft a constitution that would create an independent executive branch, stating, "I think it very material to separate in the hands of Congress the Executive and Legislative powers."[53] He continued, "the want of it has been the source of much evil than we have ever experienced from any other cause."[54] Thus, although Jefferson had a profound respect for separating the powers of government, whether he intended for the executive to have broad power during emergency remains unclear.

Scholars have suggested that Jefferson envisioned emergency powers to be "extra-legal," or outside the boundaries of the Constitution.[55] Jefferson's view of emergency power and whether it would be in the Constitution, scholars claim, contrasted with the Federalists' argument to construe emergency powers as inherently in Article II of the Constitution (Hamilton's idea). Rather, Jefferson favored a "pure form" of Locke's idea of executive prerogative power in times of emergency.[56] Bailey suggested that Jefferson perceived "prerogative" power to be completely external to the Constitution and that this view was the closest to Locke's idea of prerogative power.[57]

Jefferson held a slightly different view about the president's powers during an emergency. Instead of suggesting that emergency powers were implicit in the Constitution, he believed that such powers were not in the Constitution whatsoever. Therefore, according to Jefferson, the powers of the presidency to act with discretion and according to the executive's prerogative during an emergency were completely outside of the boundaries of the Constitution. However, the president did have emergency power, but such power was not explicitly stated within the Constitution. Instead, in order to determine the constitutionality of emergency power, Jefferson would argue that the public would determine the constitutionality of presidential emergency power by checking the president's prerogative by either reelecting or voting out the president during the next presidential election cycle. According to Jefferson, if the public reelected the president, then his use of emergency powers were constitutional, and vice versa would be equally true. Thus, although Jefferson was a strong defender of Locke's prerogative power, he agreed with the Federalists' argument that the powers of the presidency are expanded during emergency. For Jefferson, the power of prerogative lies outside the Constitution, and this contrasted with Hamilton's claim that executive emergency powers are inherent to the Constitution.

As a case in point, although the purchase of the Louisiana Territory constituted a major crisis for President Jefferson to oversee, it also provided the opportunity for him to implement his beliefs regarding presidential prerogative and emergency powers. Because controlling the Mississippi River and securing its trade routes was vital to America's long-term economic prosperity, Jefferson believed that the United States needed to claim the territories around the Mississippi, which, at the time, France controlled.[58] As such, he saw that because controlling the Mississippi delta and tributaries were critical to America's future, seizing that area was akin to an emergency.[59] American settlers both demanded to control the trade waters and sought to cultivate the rich fertile land surrounding it. President Jefferson was convinced that purchasing the Louisiana Territory was not only of great national interest economically but was also vital to national security because hostile neighbors controlled the fertile land surrounding the Mississippi River.[60]

Exports using the Mississippi had to pass through Spanish-controlled New Orleans, and without access to the Mississippi, transporting goods back east through the Ohio Valley took much longer. The British Empire, American's primary trading partner, controlled the Atlantic with the Royal Navy, and France, America's secondary trading partner, controlled most of the land to the west. As a resultant, antagonistic neighbors surrounded Americans, who were dependent on trading with those hostile elements.[61] Cognizant of both the vital economic interest of trading with Britain and France as well as national security, Jefferson was confronted with a unique situation: he had to figure out a way to maintain economic ties with two antagonistic neighbors while also maintaining national security.[62] For Jefferson, the best solution was to convince France to sell the Louisiana Territory to the United States.[63]

So in 1802 President Jefferson sent an envoy to Paris to negotiate a deal to purchase the territory, specifically New Orleans (by this time Spain had transferred control back to France), and West Florida (portions of present-day Mississippi, Alabama, and parts of Florida and Louisiana). A secret congressional allocation of money, not to exceed $2 million, financially supported the envoy.[64]

When the American ministers arrived in Paris, they received an extraordinary gift. Napoleon, in need of financial means to continue to wage his wars with Britain, was very willing to sell the territory—and not only New Orleans; he was now willing to sell all of the Louisiana Territory.[65] Initially, Ambassador Robert R. Livingston was dubious of Napoleon's offer, but by the time the second U.S. envoy arrived, which included James Monroe, the Americans quickly agreed to the deal. They settled on the amount of $15 million, which far exceeded their limited $2 million Congressional allocation.[66] In all, the Louisiana Purchase doubled the size of the United States and gave the country permanent control over the Mississippi and New Orleans. Perhaps most importantly, however, it removed France and Spain as "serious threats to American national security in the West."[67] When Jefferson heard of the deal, he wrote in a letter to his son-in-law that "this removes from us the greatest source of danger to our peace."[68]

Jefferson's purchase of the Louisiana Territory defused a potentially hazardous situation, thereby avoiding war with France and Spain while simultaneously doubling the size of the nation.[69] The purchase would help Jefferson accomplish three primary goals: (1) conquer the western territory without war, (2) open settlement to the west by controlling the Mississippi, and (3) maintain the United States' neutral status.[70]

Jefferson's major hurdle in purchasing the territory was whether or not the action would be declared constitutional. In fact, scholars noted that Jefferson did not initially believe that the Constitution permitted the "acquisition of new territory or its incorporation into the Union as new states" (the Constitution does not have any provision within it providing for the addition of new territory).[71] Scholars have also suggested that Jefferson doubted whether new territories could become states; the Constitution does provide for adding new states, upon congressional approval, although it prohibits the formation of new states beyond the borders of existing states.[72] Scholars have argued that this latter provision was the cause of Jefferson's concerns that the prohibition applied to the "creation" of new states from the territory of existing states. For this reason, he sought legal advice from Attorney General Levi Lincoln, who agreed with Jefferson's concerns; their first solution was to enlarge the existing states to include the Louisiana Purchase.[73]

Secretary of State Albert Gallatin advised the president that his administration's position could find refuge in the earlier Neutrality Proclamation, which was approved during the Washington administration.[74] Gallatin argued that the nation had a right to (1) acquire new territory and (2) sanction the acquisition whenever that acquisition comes by treaty. Further, whenever a territory has been acquired, Congress should have the power to either admit the territory into the Union as a new state or make regulations for the government of such territory.[75]

Scholars have demonstrated that Gallatin argued that the federal government should have powers that "may extend" beyond those explicitly stated in the Constitution.[76] These powers, Gallatin suggested to the president, would be heightened during an emergency.[77] Finally, he would conclude that the citizenry had implicitly "delegated authority" over territory acquisition to the national government by "vesting" it with "powers to make war and treaties, and govern the territories."[78]

Jefferson initially accepted Gallatin's reasoning, but once he learned of Monroe's success in brokering a deal with the French to buy the territory, his doubts regarding the constitutionality of acquiring new territory resurfaced. In a letter to John Dickinson (a Pennsylvanian Quaker and signer of the Constitution) in August of 1803, Jefferson stated, "our confederation is certainly confined to the limits established by the revolution. The general government has no powers but such as the Constitution has given it; and it has not given it a power of holding foreign territory, and still less incorporating it into the Union." Jefferson went on to confess that "an amendment to the Constitution seems necessary for this acquisition."[79]

Jefferson, however, believed that Congress and the citizenry held in check the presidential power of prerogative in relation to emergency. In a letter to Senator John Breckinridge of Kentucky, Jefferson stated, "The Executive in seizing the fugitive occurrence which so much advances the good of the country, have done an act beyond the Constitution. . . . The Legislature, in casting behind them metaphysical subtleties and risking themselves like faithful servants, must ratify and pay for it and throw themselves on their country for doing for them, unauthorized, what we know they would have done for themselves had they been in a situation to do it."[80] Thus, even though the nation's security depended on this transaction, Jefferson was nonetheless concerned that his use of emergency power in acquiring the territory was unconstitutional.[81] He did not agree with Hamilton, as did the other Anti-Federalists, that executive emergency powers were implicit in Article II of the Constitution. This view was consistent with Locke's principles of "prerogative power," in which executive prerogative determines when and how emergency powers are exercised and that power may or may not be an inherent constitutional power lawfully granted to the executive under authority given to him in Article II of the Constitution. Jefferson maintained that the American people, through their will of election, would determine whether his actions were unconstitutional. He stated, "We shall not be disavowed by the nation. . . . The people's act of indemnity will confirm and not weaken the Constitution, by more strongly marking out its lines."[82]

Then, in 1807, Jefferson's response to the infamous firing upon the *Chesapeake* further demonstrated how he justified emergency powers. British ships enforcing a blockade along the coast of Norfolk, Virginia, barred the *Chesapeake* from entering the waters and required the ship to leave the area. The *Chesapeake*, however, did not heed the British requests, and this led the British naval ship, the *Leopard*, to fire on the *Chesapeake*, killing several American sailors and leading to American hostages.[83]

In response to this skirmish, the American public was outraged and concerned about national security. President Jefferson acted quickly to assert American primacy over the waters and defend the coast, remarking, "Never since the Battle of Lexington have I saw this country in such a state of exasperation."[84] In response to the attack, he immediately ordered Secretary of State James Monroe to "demand" the British to disavow the deed, return all sailors taken hostage, and leave all U.S. waterways.[85] In addition, Jefferson deployed the Navy to "monitor" the Norfolk coast and ordered that additional military supplies be purchased to aid them.[86]

In 1810, in a letter to Senator Breckinridge, President Jefferson urged the senator to support the president's response, arguing that the American people would indemnify the president's actions through their representatives in Congress. In this letter, Jefferson addressed the question of whether "circumstances do not sometimes, occur, which make it a duty in office of high trust, to assume authorities beyond the law."[87] In answer to his own question, Jefferson stated, "A strict observance of the written laws is doubtless one of the high duties of a good citizen, but it is not the highest. The laws of necessity, of self-preservation, of saving our country when in danger, are of higher obligation. To lose our country by a scrupulous adherence to written law, would be to lose the law itself, with life, liberty, property and all those who are enjoying them with us, thus absurdly sacrificing the end to the means." As we can see, Jefferson believed that although the president is beholden to the strict observance to the law, the laws of "necessity, of self-preservation, of saving our country when in danger are of higher obligation."[88]

In order to determine whether Jefferson's actions were constitutional, either Congress would need to enact laws supporting his actions or it would need to rebuke his behavior. In response to the attacks of 1807 Congress adopted measures to denounce British naval hostilities, which scholars have argued was the beginning of laying the foundation for the War of 1812.[89]

In conclusion, Washington and Jefferson clearly disagree over the interpretation of executive emergency power. Washington applied Hamilton's theory of executive emergency power, or the Energy in the Executive approach, in which executive prerogative determines how and when to exercise executive emergency power and is an inherent constitutional power lawfully granted to an executive under authority given to him in Article II of the Constitution. Through it, the president acted swiftly, with the army, in order to disband the dissenters during the Whiskey Rebellion. Jefferson, however, when handling the settler issues in the early 1800s—unlike Washington's quick and assertive response—was torn as to what he could and could not do constitutionally. Jefferson presented an argument closely favoring Locke's theory of a pure prerogative power, in which executive prerogative power determines how and when to exercise emergency power and may go beyond the scope of law. Jefferson becomes increasingly interesting in his writings, where he clearly suggests that executive emergency power is potentially beyond the scope of law, but as evidenced earlier, Jefferson wrote that elections legitimize or de-legitimate whether an executive prerogative to exercise emergency power was lawful.

This finding is supported when we further examine how Jefferson handled the attacks on the *Chesapeake* naval ship. Jefferson, as demonstrated in this chapter, acted without congressional approval but wrote that he believed his actions, unless the people (who are sovereign) determined his actions to be otherwise, were constitutional. According to Jefferson, in order to know if the people supported Jefferson's actions as constitutional, they would reelect him. In hindsight we know that Jefferson won a landslide election in 1804, thus confirming for Jefferson that his actions during the *Chesapeake* crisis were constitutional.

With just these two presidents, both contemporaries, we are able to see how executive emergency power is open to presidential interpretation. In the chapters that follow, I will investigate how presidents following Washington and Jefferson would support either Washington's and Hamilton's interpretation of executive emergency power, in which an executive prerogative is an inherent power within Article II of the Constitution, or Jefferson's, in which the power is wholly an executive prerogative, potentially beyond the scope of law, with the public determining whether presidential actions will be deemed constitutional.

NOTES

1. Alexander Hamilton to George Washington, September 1, 1792, and Hamilton to John Jay, September 3, 1792, in Harold Coffin Syrett, ed., *The Papers of Alexander Hamilton* (New York: Columbia University Press, 1961), 316–17.

2. Drawn from several perspectives. See John Howe, "Republican Thought and the Political Violence of the 1790s," *American Quarterly* 19, no. 2 (Summer 1967): 147–65; Marshall Smelser, "The Jacobin Phrenzy: Federalism and the Menace of Liberty, Equality, and Fraternity," *The Review of Politics* 13, no. 4 (October 1951): 457–82; J. Wendell Knox, *Conspiracy in American Politics, 1787–1815* (New York: Arno Press, 1972).

3. Forrest McDonald, *Presidency of George Washington* (Lawrence: University Press of Kansas, 1974), 145–47.

4. Henry M. Brackenridge, *History of the Western Insurrection, 1794* (New York: Arno Press, 1969), 79–151; Leland D. Baldwin, *Whiskey Rebels: The Story of a Frontier Uprising* (Pittsburgh: University of Pittsburgh Press, 1939), 129–71.

5. Richard Kohn, "The Washington Administration's Decision to Crush the Whiskey Rebellion," *Journal of American History* 59, no. 3 (December 1972): 567–84; Baldwin, *Whiskey Rebels*, 185; Alexander Hamilton to George Washington, September 1, 1792, and Hamilton to John Jay, September 3, 1792, Syrett, *The Papers of Alexander Hamilton*, 316–17.

6. U.S. Constitution, Article II, sec. 9.

7. McDonald, *Presidency of George Washington*; Edward Samuel Corwin, Randall Walton Bland, Theodore T. Hindson, and J. W. Peltason, *The President: Office and Powers, 1787–1984: History and Analysis of Practice and Opinion* (New York: New York University Press, 1984).

8. Ibid.

9. McDonald, *The Presidency of George Washington*, 145–47.

10. "Proclamation," from John C. Fitzpatrick, ed., *The Writings of George Washington from the Original Manuscript Sources, 1745–1799*, 39 vols. (Washington, DC, 1944), 15–20. Although Hamilton wrote the declaration, Washington did indeed sign and, thus, take authorship.

11. Steven R. Boyd, *The Whiskey Rebellion: Past and Present Perspectives* (Westport, CT: Greenwood Press, 1985), 122.

12. *Writings of George Washington*, 16–18.

13. Taken from Thomas Slaughter, *The Whiskey Rebellion: Frontier Epilogue to the American Revolution* (New York: Oxford Press, 1986). Originally appeared in "Claypoole's Mail," *Pittsburgh Gazette*, November 28, 1792.

14. McDonald, *The Presidency of George Washington*, 149.

15. Saikrishna B. Prakash and Michael D. Ramsey, "The Executive Power over Foreign Affairs," *Yale Law Journal* 111, no. 2 (November 2001): 299–300.

16. "Errors of Government Towards the Indians," February 1792, in Fitzpatrick, ed., *The Writings of George Washington*, vol. 31; Glenn Phelps, *George Washington and American Constitutionalism* (Lawrence: University Press of Kansas, 1993), 44–46.

17. David Currie, "Rumors of War: Presidential and Congressional War Powers," *University of Chicago Law Review* 67, no. 1 (2000): 1–40, 2.

18. Ibid., 5–12.

19. Richard Kohn, *Eagle and Sword: The Federalists and the Creation of the Military Establishment in America, 1783–1802* (New York: Free Press, 1975), 92–93.

20. Ibid., 94.

21. James Madison, *The Papers of James Madison* (Chicago: University of Chicago Press, 1962).

22. Phelps, *George Washington and American Constitutionalism*, 44–46.
    Currie, "Rumors of War: Presidential and Congressional War Powers," 2–5.

23. Kohn, *Eagle and Sword*, 94–115.

24. Ibid., 95.

25. Ibid., 97.

26. Ibid., 94–115, 98.

27. Phelps, *George Washington and American Constitutionalism*, 103.

28. Ibid., 103.

29. Baldwin, *Whiskey Rebels*, 71–72.

30. Jeremy Bailey, *Thomas Jefferson and Executive Power* (Cambridge, New York: Cambridge University Press, 2007).

31. Ibid., 109–12.

32. Slaughter, *The Whiskey Rebellion*, 23–26.

33. Ibid., 114–16.

34. Ibid., 116–17,

35. Abraham Sofaer, *War, Foreign Affairs and Constitutional Power: The Origins* (Cambridge, MA: Ballinger Publishing Co., 1976), 65–71.

36. Ibid., 65–68.

37. Ibid., 68–71.

38. Corwin, Bland, Hindson, and Peltason, *The President*.

39. Ibid., 45.

40. Kohn, *Eagle and Sword*, 116.

41. Ibid., 117.

42. Ibid., 118.

43. Ibid., 119.

44. Ibid.

45. Steven G. Calabresi and Christopher S. Yoo, *The Unitary Executive: Presidential Power from Washington to Bush* (New Haven, CT: Yale University Press, 2008).

46. Dumas Malone, *Jefferson the President: The First Term, 1801–1805* (Boston: Little, Brown, 1970), and *Jefferson the President: The Second Term, 1805–1809* (Boston: Little, Brown, 1974).

47. Bailey, *Thomas Jefferson and Executive Power*, 15–22.

48. Noble E. Cunningham, *The Process of Government under Jefferson* (Princeton, NJ: Princeton University Press, 1978), 13–17.

49. McDonald, *The Presidency of Thomas Jefferson*, 36–38.

50. Gary Schmitt, "Jefferson and Executive Power: Revisionism and the Revolution of 1800," *Publius* 17, no. 2 (Spring 1987): 7–25.

51. Malone, *Jefferson the President: The First Term*, and *Jefferson the President: The Second Term*.

52. Bailey, *Thomas Jefferson and Executive Power*, 28, 15–22.

53. Cunningham, *The Process of Government under Jefferson*, 13–17.

54. Bailey, *Thomas Jefferson and Executive Power*, 15–22.

55. Ibid., 28.

56. Ibid., 28–29.

57. Bailey, *Thomas Jefferson and Executive Power*.

58. Malone, *Jefferson the President: The First Term*, and *Jefferson the President: The Second Term*, 285–90.

59. Malone, *Jefferson the President: The Second Term*, 286–87.

60. Ibid., 287–89.

61. Ibid., 312–13.

62. Gary Lawson and Guy Seidman, *The Constitution of Empire: Territorial Expansion and American Legal History* (New Haven, CT: Yale University Press, 2004), 3–7.

63. Malone, *Jefferson the President: The First Term*, and *Jefferson the President: The Second Term*, 285–86.

64. Lawson and Seidman, *The Constitution of Empire*, 3–7.

65. Ibid.

66. Malone, *Jefferson the President: The First Term*, and *Jefferson the President: The Second Term*, 290–300.

67. Thomas Jefferson, Letter from Jefferson to Spencer Roane, September 16, 1801, in Thomas Jefferson, *The Writings of Thomas Jefferson*, edited by Paul Leicester Ford, vol. 140 (New York: G. P. Putnam's Sons, 1892–1899), 59–61.

68. Thomas Jefferson, Letter from Jefferson to John Dickinson, December 19, 1801, in Jefferson, *The Writings of Thomas Jefferson*, 63–65.

69. Ibid.

70. Jefferson, Letter from Jefferson to Spencer Roane, September 16, 1801.

71. Malone, *Jefferson the President: The First Term*, and *Jefferson the President: The Second Term*, 285–91.

72. Malone, *Jefferson the President: The Second Term*, 286, 287–89.

73. Lawson and Seidman, *The Constitution of Empire*, 3–7.

74. Malone, *Jefferson the President: The First Term*, and *Jefferson the President: The Second Term*, 285–95,

75. Ibid., and Lawson and Seidman, *The Constitution of Empire*, 3–7.

76. Malone, *Jefferson the President: The First Term*, and *Jefferson the President: The Second Term*, 285–91.

77. Malone, *Jefferson the President: The Second Term*, 290–93.

78. Lawson and Seidman, *The Constitution of Empire*, 3–7.

79. Jefferson to Dickinson, August 9, 1803, in Jefferson, *The Writings of Jefferson*, 302.

80. Jefferson to Breckinridge, August 12, 1803, in Jefferson, *The Writings of Jefferson*, 242.

81. Lawson and Seidman, *The Constitution of Empire*, 3–7.

82. Jefferson to Breckinridge, August 18, 1803, in Jefferson, *The Writings of Jefferson*, 242.

83. Lawson and Seidman, *The Constitution of Empire*, 3–7; Malone, *Jefferson the President: The First Term*, and *Jefferson the President: The Second Term*, 175–82.

84. Lawson and Seidman, *The Constitution of Empire*, 177–81.

85. Ibid., 181–83

86. Ibid., 182–84.

87. Ibid., 182.

88. Letter from Jefferson to John Breckinridge, 1810, in Jefferson, *The Writings of Jefferson*, 242.

89. Ibid.

Chapter Four

Presidents James Madison's and Andrew Jackson's Interpretations and Applications of Executive Emergency Power

In this chapter I explore the presidencies of James Madison and Andrew Jackson in order to demonstrate their interpretations of executive emergency power, as seen through their rhetoric as well as critical domestic emergencies faced during their presidencies. Both presidential interpretations are critical in understanding executive emergency power because, like their predecessors, both offer contemporaneous yet divergent interpretations of the power. Thus, they provide a way to understand not only the meaning of executive emergency power at the founding of the nation but also the impacts of this power on early liberal democratic thinking.

Madison, while combating the first major war in the republic's history, the War of 1812, provides substantial evidence of his interpretation of executive emergency power. Conversely, Jackson, although he does not declare war, actively pursued warlike actions against the Native Americans. As such, by examining both applications of emergency power we can further help delineate American conceptions of executive emergency power as the nation began to establish itself as a sovereign power.

JAMES MADISON AND EMERGENCY POWER

In the following section I examine President James Madison's writings to indicate his interpretation and exercise of executive emergency powers during the War of 1812. Specifically, I explore his words and actions in response to the emergency, his interpretation of executive emergency powers, and any actions taken after the emergency passed to reset Madison's emergency powers.

Madison's Interpretation of Emergency Power

President Madison—along with his words and actions in response to crisis during his presidency—offers a perspective and example to help us better understand fully the complex considerations that accompany executive emergency power. Both prior to and during his presidency, which encountered the crisis that resulted in the War of 1812, Madison believed that presidential power should be limited. In fact, in response to the overzealous Hamilton, Madison argued that, if Hamilton had his way, the presidency would devolve into a monarchy, especially if "there was incompetency of one legislature to regulate all the various objects belonging to the local governments [this] would evidently force a transfer of many of them to the executive department."[1] To prevent strength in the executive, according to Madison, meant increasing the powers of the legislature, even in times of crisis.

Madison was concerned that if the legislature did not sufficiently regulate all objects of its domain, "the increasing splendor and number of its [executive] prerogatives supplied by this source [incompetency of the legislature], might prove excitements to ambition too powerful for a sober execution of the executive plan, and consequently strengthen the pretext for a hereditary designation of magistrate."[2] We can gather from the long debate over presidential emergency powers that Madison clearly opposed the Hamiltonian position. He distrusted the nature of power and its corruptive elements if they are overly concentrated; consequently, he strongly advocated for limited presidential powers.

Because he understood that concentration of executive power would most likely occur during times of emergency, Madison worried about how the government responded to emergencies. In fact, in reply to Federalist paper No. 70, he stated that "foreign policy was not naturally a function of the executive"[3] and that "the tasks of foreign policy, declaring war, making treaties, and concluding peace, were among the highest acts of sovereignty of which the legislative power must at least be an integral and preeminent part of."[4] In other words, foreign policy and emergency powers should not be relegated solely to the realm of the executive. Instead, Madison asserted, the power to combat crisis and/or wage combat in foreign arenas must be a "legislative power."

At the very least, Madison averred, the legislature should play an "integral" part in foreign affairs and combating crisis; therefore, he asserted that emergency power should be a shared power, thus opposing Hamilton's position that emergency power rests inherently with the executive. Further, he also contested the larger Lockean concept of executive prerogative power, claiming, "to suggest executive emergency powers and foreign policy are within the proper definition of executive power is in theory an absurdity, and in practice a tyranny."[5] Based on these statements, concluding whether Madison advocated for an American model for exercising emergency power is unclear; rather, his words indicate a possible departure from other presidents advocating the American model. Instead, Madison might be advocating a model in which determining the how and when to exercise emergency power might be a shared power between the branches of government and only within the boundaries of explicit written constitutional provisions authorizing the how and when to exercise that power.

Madison and the War of 1812

As we've seen, the pre-presidential Madison robustly favored rigidly defining executive emergency powers and balancing them with legislative powers, and this view did not change dramatically after he became president. One might think that the War of 1812, a real emergency, would have altered Madison's views of his presidential authority in response to the crisis, but, in fact, it did not. Instead, his request to Congress in June of 1812, when he asked for a declaration of war, was precisely that: a very polite encouragement to engage with Britain. Historian Gaillard Hunt, a Madison biographer, described Madison's war leadership nicely: "The hour had come but the man was wanting. Not a scholar in governments ancient and modern, not an unimpressed writer of careful messages, but a robust leader to rally the people and unite them to fight was what the time needed, and this it did not find in Madison."[6] The fact that Madison did not change his view of emergency power during the lead-up to the War of 1812 has baffled many historians. Many presidents hold ideals that, when faced with the realities of necessity, alter and become tempered once they are in office. Scholars have questioned whether Madison was so committed to his position that emergency power was not the sole domain of the executive that he was willing to watch the republic lose a war simply because he believed that he alone should not hold the power to conduct that war. In order to better understand his position, however, we need to examine Madison's actions and rhetoric both before and during the War of 1812 to see how he applied his interpretation of emergency power.

The War of 1812 was the first significant emergency to confront the republic—although it was the second war against the British Empire, it was the United States' first conflict as an independent nation. Prior to Madison's presidency congressional Republicans had been concerned about British actions north of U.S. borders. In particular, British blockades had been impeding American and French trading in order to aid their war against the French.

The United States, especially congressional Republicans from the northern border states, wanted Britain to withdraw the trade restrictions and release any prisoners taken during the blockades. In response, Britain formally declared its policies in the matter as Orders in Council and Continental Decrees. Orders of Council were specific British King orders that outlined the British response to the American assertions regarding trade restrictions. A continental decree was a statement from the British King regarding foreign policy toward, in this case, another continent. Both measures specifically declared Britain's authority to construct a blockade and formally announced the latitudes of the Crown's foreign policy in relation to U.S. trade in North America with the French, Britain's enemy in war.[7] Republicans had hoped that Britain would withdraw or repeal the Orders of Council so in return, the United States would not entertain the idea of waging war with Britain.[8] However, the British never withdrew the Orders, and so the War Hawks, as Virginia Congressman John Randolph called members of Congress who advocated war in response to the British actions, pressured the new president to deal with the hostilities confronting the Northern borders. Madison, who agreed with the Hawks that the British actions were hostile and threatened U.S. trade interests, decided to support a declaration of war against Britain.

On June 1 Madison sent a secret message to Congress concerning Anglo-American relations.[9] He presented an organized indictment of Great Britain for acts "hostile to the United States." The British were charged with impressing American seamen; violating American waters; establishing illegal blockades, particularly the "sweeping system of blockades under the name of the Orders of Council"; employing a secret agent to controvert the Union; and "exerting" a "malicious" influence over the native tribes in the Northwest Territory.[10] Madison believed that all of these actions constituted an emergency for the United States, one that demanded action, and that this would lead to America declaring war against Britain.[11]

Some historians have suggested that as the first president to address and face such a crisis, Madison "would be required to lead the nation by inspiring them to up the popular cause." However, according to scholars, he "would not fare well at 'rallying the country' behind the war effort"[12] and that his "scholarly disposition made the engineer's tasks of war a challenge; his retiring personality made him wholly unsuited for the role of inspirational leader."[13] Thus, based on the historical accounts of his leadership style prior to and during the war, Madison maintained his pre-presidential interpretation of emergency power—that such power was not the sole domain of the executive. This might explain why he was such an "uninspiring leader" during the War of 1812.

Nonetheless, Madison did urge Congress to declare war against Britain. Historian David Hickey, a leading Madison biographer, has noted that Madison's message "echoed that of the Declaration of Independence, which was a reflection of the Republican view of a second war of independence necessary to end Britain's quasi-colonial control of North America and its seaways."[14] However, although Madison believed that Britain's continued aggression was hostile to the United States' prosperity and sovereignty, he was nonetheless deferential regarding the power of the executive. He did not want to overstep his executive authority, and as a result, he did not explicitly recommend a declaration of war, though the thrust of his message was quite clear: "We behold . . . on the side of Great Britain a state of war against the United States, and on the side of the United States, a state of peace towards Britain."[15]

Moreover, the fact that Madison encouraged Congress to declare war did not motivate him to become a successful commander in chief during the war. As Irving Bryant has shown, as president, Madison never controlled Congress—or even his own cabinet. His continual deference, based on his insistence that the president is not to wield unlimited power, even during war, made Madison a failure as a commander in chief. The repudiation of Madison by Congress and the press was so austere that in the spring of 1812, the congressional delegation from Mississippi declared, "the executive is much censured by all parties for the tardiness of its advances to meet the tug of war, and the tenure of Mr. Madison's continuance in the presidential chair, in my opinion, depends upon the success of our hostile preparations."[16] Yet the president, through his passivity, allowed America to lose the war, as Bryant went on to state, "Madison reigned, but he did not rule. . . . The war came, not because of the President, but despite him. The war came, not for any single reason, but from the interplay of many."[17]

His handling of the War of 1812—his decision to act only with Congressional consent—proved to be disastrous. Based on Madison's words stated earlier, concluding whether Madison advocated for an American model for exercising emergency power is unclear; rather, Madison's words indicate a possible departure from other presidents' who advocated the American model. Instead, Madison might be advocating a model in which determining the how and when to exercise emergency power might be a shared power between the branches of government and only within the boundaries of explicit written constitutional provisions authorizing the how and when to exercise that power.

Madison's restraint prompts us to examine the reality of weighing the needs of the nation during a time of war or emergency with philosophical ideals regarding the tenuous balance of governmental power, particularly executive power. We must ask ourselves, do we want a leader to do whatever it takes during an emergency to ensure we prevail? In this case Madison was true to his beliefs of limited presidential authority, even during an emergency. He followed the written law and pursued action against the British only after receiving a full declaration of war from Congress. His actions were completely constitutional; however, throughout the war his enthusiasm and leadership were missing. It is debatable whether his lack of leadership is attributable to being handicapped to lead the war effort because he did not believe the president should have the authority to wage war, because he did not feel that the war effort was a worthy endeavor, or perhaps because he simply was a weak leader.

Making sense of the complex issue of his poor leadership in a time of crisis is difficult; however, based on his own words and actions, we can conclude that Madison's belief that the president should not wage war alone may have hampered the army's ability to act quickly and decisively against the British invasion. For every action Madison pursued during the war, he always made sure to first receive congressional approval, and this may have delayed the response time during the crisis. There is no doubt that his actions followed the tenets of the Constitution explicitly; yet the outcome of the war was not successful. Thus, Madison's adherence to constitutionality may have jeopardized the fate of the nation.

Possibly the lesson learned from the Madison presidency is that a president must be bold, assertive, and decisive during a crisis, even if doing so means he must act without congressional approval; otherwise, the country may lose a war, or perhaps the next insurrection will be of such magnitude that the necessity to respond will not allow for any hesitation or deliberation before acting. This lesson becomes even more imperative when we examine the Civil War and Lincoln's actions to combat Southern rebels. During that crisis Lincoln did not wait for Congress to approve his actions but instead just acted. As a result, although the Civil War was immensely bloodier than the War of 1812, the Federal Army—and the Union—prevailed. Therefore, one cannot help but be grateful that Madison was not president during the Civil War. Through the contrast of these two wars and their attending presidents, we see how at times the need to preserve the Union can be at odds with the demand to maintain the written law as prescribed in the Constitution. In chapter 5 I will examine further Lincoln's actions during the Civil War, which provides the most pronounced example of this dilemma.

ANDREW JACKSON AND EXECUTIVE EMERGENCY POWER

I now move to discuss the presidency of Andrew Jackson and his policy of Indian removal in the early nineteenth century, examining Jackson's (1) interpretation of emergency power, (2) application of emergency power, and (3) reaction to the use of emergency power as well as how the Court reset such power.

Although recently some historians and biographers, particularly Jon Meachem, have reassessed Jackson's presidency, drafting more laudatory biographies of him that often focus on his appeals to the "people" and his outward interest in "reducing the national debt,"[18] these accounts also deemphasize the atrocities of his Indian removal policy. In respect to executive emergency power, therefore, addressing Jackson's policy toward Native Americans is important because (1) Jackson exerted his executive prerogative and pressured Congress to draft legislation in order to begin the removal of Indians, and (2) Jackson's removal of the Indians demonstrates that executive emergency power not only is limited to military insurrections or wars; it is also applicable to varying presidential prerogatives and, as noted throughout this book, the president's prerogative is entirely his discretion. Because Jackson's presidency offers an illuminating perspective on executive emergency powers that defines the power more broadly—not limited only to wars or insurrections but also to domestic policy—analyzing his interpretation of executive emergency power is important in order to determine whether his interpretation is congruent with earlier presidential interpretations; thereby creating a cavalier presidency.

Jackson's Perspective on Emergency Power

Although Jackson lost a very contentious election in 1824, in 1828 he would reemerge and forever change the presidency. The contentious loss, however, made Jackson aware of the "corruptive" element of government, particularly when people are not "represented."[19] Scholars have suggested that Jackson's vision of the president as the "voice" of the people is critical to understanding the transformation of the presidency, because "he reconstructed the office into the direct representative of the American people."[20] Robert Remini observed that, after winning the election of 1828, Jackson embarked to transform the political system and the presidency. He sought to advance the "cause of democracy," and most importantly, he "made an expanded executive power his tool in that great project."[21]

Jackson's critics called him "King Jackson" because he used presidential prerogative in exercising executive power.[22] Thus, he was the first "imperial president," a "transformative president," and the "peoples' president."[23] Such titles speak directly to Jackson's interpretation of presidential authority and are crucial to grasping his concept of presidential prerogative power as related to emergency power.

To begin, Jackson had a broad and expansive interpretation of presidential power (which he later applied to his interpretation of executive emergency power). In 1830 the Senate censured President Jackson in response to his attack on the National Banks; Jackson countered the Senate's disapproval by declaring that "the President is the direct representative of the American people" and that any censure was "wholly unauthorized by the Constitution, and in derogation of its entire spirit."[24]

Next, Jackson's view of his presidential prerogative would provoke him to first rebuke the Senate and then go on to rebuke the Court as well. In his response to Marshall's decision in *Worcester v. Georgia* (31 U.S. 515, 1832), which struck down a Georgia law that allowed for the removal of the Cherokee Indians, Jackson retorted, "Well, John Marshall has made his decision, now let him enforce it."[25] Jackson's assault on Marshall did not stop there; he also criticized Marshall for his holding in *McCullough v. Maryland* (17 U.S. 316, 1819). Further, he then rebuked the Congress for reauthorizing the National Bank in a formal veto. In his veto message Jackson declared that as the president, at times he understood the Constitution better than the Court and the Congress.[26]

Furthermore, in response to Congress reauthorizing the National Bank, Jackson issued a message in addition to his veto, stating that the Bank was a threat to the economic prosperity of the republic and could pose economic perils in the future, becoming the first president to suggest that government's role in the economy could lead to monumental perils in the future. Through these two actions Jackson exhibited his exercise of prerogative power.

All of these actions demonstrate that Jackson favored a robust interpretation of presidential behavior and executive emergency powers. He had a broad view of what it meant to represent the people, protect the state from crisis, and do what was within his "prerogative" to ensure that a crisis would be dealt with accordingly and swiftly. Jackson applied this concept of emergency power when he removed the Indians from the U.S. Southeast.[27]

Jackson and the Indian Removal

After the Supreme Court rebuked Jackson in the *Worcester* case, as part of his support for western expansion, Jackson orchestrated a policy for the removal of the Indians from the frontier by pushing Congress to pursue his Indian removal policy and ordering his generals to "pressure" the Indians to move southwest. His policy was a combination of his own "personal feelings towards Indians" and his early encounters with the Cherokee Indians in Northern Florida.[28]

Although federal treaties guaranteed millions of acres in the Southwest to the native tribes and federal policy recognized them as self-governing sovereigns, the U.S. government nonetheless encouraged missionaries to "civilize" them.[29] This idea of civilizing the natives was, as scholar Roy Harvey Pearce has argued, a consequence of "the westward travelers' fear of the savage nature of the Indians." These feelings were so strong that many people "living on the outer fringes of the Republic feared interactions with the Indians" because those interactions were often injurious altercations that produced casualties, all of which "led to a depiction of Indians that was not fair, nor accurate." Ignorance leads to fear, and fear in turn leads to brash and even "outrageous policies" that were, unfortunately, directed against the native tribes.[30]

The Cherokee had their own constitution, laws, and more than six million acres of land in Georgia. However, when the Georgia legislature adopted laws "forcing the Cherokee to leave and prohibiting white Americans from assisting them,"[31] Jackson did not disagree with its actions to remove the Indians. Scholars have argued that Jackson viewed the removal of the native tribes as "advancing America's economic development and enhancing its strategic position in the Southwest."[32] Furthermore, he possibly favored Indian removal so that "white Americans" could settle on the fertile lands of the Southwest without "fear of attacks along the borders."[33] Further, scholars have suggested that Jackson believed "whites and Indians could not live together, therefore it was better to keep them apart."[34]

In his first inaugural address on March 4, 1829, President Jackson delineated his goals for his presidency, including his goals for the Indian tribes: "It will be my sincere and constant desire . . . to observe toward the Indian tribes within our limits a just and liberal policy, and to give that humane and considerate attention to their rights and their wants which is consistent with the habits of Our Government and the feelings of our people."[35] In Jackson's opinion, however, allowing the Cherokee to administer their own laws "would create an independent state within the borders of Georgia." Thus, he told Congress that he had "informed the Indians that their attempt to establish an independent government would not be countenanced by the Executive of the United States." Jackson continued to advise the Cherokee to "emigrate beyond the Mississippi or submit" to state law.[36] Scholars suggest that he knew that the Indians had little option but to emigrate.[37]

Prior to Jackson taking office, the Georgia legislature began to pass laws to remove the Cherokee from the state. In response to the Cherokee adopting their own constitution, the legislature, with the full support of President-elect Jackson, decreed on December 20, 1828, that "all Indian residents within the state's boundaries would fall under its jurisdiction after six months."[38] Interestingly, the Georgia legislature moved so broadly and quickly to remove the native tribes because it "had lost patience with the Federal government for its failure to keep the promise it made in 1802 to extinguish Indian land titles within Georgia."[39]

In light of Georgia's actions as well as the likelihood that Alabama and Mississippi would follow suit, Jackson decided to take action against the native tribes himself. He "dispatched two Tennessee Generals, John Coffee and William Carroll,"[40] ordering them to visit the Creeks and Cherokees and attempt to persuade the natives to "remove peacefully" from the Southeast to the West. This order for the generals to "persuade" the natives to leave peacefully constitutes Jackson's first explicit use of emergency power because he told the generals to "inform the tribes that the President agreed with the laws of Georgia."[41] Specifically, Jackson directed them to say, "the President is of the opinion that the only mode left for the Indians to escape the effects of such enactments, and consequences more destructive . . . is, for them to emigrate. . . . He is sincerely anxious . . . to save his people and relieve the States."[42] Scholars have claimed that Jackson was concerned about the "well being" of Southerners living on the fringes of the Republic who must be "saved" from the "savages"; for Jackson, this was of "national importance."[43]

Through his generals Jackson communicated to the Indians that "the Federal Government could and would protect them fully in the possession of the soil [which was described as 'fertile and abundant country'] and their right of self government." However, he was very clear that if the Indians refused to move, "they must necessarily entail destruction upon their race."[44]

In order to push the removal of the natives, who would not leave upon Georgia's or Jackson's requests, the president pursued congressional legislation so that the federal government could legally remove the native tribes from the Southeast. Jackson placed the *Indian Removal Bill*, which formally set aside land for the Cherokee should they voluntarily leave Georgia, at the top of his legislative agenda in his first year of office.[45] To force the issue, he insisted the bill state unequivocally that the Cherokee had no claim to sovereignty and were subject to state laws. Overall, the bill was very consistent with Jackson's view that the states were allowed to regulate all matters not specifically given to the federal government.[46]

Public reaction to the bill was split. Although Georgians, and not only those fringe communities closest to the Indian communities, fully supported the bill,[47] northern Christian groups accused Georgia of violating federal treaties and attacked the administration for racism.[48] The public's reaction to the bill came as a surprise to Jackson.[49] In particular he was overwhelmed by the public outcries, which came mostly in the form of petitions opposing the removal and protesting the "betrayal" of Native Americans and the many promises made to them in the past.[50] The northern Christians would ask, "How could civilized men thrust aborigines into a wasteland and not see the act as evil and contemptible?"[51]

Jackson reacted with defiance to the public's outcry and continued to express his support for Georgia. Further, in order to secure the successful passage of a removal bill, he actively intervened in Congress to ensure that committees in the House and Senate charged with creating the bill were composed of people who could be relied upon to support his position.[52] Not only were Jackson supporters Hugh Lawson and John Bell, both of Tennessee, assigned to chair the committees, but most of the members on each committee were southerners committed to the removal.[53] Further, Jackson called on the Speaker of the House Henry Clay to support the legislation. Thus, his intervention and influence over the congressional process to draft and pass the bill indicate that he used executive prerogative broadly.[54] Jackson viewed his actions to remove the Indians as "necessary" and that he "needed" to protect the nation from future problems and incursions.[55]

Nonetheless, the ensuing debate on the Senate floor over the Removal Bill was controversial and intense. The debate began on April 6, 1830. Senator Theodore Frelinghuysen of New Jersey led the main opposition to the bill, speaking for three days on the subject, for at least two hours straight each day.[56] Frelinghuysen objected not only to the Removal Bill but also to Jackson's intervention into the legislation process. He called the president's interventions "intrusive" and criticized the fact that they were done "without the slightest consultation with either House of Congress, without any opportunity for counsel or concern, discussion or deliberation, on the part of the coordinate branches of the Government, to dispatch the whole subject in a tone and style of decisive construction of our obligations and of Indian rights."[57] Frelinghuysen was most concerned with Jackson's view of presidential authority and his "brash" nature of getting his way.[58]

Senator Frelinghuysen would go on to rebuke Jackson's prerogative in the matter of removing the Indians, declaring, "we must firmly protest against the Executive disposition of these high interests and of his authority. . . . He has no business intruding on congressional affairs."[59] The senator insisted that the president's concern for the welfare of the citizens of Georgia and his belief that it was a "grave emergency" for the nation did not give him the right to "intervene" in congressional affairs.[60]

Jackson's policy did garner some support, however. Senator John Forsyth from Georgia attacked Senator Frelinghuysen's comments, "screaming back" that "the North can do what they wish with tribes within their borders, but southerners are denied the same rights." Senator Forsyth went on to uphold Jackson's intervention and policy: "President Jackson is simply defending a state's right to administer the law within her boundaries."[61] In the end, the bill passed "handily in the Senate, but by only 102–97 in the House in 1830."[62] President Jackson signed the bill on May 28, 1830, a victory for Jackson in his direct attempt to quell what he deemed a "national issue."

He and Congress alone did not decide the issue of the president's prerogative to remove the natives. The Indians, along with their northern allies, brought suit against the federal government, claiming that the government's actions violated the sovereignty of the native tribes and their treaties with the United States. The result was *Worcester v. Georgia*, heard before the Supreme Court.

Resetting Jackson's Emergency Power: *Worcester v. Georgia*

In *Worcester v. Georgia* the Supreme Court attempted to restrain President Jackson's prerogative power; however, Jackson defied the Court's ruling and moved forward with his plans. In this example of presidential interpretation of executive emergency power, Jackson's defiance of the Court speaks directly to the concerns of how to reset these powers, especially if the president denies the legitimacy of the Court, which, I suggest, is responsible for reining in executive powers.

Unhappy with the actions of the federal government, the native tribes and their allies challenged Jackson in the courts, and their case made its way to the U.S. Supreme Court. The Court rejected the natives' initial challenge to prevent Georgia from enforcing its laws, stating that the tribes were not a "foreign nation" that could appear in federal court.[63] Meanwhile, Georgia had already clearly maintained that it would not support any Court ruling in favor of the native tribes. Further, Jackson supporters in Congress echoed Georgia's resolution, introducing a bill to repeal section 25 of the Judiciary Act of 1789, which had given the Court jurisdiction over state court judgments.[64]

However, the breaking point arose for the Cherokee when Georgia arrested and jailed Christian missionaries for refusing to leave Cherokee lands. Two missionaries, Samuel Worcester and Elizur Butler, challenged their imprisonment before the Supreme Court. The missionaries were arrested on the grounds that they had violated Georgia state law, which required all whites to have a license if they chose to live within the Cherokee lands. In *Worcester v. Georgia* (31 U.S. 515, 1832) Chief Justice Marshall struck down Georgia's Cherokee laws not because they violated treaties but because Georgia's laws violated the Constitution. According to Marshall, "the Indian nations had always been considered as distinct, independent political communities, retaining their original natural rights, as the undisputed possessors of the soil, from time immemorial."[65] Therefore, according to the Court, the Constitution gave exclusive control over all relations with the tribal nations to the federal government; the states could not disregard a federal treaty.

Georgia officials refused to appear before the Court and defied the Court's ruling; more importantly, Jackson made no effort to enforce the ruling. Instead, allegedly Jackson responded to the ruling by stating, "Well, John Marshall has made his decision, now let him enforce it."[66] Daniel Howe, a leading historian on Jackson and the Indian Removal, suggests that this caustic remark is "consistent with Jackson's behavior and quite in character with his view of authority and crisis" and illustrates Jackson's "pugnacity, his Indian policy, and his view of the President's position in the constitutional system."[67] Regarding the removal of the natives, Jackson believed that the federal government did have "sole prerogative" to handle issues among the states, the native tribes, and the federal government; Jackson clearly stated his ill opinion of the Court's ruling, as seen in the alleged statement above.[68]

Rather than defying the Supreme Court outright, however, the Georgia courts simply did not acknowledge the ruling, and Jackson did not feel compelled to even respond to it.[69] Without a clear objection or formal acceptance of *Worcester* from the state, the Court had no formal or legal authority to order Georgia to obey the decision.[70] With the Court unable to enforce its own decision, Jackson declared, "the decision of the Supreme Court has fell still born, and they find they cannot coerce Georgia to yield to its mandate."[71]

In his reelection bid in 1832, states in the South, where the issue of Indian Removal was much relevant, aided Jackson to victory, even as the issue—and Jackson—remained unpopular in the North. In his second term Jackson moved quickly to remove the native tribes from the Southeast, moving them west to Oklahoma by purchasing on behalf of the U.S. government the Cherokee land for $5 million, in exchange for the land in Oklahoma. By 1838 some twelve thousand Cherokee had been forced to migrate west along the "trail of tears," where an estimated four thousand or more died along the way. Thus, Jackson maintained his belief that he had the executive authority and initiative to act in accordance with the will of the people and to prevent future skirmishes between the natives and westward travelers. For Jackson, the Indian Removal was a "legislative achievement" as well as an achievement of his "prerogative" to both secure expansion for U.S. settlers and prevent future incursions.[72]

Remini has argued that this "tarnished monumental event in American History brought the entire government into the process of expelling Indians from their southern homelands . . . all at the expense of Jackson's executive initiative." What is more surprising is that the "majority of the voting public was in favor of the removal, hence reelecting Jackson in 1832 . . . but the removal was clear evidence of a policy that was harsh, arrogant, racist, and at the time, inevitable."[73]

There is little doubt that Jackson's actions were controversial, racist, and ill spirited. Historically, this interpretation of executive emergency power demonstrates clearly that it should never be used for personal or domestic political agendas. According to the evidence presented here, the native tribes were not a national threat equal to earlier rebellions, nor were they as much of a threat to national security as the hostilities of the British Navy leading up to the War of 1812. Yet Jackson proceeded to remove the natives, justifying his actions by arguing that if the United States did not remove the Indians, it would become vulnerable and weak, claiming that the natives were as much a threat to America as international threats—that is, the Spanish, French, or British.

Thus, because the threat—if any—that the native tribes posed to the United States was not comparable to that from the European nations, Jackson's interpretation of executive emergency power has lasting implications. He expanded the definition of emergency and, therefore, increased the emergency powers to fit his own political and personal domestic agenda. Consequently, Jackson's use of executive emergency power constituted an abuse of that power; it was not in the spirit of what Locke called "prerogative" power or what Hamilton argued for in Federalist No. 70. Locke stated very clearly in his *Second Treatise on Civil Government* that "prerogative power is only to be used for the public good."[74] Jackson's actions to remove the natives were not in the larger public's best interests.

Furthermore, Jackson manipulated public opinion in order to scare people into believing that the native presence was tantamount to a national emergency. He used his generals to coerce the tribes into ultimatums that were not beneficial for them, and he allowed his generals to make the natives believe that if they did not agree to the terms of the Indian Removal Bill, the Federal Army would forcibly remove them. Yet Congress never agreed to the president's general statements; therefore, Jackson never had the authority to instruct his generals to say anything to the native tribes about what the Federal Army may or may not do. Because of this deception, however, the Indians were intimidated and forced into the agreement. Jackson misused the powers of his office to force the tribes into leaving their native lands.

Jackson's behavior is instructive; it shows us just how easily a president may manufacture an emergency to suit his own domestic agenda. Specifically, once a president declares something an emergency, then he is enabled with broader powers to combat that emergency. If the emergency is not legitimate, however, but rather manufactured—as was the case with the Indians Removal—then the use of that power is illegitimate.

The risk that presidents may manufacture emergencies to benefit their own ends is one that a populace must guard against because the executive may use that power for undemocratic or ignoble purposes. These are not the intent of executive emergency powers; rather, the function of executive emergency power is to preserve the state, not discard people within the state whom the majority deems unworthy. Although the powers may be used to combat rebels, prevent domestic criminal activity against the state, and suspend habeas corpus in order to preserve and defend the state against internal conflict, the power should not be used simply to exploit minorities or groups of people within the state because of racist prejudices.

Jackson's actions exposed the inherent weakness in the liberal democratic interpretation of executive emergency power—that the power is discretionary and built on the implicit notion that the executive will use the power only to do good things aimed at preserving the state; this is made clear by Jackson's mobilization of the military to address the Cherokee Indians in Georgia without congressional approval. Jackson appears to support Hamilton's executive emergency power theory that executive prerogative determines how to exercise that power and emergency power is an inherent constitutional power lawfully granted to him under his authority in Article II of the Constitution.

However, in practice, no ruler is perfect and absolutely honest. Consequently, the state must protect against the possibility that an executive will seize these powers for ignoble reasons and outcomes. In the conclusion I will explore possible mechanisms to prevent abuse of executive emergency power; thereby creating a cavalier presidency.

Thankfully, not all presidents will be as disingenuous with their executive power as Jackson was, and some will agree that the power is inherent within the Constitution and can be used only as long as an emergency exists. In chapter 5 I will explore this type of leader—Abraham Lincoln—who is the type of leader liberal democratic theorists likely had in mind when they conceived of executive emergency powers as discretionary. Unlike Jackson, Lincoln used the power to preserve the Union as well as the sovereignty of the American people and their Constitution.

NOTES

1. Gaillard Hunt, *The Life of James Madison* (New York: Russell & Russell, 1968), 325. Also see James Madison, *Writings*, edited by Jack N. Rakove (New York: Library of America, 1999), 6:67. As part of the larger debate between Hamilton and Madison, after simply reading the Federalist Papers credited to Hamilton, Madison considered Hamilton a *monocrat* or a *monarchist*.

2. Hunt, *The Life of James Madison*, 318–19.

3. Ibid., 321–22.

4. Herbert J. Storing and Murray Dry, "Letters of Pacificus and Helvidius," in *The Complete Anti-Federalist* (Chicago: University of Chicago Press, 1981), 53–64. In these letters Madison again advocates the diffusion of executive power, and this is in direct opposition to the monarchist Hamilton, who seems to be advocating for a constitutional monarchy, at least in Madison's opinion.

5. Ibid., 53–64.

6. Hunt, *The Life of James Madison*, 146–47.

7. Donald Hickey, *The War of 1812: A Forgotten Conflict* (Urbana: University of Illinois Press, 1989), 43.

8. Ibid., 44.

9. Ibid.

10. James Madison, "Proclamation on Anglo-American Affairs," June 1, 1812, in Madison, *Writings*.

11. Ibid., 34.

12. Hickey, *The War of 1812*, 44; Hunt, *The Life of James Madison*, 146–47.

13. David S. Heidler and Jeanne T. Heidler, *The War of 1812* (Westport, CT: Greenwood Press, 2002), 47–49.

14. Hickey, *The War of 1812*, 44.

15. Ibid., 45–46.

16. Heidler and Heidler, *The War of 1812*, 47–49.

17. Irving Bryant, "Madison Encouraged the War Movement," in *The Causes of the War of 1812: National Honor or National Interest?*, edited by Bradford Perkins, 104–7 (New York: Holt, Rinehart and Winston, 1962).

18. Jon Meacham, *American Lion: Andrew Jackson in the White House* (New York: Random House, 2008), 10.

19. Robert Remini, *Andrew Jackson and the Course of American Freedom* (Baltimore, MD: Johns Hopkins University Press, 1998), 305–21; Robert Remini, *Andrew Jackson and His Indian Wars* (New York: Viking, 2001), 20–35.

20. Robert Remini, "The Constitution and the Presidencies: The Jackson Era," in *The Constitution and the American Presidency*, edited by Martin L. Fausold and Alan Shank, 34–56 (Albany: State University of New York Press, 1991). In this chapter I draw on the wealth of many Jackson histories: principally Remini's works, part of a three-volume series titled *The Life of Andrew Jackson* (New York: Harper & Row, 1988); H. W. Brands, *Andrew Jackson: His Life and Times* (New York: Doubleday, 2005); Sean Wilentz, *Andrew Jackson* (New York: Times Books, 2005); Daniel Walker Howe, *What Hath God Wrought: The Transformation of America 1815–1848* (New York: Oxford University Press, 2007); Arthur Schlesinger Jr., *The Age of Jackson* (Boston: Little, Brown, 1945). Remini, *Andrew Jackson and the Course of American Freedom*, 305.

21. Remini, *Andrew Jackson and the Course of American Freedom*, 347.

22. Ibid., 351–64.

23. Ibid., 367–74.

24. James D. Richardson, *A Compilation of the Messages and Papers of the Presidents, 1789–1897* (Washington, DC: Government Printing Office, 1896–1899), 1154; Remini, *Andrew Jackson and the Course of American Freedom*, 367–74.

25. There is debate regarding the legitimacy of Jackson's words following the McCullough Decision. Some suggest it is valid, whereas others do not. I will note, however, that Robert Remini, considered by most as the prominent Jackson biographer, believes the quote is valid.

26. In his veto message Jackson elaborated his concerns about the Congress and the Court declaring the constitutionality of actions without consent from the president, found in Andrew Jackson, *Narrative and Writings of Andrew Jackson . . .* (Miami, FL: Mnemosyne Publishing, 1969).

27. Remini, *Andrew Jackson and the Course of American Freedom*, 371–73; Remini, *Andrew Jackson and His Indian Wars*.

28. Remini, *Andrew Jackson and the Course of American Freedom*, 371–73; also see Howe, *What Hath God Wrought*, 342–57.

29. Remini, *Andrew Jackson and the His Indian Wars*, 373.

30. Roy Harvey Pearce, *Savagism and Civilization: A Study of the Indian and the American Mind* (Berkeley: University of California Press, 1988), pt. I, 3–34.

31. Remini, *Andrew Jackson and His Indian Wars*, 373.

32. See Howe, *What Hath God Wrought*; Remini, *Andrew Jackson and His Indian Wars*; Pearce, *Savagism and Civilization*.

33. Remini, *Andrew Jackson and the Course of American Freedom*, 373; Remini, *Andrew Jackson and His Indian Wars*.

34. Remini, *Andrew Jackson and the Course of American Freedom*, 370–73.

35. Andrew Jackson, "First Inaugural Address," in *A Compilation of the Messages and Papers of the Presidents, 1789–1897*, vol. 2, edited by James Daniel Richardson, 436–38 (Washington, DC: U.S. Government Printing Office, 1896), 438.

36. Andrew Jackson, "First Annual Message," in *A Compilation of the Messages and Papers of the Presidents, 1789–1897*, 442–62, at 458.

37. See Remini, *Andrew Jackson and the Course of American Freedom*, 145; Howe, *What Hath God Wrought*, 301.

38. *Cherokee Nation v. Georgia*, 30 U.S. 1, 1831.

39. Ibid. This point sounds eerily similar to the contemporary debate regarding Arizona's immigration law, which was a response to frustrations with the Federal government's lack of enforcement, according to Arizona lawmakers.

40. Remini, *Andrew Jackson and the Course of American Freedom*; Remini, *Andrew Jackson and His Indian Wars*, 125–28.

41. Howe, *What Hath God Wrought*, 412–16.

42. Ibid., 414–21; Remini, *Andrew Jackson and His Indian Wars*.

43. Howe, *What Hath God Wrought*, 414–21, 423–25.

44. Ibid.

45. Remini, *Andrew Jackson and the Course of American Freedom*; Remini, *Andrew Jackson and His Indian Wars*, 305–11.

46. Howe, *What Hath God Wrought*, 414–21.

47. Remini, *Andrew Jackson and the Course of American Freedom*; Remini, *Andrew Jackson and His Indian Wars*, 125–28.

48. Ibid., 423.

49. Remini, *Andrew Jackson and the Course of American Freedom*; Remini, *Andrew Jackson and His Indian Wars*, 305–11.

50. Remini, *Andrew Jackson and His Indian Wars*, 313–20.

51. Remini, *Andrew Jackson and the Course of American Freedom*; Remini, *Andrew Jackson and His Indian Wars*, 315.

52. Remini, *Andrew Jackson and His Indian Wars*, 318–22.

53. Remini, *Andrew Jackson and the Course of American Freedom*; Remini, *Andrew Jackson and His Indian Wars*, 305–25.

54. Remini, *Andrew Jackson and the Course of American Freedom*, and *Andrew Jackson and His Indian Wars*; Howe, *What Hath God Wrought*, 55.

55. Remini, *Andrew Jackson and the Course of American Freedom*; Remini, *Andrew Jackson and His Indian Wars*, 305–30.

56. Remini, *Andrew Jackson and His Indian Wars*, 324–27.

57. Remini, *Andrew Jackson and the Course of American Freedom*; Remini, *Andrew Jackson and His Indian Wars*, 325.

58. Remini, *Andrew Jackson and His Indian Wars*, 325–32.

59. Howe, *What Hath God Wrought*, 414–21; Remini, *Andrew Jackson and the Course of American Freedom*; Remini, *Andrew Jackson and His Indian Wars*, 305–30.

60. Howe, *What Hath God Wrought*, 55, 63.

61. Ibid., 63.

62. Ibid., 414–21; Remini, *Andrew Jackson and the Course of American Freedom*; Remini, *Andrew Jackson and His Indian Wars*, 305–30.

63. Remini, *Andrew Jackson and the Course of American Freedom*; Remini, *Andrew Jackson and His Indian Wars*, 305–6. Although the Court never acknowledged that the tribes are foreign nations, it did state that they are independent political communities that could enter into treaties with the United States; hence, only Congress could enact laws or treaties with the tribes, not a state (in this case Georgia).

64. Remini, *Andrew Jackson and the Course of American Freedom*; Remini, *Andrew Jackson and His Indian Wars*, 305–15.

65. *Worcester v. Georgia*, 31 U.S. 515 (1832).

66. Howe, *What Hath God Wrought*, 414–21; Remini, *Andrew Jackson and the Course of American Freedom*; Remini, *Andrew Jackson and His Indian Wars*, 155–70, 305–30. The validity of Jackson's remark is disputed among historians.

67. Ibid., 155.

68. Ibid., 155–70, 305–30.

69. Ibid., 156.

70. Ibid., 155–70, 305–30.

71. Meacham, *American Lion*, 204.

72. Howe, *What Hath God Wrought*, 414–21; Remini, *Andrew Jackson and the Course of American Freedom*; Remini, *Andrew Jackson and His Indian Wars*, 155–70, 305–30.

73. Ibid., 305–30.

74. John Locke, *Second Treatise on Civil Government*, in Michael Morgan, ed., *Classics of Moral and Political Theory*, 765–87 (Indianapolis, IN: Hackett Publishing Co., 1992).

Chapter Five

President Lincoln's Interpretation and Application of Executive Emergency Power

In this chapter I will examine Abraham Lincoln's approach to handling crisis, relying on his own words in order to understand his philosophy of executive emergency power. This methodology will provide a fresh look at Lincoln's conception of his role and duty in light of the greatest emergency the United States had ever faced, the Civil War. After reviewing Lincoln's thoughts and reflections on executive emergency power, which I will examine alongside his actions during the war, I will then discuss where Lincoln's philosophy fits in with the philosophers discussed in chapter 1.

Americans widely regard Abraham Lincoln as one of the most important presidents in U.S. history; indeed few U.S. presidents stand higher in the nation's executive pantheon than Lincoln. In fact, Edward Corwin has remarked that Washington founded the nation; Lincoln saved it. [1] Without Lincoln, the United States might have lost eleven of its thirty-six states—composing approximately a third of its thirty million inhabitants. [2] Although he did not choose the Civil War that engulfed his presidency, Lincoln stared into the face of that enormous crisis and resolved to overcome it—unlike future presidents, who, after taking the Office, would sour the mood of the nation by chiding that they "inherited" the current crisis. [3] But Lincoln envisioned the Constitution as serving the entire nation, not a document designed to protect the abhorrent institution of slavery, and preceded accordingly.

Although Lincoln knew that war was inevitable, knowing that did not ease Lincoln's burden when the country became embroiled in a civil war. Victory over the South came at an enormous price; historians have estimated that out of a population of thirty-one million approximately six hundred thousand Americans lost their lives. This was a war between fathers and sons, brothers and neighbors. One-quarter of the South's white male population of military age were either killed or injured. And whereas the total value of northern wealth rose during the 1860s, southern wealth declined significantly.[4]

Lincoln remarked that the human cost of the war was troubling to his conscience and even his soul, but he vowed he would stay the course, knowing as he did his obligation and the country's need to atone for slavery, remarking, "Fondly do we hope, fervently do we pray, that this mighty scourge of war may speedily pass away."[5] Furthermore, in his Second Inaugural Address Lincoln commented that the nation had to atone for its sin— the sin of slavery—and that the war was the only way to do so: "Yet, if God wills that it continue until all the wealth piled by the bondsman's two hundred and fifty years of unrequited toil shall be sunk, and until every drop of blood drawn with the lash shall be paid by another drawn with sword." He then continued, "as was said three thousand years ago, so still it must be said 'the judgments of the Lord are true and righteous altogether.'"[6] Ultimately, one of the lives lost as a result of the most devastating war on U.S. soil would be Lincoln's—the first U.S. president to be assassinated.

Before his ultimate sacrifice, however, when he was confronted with the crisis of a dissolving union, Lincoln needed to determine what power he had—if any—to handle the calamity. Therefore, understanding his interpretation of the Constitution and emergency power is tremendously important when analyzing his actions during the crisis. Lincoln turned to the Commander-in-Chief clause of the Constitution, using it during the beginning of the war as his power to conduct war without the consent or declaration from Congress. He would see the entire South as the battlefield and would understand his powers to attack anything that would help the Confederacy win the war. In this chapter I will analyze all of Lincoln's actions during the war in order to determine (1) Lincoln's interpretation of emergency power, (2) the constitutional merit for such actions, and (3) Lincoln's defense for his actions.

Some scholars have argued that part of Lincoln's tragedy—if his life can be considered a tragedy—is that he had to exercise such "unconstitutional" powers in order to save the Union.[7] In his classic study of Lincoln, Arthur Schlesinger called Lincoln a "despot," and both Edward Corwin and Clinton Rossiter made the bold claim that during the war, Lincoln assumed the mighty powers of a "dictator."[8] There were some Republicans during the war who were concerned about the powers Lincoln invoked; they believed the Constitution did not afford him such power.[9] However, these people did not convince Lincoln otherwise; instead, he believed he had the authority to combat the Southern rebels with the full force of the Constitution and the Federal Army. Lincoln wrote to a Kentucky newspaper editor in 1864, asking, "Was it possible to lose the nation, and yet preserve the Constitution?" Lincoln's profound answer to his own question was, "By general law life and limb must be protected; yet often a limb must be amputated to save a life; but a life is never wisely given to save a limb." [10] In other words, Lincoln argued, necessity could justify unconstitutional acts. In the same letter Lincoln stated, "I felt that measures, otherwise unconstitutional, might become lawful, by becoming indispensable to the preservation of the Constitution, through the preservation of the nation." [11]

Considering Lincoln's actions and philosophy regarding emergency power, scholars have tended immediately to ponder whether he was a constitutional dictator. [12] Yet there is little to no scholarly dialogue that considers how Lincoln's philosophy agreed or disagreed with the intellectual history and previous thinkers' contributions on the subject. In this chapter I review only Lincoln's words—both written and spoken—to determine how he interpreted executive emergency power; I then consider how Lincoln's philosophy agreed or disagreed with previous thinkers concerning executive emergency power.

The question of whether Lincoln was a dictator should be easily refuted by reviewing both Lincoln's actions and his own words regarding emergency power. Although I grant that during the war he used more power and did so more broadly than any previous president, I argue that he was responding to a crisis of unprecedented caliber and enormity; the very life of the nation depended on his determination and ability to act. This chapter will shed light on how Lincoln's interpretation of executive emergency power rejected Locke's prerogative power and favored Hamilton's theory of energy in the executive and that executive emergency power is inherent within Article II of the Constitution. Lincoln drew heavily on his predecessors' actions and interpretations of emergency power, and, as they had, he concluded that his constitutional duty to execute the laws, his role as chief executive, and his presidential oath granted him power to use force, if necessary, against those who opposed the authority of the U.S. government. Lincoln correctly understood that preserving the nation was the president's fundamental responsibility, stating, "my oath to preserve the constitution to the best of my ability, imposed upon me the duty of preserving, by every indispensable means, that government, that nation, of which that constitution was the organic law." [13]

This book argues that Lincoln believed that the Constitution upheld inherently executive emergency power and that this power should be used only for preserving the Union and the Constitution. Although he had the option to exercise a pure form of prerogative power, an extralegal approach to executive emergency power, he considered executive emergency power to be inherent in the Constitution. As he understood the Constitution, his right to act and use emergency power was included under the Commander-in-Chief clause and this granted him the ability to raise an army, invade and blockade the South, establish a military government of captured territory, suspend the writ of habeas corpus, and employ tough internal security measures. As Rossiter stated, "Lincoln's political rhetoric may have invoked or sounded of Jefferson's idea of prerogative, but his constitutional logic followed that of Alexander Hamilton."[14]

In response to scholars, such as Rossiter and Corwin, who have argued that Lincoln displayed characteristics of a "dictatorship" during the Civil War, I aver that such a claim neglects the fact that Lincoln took very important measures and actions to reinforce the principles of democracy: the normal political processes continued to operate in the North throughout the war; a formal opposition party continued to challenge Lincoln's wartime policies; and regular elections continued to be held. This last example is especially important to note because in 1864 voters were given the opportunity to choose between Lincoln's war policies and those of his critics; Lincoln was reelected. In fact, he even spoke to his cabinet secretaries about his concerns that the presidency may fall into the hands of retired war general George McClellan. Here, I use remarks and writings from Lincoln himself to demonstrate clearly his constitutional reasons for actions and refute the notion that he was a self-seeking, power-hungry dictator. As Rossiter stated so astutely, in order to understand the idea of crisis government in America, one must understand "that the story of crisis government in the Civil War is the story of Abraham Lincoln."[15]

LINCOLN AND THE WAR

Lincoln began his political career as a member of the Whig party. The Whigs responded to what they considered the overzealous nature of President Andrew Jackson, with some even suggesting that Jackson thought himself a "king." Ironically, Lincoln's Whig affiliation in the beginning of his political career indicates that he stood for limiting government power and, most importantly, restraining political leaders' ambitions. With this in mind, some might see as ironic the fact that Lincoln would forever change the executive office and possibly become the most powerful president in the history of the country.

In 1838 Lincoln spoke before the Springfield Young Men's Lyceum in which he delivered a vitriolic speech railing against political ambition. The twenty-nine-year-old politician warned that the "perpetuity of our free institutions" and the survival of the Constitution "would be threatened by other leaders of great ambition who would not be content simply to uphold the work of the founding generation." He worried that "such men would disdain the well-worn path of the constitutional government." Lincoln then went on to state that these men would be members of the "family of the lion, or the tribe of the eagle, and such men would seek to use the Office to remake politics and government in their own image."[16] Lincoln expressed a clear respect for the Constitution, proclaiming that "a reverence for the constitution and the laws has become the civil religion of the nation and thus serve as a bulwark against immoderate political ambition."[17] Based on these comments, it is not surprising that when he was elected president, he remained very beholden to the Constitution and the powers explicit and implicit to the presidency.

Furthermore, as a Whig, Lincoln criticized President Polk's actions during the Mexican War. While serving in the House of Representatives Lincoln argued that the Constitution gave "the war making power to Congress . . . and that the will of the people should produce its own result without executive influence."[18] Thus he expressed profound respect for the limitations of presidential power, especially during war and emergency, as well as for the Constitution. Yet, as we know, Lincoln would come to evolve his point of view, not out of convenience or as a result of his own ambition but rather out of dire necessity to preserve the principles and laws of the country he loved. Lincoln's famous nomination acceptance speech for the Senate in 1858 exemplifies his reverence for preserving the Union and upholding the Constitution: "A House divided against itself cannot stand. I believe this government cannot endure, permanently, half slave and half free. I do not expect the Union to be dissolved, I do not expect the House to fall, but I do expect it will cease to be divided. It will become all one thing, or all the other."[19]

Unlike his predecessor James Buchanan, Lincoln could not avoid the secession of the Southern states. Although Buchanan agreed that secession was unconstitutional, he still did not believe that he had the constitutional authority to stop it. In the waning days of his administration, Buchanan defended the federal government's right to protect federal property, but this did not include granting the government the authority to wage war against a state or group of states. In his 1860 address to Congress, Buchanan argued a state could not secede legally, but he qualified this by stating that the president could not "make war against a state . . . and that the only human tribunal under Providence possessing the power to meet the existing emergency was that of Congress."[20]

Lincoln interpreted the Constitution quite differently from his predecessor. Lincoln believed that the Constitution afforded him greater power to address the Southern secession than politely asking them to return to the Union. South Carolina's bold seizure of federal property and attack on Fort Sumter in April of 1861 justified Lincoln's interpretation of executive power. To him, it was clear that the Confederate states were "frustrating the constitutional system" and denying the results of nationwide democratic elections.[21] Lincoln issued a clear ultimatum to the Southern rebels, reminding them that he was president, that the Constitution was to be defended, and "that the laws of the Union be faithfully executed in all the States."[22] He went on to tell the rebels that "you have no oath registered to heaven to destroy the government . . . while I shall have the most solemn one to preserve, protect, and defend it."[23] In his farewell address to the loyal citizens and voters of Illinois, Lincoln acknowledged the great task before him: "I now leave, not knowing when, or whether ever, I may return, with a task before me greater than that which rested upon Washington."[24]

In Lincoln's first inaugural address he promised "not to interfere with the bargain reached in the Constitution that the Southern states could decide on slavery as a matter of their own domestic institution."[25] However, the issue of secession was different from slavery; he saw secession as unconstitutional and a blatant defiance of the democratic process, declaring, "I hold that in contemplation of universal law and of the Constitution the Union of these states, is perpetual . . . that no state upon its own mere notion can lawfully get out of the Union."[26] In other words, the Union pre-existed the Constitution, which is further evidenced in the Preamble, as it states that it aims "to form a more perfect Union." Because Lincoln believed secession was illegal and unconstitutional, the Southern states were still part of the nation, and "the Union was unbroken."[27] Using Lincoln's logic, a state may not dissolve the Union; in order to dissolve the Union, every state must first vote to disband the Constitution.

In describing Lincoln's actions, I, like scholars Rossiter and Corwin, suggest that the period can be divided into two distinct parts: those actions taken at the outbreak of armed rebellion on April 12, 1861, and the subsequent meeting of Congress on July 4, 1861, and those actions taken throughout the remainder of the war.

Confronted with southern secession in December of 1860 and the rebel attacks on Fort Sumter only one day after taking office, Lincoln had little time to react to the worst emergency in U.S. history. He was mindful of the rebels' illegal actions; a letter written in late 1864 exhibits his underlying mindset and rationale that guided his actions during the war, making clear his constitutional interpretation supporting his position to use federal power broadly to respond to the crisis. Lincoln stated, "It became necessary for me to choose whether, using only the existing means, agencies, and processes which Congress had provided, I should let the Government fall at once into ruin or whether, availing myself of the broader powers conferred by the Constitution in cases on insurrection, I would make an effort to save it, with all its blessings, for the present age and for posterity."[28]

Lincoln's first action was to issue a stern executive proclamation (April 15, 1861) in which he declared "that the executive of the laws of the United States were being forcibly obstructed in the seven southernmost states." He argued that his constitutional duty was to uphold the Constitution, an oath he considered "registered to Heaven," and to dispel the rebels, an "unruly" gigantic mob. In the proclamation Lincoln called forth "the militia of the several States of the Union to the aggregate number of 75,000" to "suppress the rebellion . . . and guarantee the execution of the laws." In the same proclamation, he also requested both Houses of Congress to convene in a special session on July 4 "to consider and determine such measures as, in their wisdom, the public safety and interest may seem to demand."[29] Scholars have questioned why Lincoln did not call for a joint session of Congress sooner; Rossiter and Corwin suggest Lincoln delayed the session because he believed the war would be over by July 4, 1861. Thus, by combating the crisis himself rather than calling a session, Lincoln avoided potential bickering and delays as well as a weakened war effort that Congress would bring forth; he addressed the crisis he saw best fit, thereby reducing delays and strengthening the war effort.[30]

With a proclamation on April 19, Lincoln created a blockade on the ports of the seceded states. On April 20 he ordered a total of nineteen vessels to be added immediately to the Navy, stating that "this is for the purposes of public defense."[31] Just a few days later the blockade was extended to the ports of Virginia and North Carolina.[32] Lincoln would describe his reasons for imposing the blockade as "necessary" because criminals—otherwise known as the Southern rebels—threatened the United States:

> Now, therefore, I, Abraham Lincoln, President of the United States, with a view to the same purposes before mentioned, and to the protection of the public peace, and the lives and property of quiet and orderly citizens pursuing their lawful occupations, until Congress shall have assembled and deliberated on the said unlawful proceedings, or until the same shall ceased, have further deemed it advisable to set on foot a blockade of the ports within the States aforesaid, in pursuance of the laws of the United States, and of the law of Nations, in such case provided.[33]

Thus, Lincoln was justified in imposing the blockade because he was protecting lives, property, and the public peace. According to him, all of these actions were a necessary function of government. Because he believed his primary duty was to protect the Union in light of the insurrection, Lincoln went on to explain the necessity for using "competent force" to deal with ships or those who violate the blockade:

> For this purpose a competent force will be posted so as to prevent entrance and exit of vessels from the ports aforesaid. If, therefore, with a view to violate such blockade, a vessel shall approach, or shall attempt to leave either of the said ports, she will be duly warned by the Commander of one of the blockading vessels, who will endorse on her register the fact and date of such warning, and if the same vessel shall again attempt to enter or leave the blockaded port, she will be captured and sent to the nearest convenient port, for such proceedings against her and her cargo as prize, as may be deemed advisable.[34]

The previous quotations demonstrate Lincoln's logic for imposing a blockade on the Southern rebel ports, by which he used executive emergency power by interpreting that power as based on the executive's need to respond to a crisis that threatens the Union.

On May 3 Lincoln pursued further action, using power that, under normal circumstances, would be reserved to the Congress, such as the power to "raise and support an army" and "provide and maintain a navy," both provisions granted to Congress in Article I of the Constitution. In his proclamation he reasoned that his authority to organize an army is derived from necessity and emergency. Although his authority for raising a militia was based on statutory law, enlarging the military—Lincoln called for "42,034 volunteers to serve for the period of three years and to enlarge the regular army by 23,000 and the navy by 18,000"[35]—and commanding it to combat without congressional consent were not based on statutory provisions.

In addition to usurping congressional authority to enlarge and command the military, Lincoln also pursued ways to fund the war. On April 20 he directed Secretary of the Treasury Salmon P. Chase to advance $2 million of unappropriated funds in the Treasury to three private citizens of New York who had the sole responsibility to use the money to finance governmental military operations. This was done without congressional approval. Lincoln stated that the funds were to be "used by [the three New Yorkers], in meeting such requisitions as should be directly consequent upon the military and naval measures necessary for the defense and support of the Government." He realized he did not have power to appropriate funds, but he reasoned that he needed to take such extraordinary measures because he questioned the loyalty of some government officials in various departments and was concerned that certain "disloyal" people might act to prevent the government from financing the war. He stated, "I only confided in private citizens to conduct official duties because they were favorably known for their ability, loyalty and patriotism."[36]

Suspending habeas corpus was possibly Lincoln's most controversial action. To maintain public order and suppress open treason in the Union, Lincoln, in a proclamation delivered on April 27, authorized the commanding general of the U.S. Army to suspend the writ of habeas corpus, stating, "at any point or in the vicinity of any military line which is now or which shall be used between the city of Philadelphia and the city of Washington."[37] He continued,

> Now, therefore, be it ordered, first, that during the existing insurrection and as a necessary measure for suppressing the same, all Rebels and Insurgents, their aiders and abettors within the United States, and all persons discouraging volunteer enlistments, resisting militia drafts, or guilty of any disloyal practice, affording aid and comfort to Rebels against the authority of United States,

shall be subject to martial law and liable to trial and punishment by Courts Martial or Military Commission. [38]

Significantly, in the proclamation Lincoln refers to the Southern secessionists as "rebels" and "insurgents," therefore classifying the secessionists as violators of the law, and this then authorized him to suspend the habeas corpus requirements of anyone abetting or aiding the forces against the legitimate Northern army. According to Lincoln, all of this power rested on the Commander-in-Chief and Oath clauses of the Constitution. From these clauses he deemed that his principal responsibility was to end the insurgency via the military. To be constitutionally permissible, suspending habeas corpus had to be aimed toward that goal.

Furthermore, Lincoln declared that anyone arrested in relation to the rebellion would face military tribunals, stating, "Second. That the Writ of Habeas Corpus is suspended in respect to all persons arrested, or who are now, or hereafter during the rebellion shall be, imprisoned in any fort, camp, arsenal, military prison, or other place of confinement by any military authority of by the sentence of any Court Martial or Military Commission." [39] Months later Lincoln wrote that suspending habeas corpus was only for the purpose of responding to "violence being visited by the Baltimore mobs and the rebels possibly travelling on the Washington and Philadelphia rail lines." [40] On July 2, 1861, he would extend this power to include the area between New York and Washington. [41] Furthermore, Lincoln would challenge some claims from members of Congress that such power lay only with Congress. He even went so far as to write a letter to Attorney General Bates, instructing him to resolve this particular problem and to clarify whether the president has such power during times of emergency. Bates responded that, given the magnitude and severity of the crisis, the executive would and did have the power to suspend habeas corpus. [42] Regardless, the lower federal court later admonished Lincoln for this action in the *Ex Parte Merryman* (17 F. Cas. 144) decision in 1861, a decision the Lincoln administration disregarded. [43]

Lincoln's final action before convening a joint session of Congress on July 4, 1861, was to issue a directive stating that the Post Office be closed to "treasonable correspondence" and that "persons who were represented to him as being or about to engage in disloyal and treasonable practices . . . be arrested by special civil as well as military agencies and detained in military custody when necessary to prevent them or deter others from such practices." [44] Thus, in sum, before Congress reconvened, Lincoln's executive emergency actions included ordering a naval blockade, raising an army, suspending habeas corpus, regulating the distribution of mail, and appropriating funds to private citizens as well as to the military without congressional approval. Recalling that Lincoln thought the war would be over by July, [45] by the time Lincoln reconvened Congress, he had implemented a complete program that included the executive, legislative, and judicial branches as well as the military in order to suppress the insurrection.

On July 4 Lincoln greeted Congress with a special message that outlined clearly all of the actions he had taken and defended those actions as constitutional because they were under the "war power of the Government." Lincoln, forever the republican and not the dictator, stressed to Congress that if they felt any of his measures were unconstitutional or "outside the boundaries of the Federal Government," they should consider whatever ratification was necessary to legalize them. In the message he made very clear that the executive branch holds emergency powers, stating, "such powers of crisis are inherent within the Constitution, reserved to the executive by means of the Commander-in-Chief clause and must always be aimed at the self-preservation of the Union." He clarified that his decision to take military action was based on necessity and conditions that provided no other choice: "Finding this condition of things, and believing it to be an imperative duty upon the incoming Executive, to prevent, if possible, the consummation of such attempt to destroy the Federal Union, a choice of means to that end became indispensable. This choice was made; and was declared in the Inaugural address."[46]

Furthermore, he reminded the Congress that attempts had been made to end this crisis peacefully, but the Southern rebels were not interested in peaceful resolution:

> [The Federal Government] sought only to hold the public places and property, not already wrested from the Government, and to collect the revenue; relying for the rest, on time, discussion, and the ballot-box. It promised a continuance of the mails, at government expense, to the very people who were resisting the government; and it gave repeated pledges against any disturbance to any of the people, or any of their rights. Of all that which a president might constitutionally, and justifiably, do in such a case, everything was foreborne, without which, it was believed possible to keep the government on foot.[47]

Knowing that the Southern rebels were not interested in ending the dispute without bloodshed, Lincoln concluded that he was left with no other option but to act swiftly against the Southern rebels so as to preserve the Union, stating, "So viewing the issue, no choice was left but to call out the war power of the Government; and so to resist force, employed for its destruction, by force, for its preservation."[48] Thus, Lincoln resolutely believed that, as president, he was obligated to preserve, defend, and protect both the Union and the Constitution.

I include here the following primary source material to demonstrate further Lincoln's interpretation of executive emergency power. Although he would use emergency power reluctantly, he felt that his use of that power was appropriate based on his interpretation of the Constitution, which provided him with inherent emergency power to be used only if necessary to save the Union.

In the following quotation Lincoln elucidated why he, as executive, acted properly and explained that the appropriate role of the legislator was to legitimate his actions. His words here are important because they show Lincoln's respect for the law even during a time of crisis:

> A right result, at this time, will be worth more to the world, than ten times the men, and ten times the money. The evidence reaching us from the country, leaves no doubt, that the material for the work is abundant; and that it needs only the hand of legislation to give it legal sanction, and the hand of the Executive to give it practical shape and efficiency. One of the greatest perplexities of the government, is to avoid receiving troops faster than it can provide for them. In a word, the people will save their government, if the government itself, will do its part, only indifferently well. [49]

In other words, Lincoln expected the legislature to give legal sanction to the executive's actions taken for the sake of preserving the Union. Although Lincoln does acknowledge that the work is abundant and the task of war is complicated, during a crisis the objective end of government, according to him, is to do what is necessary to preserve and defend the nation.

Lincoln also made clear that the executive is responsible for administering the laws and upholding his Oath of Office. In this way the following quotation is important because it further demonstrates Lincoln's profound respect for the law during the crisis: "He desires to preserve the government, that it may be administered for all, as it was administered by the men who made it. Loyal citizens everywhere, have the right to claim this of their government; and the government has no right to withhold, or neglect it. It is not perceived that, in giving it, there is any coercion, any conquest, or any subjugation, in any just sense of those terms."[50] Thus, Lincoln believed that he had an obligation to "preserve government" and that this was his full responsibility because of the Oath of Office he had sworn.

Lincoln even asserted that the power to suspend habeas corpus was not clearly left solely to Congress in times of emergency, arguing that "these measures, whether strictly legal or not, were ventured upon under what appeared to be a popular demand and a public necessity, trusting then, as now, that Congress would readily ratify them. It is believed that nothing has been done beyond the constitutional competency of Congress."[51] This statement is important because it establishes Lincoln's philosophy that even though he suspended habeas corpus, he did so only because he felt that the public demanded him to out of necessity.

Furthermore, Lincoln demonstrated great restraint and regret that the executive had to act, stating, "It was with the deepest regret that the Executive found the duty of employing the war-power, in defense of the government, forced upon him. He could but perform this duty, or surrender the existence of the government."[52] Clearly, he was hesitant to use executive emergency power, and he did not take lightly the responsibility of that power or desire to wield it; rather, Lincoln used the power out of necessity. Additionally, compromise could not fend off the crisis, he claimed, because "No compromise, by public servants, could, in this case, be a cure; not that compromises are not often proper, but that no popular government can long survive a marked precedent, that those who carry an election, can only save the government from immediate destruction, by giving up the main point, upon which the people gave the election."[53] Again, we see that Lincoln's actions were borne out of necessity—and this is the crux of Lincoln's argument and executive emergency philosophy. For Lincoln there was really no choice; if he was indifferent to the Southern hostility, both the Union and the Constitution would be lost, neither of which was acceptable to Lincoln. For him, the only option was a war of necessity, and thus the power the president would wield would be likewise out of necessity.

Lincoln felt that because his power was manifested from the people and granted by the Constitution, the executive was bound to act: "as a private citizen, the Executive could not have consented that these institutions shall perish; much less could he, in betrayal of so vast, and so sacred a trust, as these free people had confided to him. He felt that he had no moral right to shrink; nor even to count the chances of his own life, in what might follow. In full view of his great responsibility, he has, so far, done what he has deemed his duty." Thus, from this statement, we see that Lincoln felt an obligation to act, even if those actions may be contrary to the spirit or literal word of the Constitution, because, as he asserted, he had "a sacred trust [which he could not betray] . . . a great responsibility [of which he could] not let the institutions perish."[54]

In defense of republicanism, Lincoln granted that Congress must legitimate all actions already taken: "You will now, according to your own judgment, perform yours. He sincerely hopes that your views, and your action, may so accord with his, as to assure all faithful citizens, who have been disturbed in their rights, of a certain, and speedy restoration to them, under the Constitution, and the laws."[55] Further, he never implied that his actions were constitutional; in fact, in a letter circulated to Justice Chase at the beginning of the war, Lincoln wrote, "These rebels are violating the Constitution to destroy the Union. I will violate the Constitution if necessary to save the Union; I suspect . . . that our Constitution is going to have a rough time of it before we get done with this row."[56] Thus, Lincoln prescribed to a theory of executive emergency power in which, in the absence of Congress and in the face of great peril and emergency, the president has the right and duty to take measures that might be considered illegal or unconstitutional under ordinary circumstances. However, all actions are necessarily subject to subsequent congressional approval.

Furthermore, Lincoln adhered closely to Hamilton's vision of emergency power in that he believed that, in time of great peril, the energy and execution of action is the complete domain of the presidency. The strong tenor of Lincoln's actions and declarations embrace the assertion that the presidency has the absolute power of defending and preserving the Union. Lincoln stated his rational for using such power in a letter: "Are all the laws but one to go unexecuted, and the Government itself go to pieces lest that one be violated? Even in such a case, would not the official oath be broken if the Government should be overthrown when it was believed that disregarding the single law would tend to preserve it?"[57] In other words, he claimed that in times of great peril an official of a democratic, constitutional state will act more faithfully to his Oath of Office if he breaks one law so that the rest can operate unimpeded. Lincoln established that preserving the Union was the primary objective for the U.S. Republic during the Civil War, and this would, to some extent, become a doctrine of paramount necessity.[58]

From Lincoln's writings and actions I argue that he clearly adhered to an interpretation of executive power during crisis that was expansive and based on necessity. The old Roman adage *inter arma silent leges* (in war, the laws are silent) is a fine summation of Lincoln's actions and rhetoric during the Civil War. Further, in Lincoln's address to Congress on July 4, 1861, he elaborated specifically on his interpretation of executive emergency power:

> The attention of the country has been called to the proposition that one who is sworn to "take care that the laws be faithfully executed," should not himself violate them. Of course some consideration was given to the questions of power, and propriety, before this matter was acted upon. The whole of the laws which were required to be faithfully executed, were being resisted, and failing of execution, in nearly one-third of the States. Must they be allowed to finally fail execution, even had it been perfectly clear, that by the use of the tenderness of the citizen's liberty, that practically, it relieves more of the guilty, than of the innocent, should, to very limited extent, be violated?[59]

Here he explains that, in his theory of executive emergency power, the executive must act to execute the law faithfully with the intent to preserve the Union. Furthermore, he understood that in order to do so, a law or two may need to be violated so as to safeguard the rule of law. Lincoln revealed that although the faithful execution of the laws should be considered paramount in U.S. constitutional obedience, if some members of the Union do not adhere to the law and undermine the stability of the Union, the executive is forced to decide whether to be handicapped to law, bound so tightly that the Union shall cease to exist, or to compromise some laws so as to save the institution.

Lincoln likewise posed a similar question: "Are all the laws, but one, to go unexecuted, and the government itself to go to pieces, lest that one be violated? Even in such a case, would not the official oath be broken, if the government should be overthrown, when it was believed that disregarding the single law, would tend to preserve it?"[60] Clearly, he claimed that, above all, the Union had to be preserved because without it, the Constitution and the rule of law would be rendered meaningless.[61]

Moreover, in a letter to Senator Albert Hodges, Lincoln clarified his rationale for using executive emergency power during the war:

> I have never understood that the Presidency conferred upon me an unrestricted right to act officially upon this judgment and feeling. It was in the oath I took that I would, to the best of my ability, preserve, protect, and defend the Constitution of the United States. I could not take the office without taking the oath. Nor was it my view that I might take an oath to get power, and break the oath in using the power. I understood, too, that in ordinary civil administration this oath even forbade me to practically indulge my primarily abstract judgment on the moral question of slavery. . . . I did understand however, that my oath to preserve the constitution to the best of my ability imposed upon me the duty of preserving, by ever indispensable means, that government, that nation, of which the constitution was the organic law.[62]

Thus, Lincoln clearly outlined once again that, to the best of his abilities and by whatever "indispensable means" he may muster, he must act out of necessity because the Oath of Office conferred upon him as the president obligates him to preserve the Constitution, the nation, and the government of which the "constitution was the organic law." The executive may exercise these powers to suspend the normal democratic processes of law only if he is doing so to preserve the Union.

In response, on August 6, 1861, Congress, faced with the peril of war and Lincoln's initial actions to handle the conflict, registered approval of "all the acts, proclamations, and orders of the President respecting the army and navy of the United States and calling out or relating to the militia or volunteers from the United States."[63] In addition, when first faced with the question of the constitutionality of Lincoln's actions, the Court granted him support. In the *Prize Cases* of 1863 (67 U.S. 635), the Supreme Court addressed the president's authority to enforce and create a naval blockade legally and issued a general consent to Lincoln's extraordinary exercise of war power. The Court stated,

> Whether the President is fulfilling his duties as Commander-In-Chief, in suppressing an insurrection, has met with such armed resistance, and a civil war of such alarming proportions as will compel him to accord to them the character of belligerents, is a question to be decided by him, and this Court must be governed by the decisions and acts of the political department of the Govern-

ment to which this power was entrusted. . . . He must determine what degree of force the crisis demands.[64]

Thus, the Court acknowledged that the president has the constitutional power, under such circumstances as he shall deem imperative, to brand as belligerents the inhabitants of any area during a grave and perilous insurrection. The Court's interpretation therefore suggests that once an emergency has been declared and the presence of enemy combatants of the state has been established, the president has an almost unrestrained power to treat any citizen supporting the insurrection as enemies of the United States, thereby placing such citizens outside the protection of the U.S. Constitution.

Astonishingly, once Congress reconvened following their recess and the president's call to assemble, the normal democratic process of the U.S. Republic began to function again—and did so for the remainder of the war. Scholars have remarked on this because in many other regimes confronted with great peril, as executive power becomes inflated, legislative power usually deflates, typically as the result of delegating legislative power to the executive. However, this was not the case with Lincoln and Congress. Instead, Congress would continue its normal, grinding legislative process. Reflecting on the period, historical scholars have remarked that the "entire legislative program by which the Union was governed at home was done by Congress, and the armies were kept to the field."[65] Lincoln participated little in the legislative process, though he took part substantially in the military strategies and command. In this way, he did not attempt to break down the barrier between the legislative and executive branches; rather, he simply ignored it, as we can see in an annual message to Congress on July 14, 1862. Here, Lincoln outlined a rather general legislative agenda, but he included a specific proposal for compensated abolition. Some in Congress found this move to be audacious, but it nonetheless speaks to the fine balance of power between these two branches during the war: Lincoln did not completely acquiesce to Congress, nor did Congress completely capitulate to Lincoln.

The midterm elections of 1862 led to a stronger Republican Congress, which meant that Congress now showed more concern about the expanse of presidential power during the war as well as the general progression of the war to date. Some Republicans opposed Lincoln and his decisions during the war. The Joint Committee on the Conduct of War caused particular irritation for Lincoln, as it investigated everything related to the conduct of the war.[66] Led by Senators Benjamin Wade and Zachariah T. Chandler, the committee never ceased to assert to Congress its prerogative to participate in the conduct and deliberations of the war effort and maintained that it would not under any circumstances surrender this power to the presidency.[67]

The committee produced eight volumes of recommendations and critiques regarding the way the president handled the war, and these certainly caused continual exasperation for Lincoln. The reports were lengthy, at times hostile, and virtually led to the president's appointment of Edward Stanton as Secretary of War. Most scholars are ambivalent about whether the committee proved harmful in the war effort; however, they do agree that the existence of the committee proved that Congress would not be a passive observer of the war effort and that the U.S. doctrine of the separation of powers would function even during a crisis.[68]

Although Congress challenged the president on issues related to the war, this did not dampen Lincoln's resolve regarding his power during the war. In a 1862 letter to General John C. Breckinridge, Lincoln wrote that, when it came to military matters, his resolve and his interpretation of the war powers afforded him by the Constitution were better defined and more elevated than they were before the war. The letter suggests that Lincoln felt constitutionally empowered to take any necessary actions that the military situation demanded, stating, "As Commander in Chief of the Army and the Navy in time of war I suppose I have a right to take any measure which may best subdue the enemy."[69] Historian Edward Corwin has remarked that Lincoln believed the use of presidential power during the war was unlimited as long as that power was aimed at preserving the Union; thus, if Lincoln met this qualification of power, the matter was then an executive affair.[70]

Many of Lincoln's acts were executions of traditionally congressional power. In fact, after the Acts of August 6, 1861, and July 17, 1862, all future proceedings in the confiscation of rebel property could be regarded as presidential executions of congressional will.[71] This also included all presidential suspensions of the writ of habeas corpus after the Act of March 3, 1863.[72] Many of Lincoln's other actions did not merely enforce congressional statutes, however; instead, he exercised his own presidential authority based on his interpretation of the latitudes of presidential emergency power under the Constitution. The Emancipation Proclamation of September 22, 1862, and the Militia Act of 1862, for example, demonstrate Lincoln's interpretations of emergency power, as they take actions that Lincoln felt Congress lacked the resolution to execute.

Lincoln believed that the emergency and his authority as commander in chief during a war expanded his executive powers, which led him to conclude that he could take measures that, under normal circumstances, would require an amendment to the Constitution. Until this time, no president had come to such a conclusion of emergency power. Following this logic, he adopted one of his most momentous exercises of his executive emergency power, the Emancipation Proclamation of 1862. In this proclamation, Lincoln argued that "he as president could proclaim any or all of the slaves free without compensation to their owners, if such a step were regarded as indispensable to the prosecution of the war."[73] He insisted that such a step was indeed indispensable to the war; thus, Congress's discussions of assigning compensation for abolition were unnecessary. Lincoln stated, "Now, therefore I, Abraham Lincoln, President of the United States, by virtue of the power in me vested as Commander-in-Chief, of the Army and Navy of the United States in time of actual armed rebellion against the authority and government of the United States, and as a fit and necessary war measure for suppressing said rebellion."[74] This quotation is important because it makes clear Lincoln's belief that during an emergency the powers of the presidency expand beyond the limitations of Article II of the Constitution, thus enabling him to do things that he deemed necessary given the circumstances of the war—in this instance, emancipating the slaves without congressional approval.

Furthermore, he stated that "as absolute an exercise of power as the ukase of the Czar which freed the serfs, so do I have the power to free the negro." Thus, he expected that freeing the slaves in the rebel territory would transform them into an immeasurable aid to the Union cause, therefore rendering the proclamation within his powers as commander in chief. The final Emancipation Proclamation of January 1, 1863 elucidates this point further, in which Lincoln stated, "by virtue of the power in me vested as Commander in Chief, of the Army and the Navy of the United States in time of actual armed rebellion against the authority and government of the United States . . . freeing the slaves is a fit and necessary war measure for suppressing the said rebellion."[75] The emancipation, then, according to Lincoln, shows him prescribing to a theory of executive emergency power that granted him expanded power because he was the commander in chief of the military, and any action related to the war effort was thus within the presidency's domain to use for the sake of winning the war.

Under the *Militia Act of 1862,* Lincoln also took further actions without Congress's approval. In this act, he initiated a program of limited conscription, a program to create a complete code of the rules of war applicable to the armies in the field (a power reserved to Congress in Article I, section 8, clause 14 of the Constitution), and a plan to establish military and permanent governments in the conquered territories. With this Militia Act he also issued the first plans for reconstruction.[76] Lincoln justified these actions and the Act because they were related to his execution of the war effort as commander in chief. It is fair to say that Lincoln took his title as commander in chief literally and very seriously.[77]

LINCOLN AND CIVIL LIBERTIES

Lincoln's most difficult decision during the Civil War was whether or not to limit civil liberties throughout the crisis. Although he did not enact a sweeping suspension of the Bill of Rights, he did restrain liberties in order to limit the very real concerns regarding treason throughout the Union. He suspended the writ of habeas corpus during the war, and although this first only included the rail lines from Washington DC to Philadelphia, it later expanded as far north as New York City. Here I will review Lincoln's defense for these actions. In sum, he sought to prevent treason and discouragement of recruiting Union soldiers as well as to maintain peace in the North. The constitutional merit for these actions rested on his interpretation of his absolute power as commander in chief of the military during a war.

Even though Chief Justice Roger B. Taney rebuked the president for suspending habeas corpus, Lincoln never considered his action unconstitutional, partly because he believed that a component of his duty as commander in chief was to prevent further insurrections and suppress treason in the Union territories. His September 24, 1862, declaration explains his interpretation of his duties, such that he suspended the writ without even referencing Congress as the sole authority to do so, stating,

> Be it ordered, first, that during the existing insurrection, and as a necessary measure for suppressing the same, all Rebels and Insurgents, their aiders and abettors, within the United States, and all persons discouraging volunteer enlistments, resisting militia drafts, or guilty of any disloyal practice affording aid and comfort to Rebels against the authority of the United States, shall be subject to martial law and liable to trial and punishment by courts-martial and military commissions. [78]

Thus, according to Lincoln, his action to suspend habeas corpus was not for his own gain or the benefit of a malicious agenda; instead, he asserted this power to reduce the relative risk of treason and future insurrections in the North. He was interested only in using the suspension of the writ to obtain "Rebels and Insurgents, their aiders and abettors" and those who are "discouraging volunteer enlistments, resisting the militia drafts, or are guilty of disloyal practice." Therefore, Lincoln suspended habeas corpus to protect loyal, law-abiding citizens of the Union and aid in the Union's efforts to win the war.

Lincoln also stated that the federal government should handle such enemy combatants of the state, "that the writ of habeas corpus is suspended in respect to all persons arrested, or who are now or hereafter during the rebellion shall be imprisoned in any fort, camp, arsenal, military prison, or other place of confinement by any military authority, or by the sentence of any court-martial or military commission." [79]

In regard to the second component of Lincoln's address, that dealing with the suspension of habeas corpus, the Court struck down Lincoln's assertion that he could try civilian enemies of the state in military tribunal courts while civilian courts were still in operation. [80] However, this decision *Ex Parte Milligan* (71 U.S. 2 1866), was rendered long after the war was over, in 1866, so the decision had no impact on Lincoln's actions. The other key case regarding the writ suspension was *Ex Parte Merryman* (17 F Case 144 1861), a lower court decision in which Chief Justice Taney ruled against Lincoln's assertion that he held the authority to suspend the writ of habeas corpus. Taney ruled that only Congress had the authority to suspend the writ, as cited in Article I, section 9 of the Constitution. Lincoln disregarded the decision. In his address to Congress on July 4, 1861, he reasoned that he was permitted to suspend the writ, asking, "Are all the laws, but one, to go unexecuted, and the government itself go to pieces, lest that one be violated?"[81] His answer was that violating the law may be necessary in order to save the Union. The controversy over this issue was resolved when Congress passed the Habeas Corpus Act of 1863, which formally suspended the writ of habeas corpus under congressional authority.

Lincoln was remarkably tolerant of criticism during the war and upheld the principle of free press. In fact, historians have remarked that even though he placed limitations on the postal service, some seditious editors were detained, and some newspapers "deserved" suspension, in general, the liberty and the license of the Northern press suffered no restrictions.[82] Lincoln explicated his policy regarding the expression of opinion in a letter to General Schofield: "You will only arrest individuals and suppress assemblies or newspapers when they may be working palpable injury to the military in your charge, and in no other case will you interfere with the expression of opinion in any form or allow it to be interfered with violently by others. In this you have discretion to exercise with great caution, calmness, and forbearance."[83] Thus, Lincoln placed a high degree of trust in the role of the citizenry to act with calm discretion as they enforced the president's actions, in this instance, to screen mail and news that the office would deem as causing "palpable injury to the military." Apparently, to Lincoln, screening the mail and applying censure was permissible during the Civil War.

DISCUSSION

To conclude this chapter, I now explore the question of where Lincoln's approach to executive emergency powers can be situated within the philosophical field on this issue. The previous section reviewed Lincoln's words and actions to identify some of his philosophy, but it is also important to consider how Lincoln's theories fit into the larger sphere of theoretical development on emergency power. Although scholars have looked at Lincoln's words and actions so as to determine whether he was a constitutional dictator, there is little discussion that considers where he stood in relation to the intellectual history on emergency power. Here I explore previous thinkers' theories on emergency power and consider them alongside Lincoln's philosophy in order to construct a tangible argument to demonstrate that Lincoln had a unique interpretation of emergency power that combined the thoughts of Locke with those of Hamilton. In so doing, he formed an interpretation of executive emergency power as that which should be used only out of necessity to preserve the state. Furthermore, with his theory of executive emergency power he held that the power may be used only out of necessity to (1) preserve the state through quick response to threats, (2) provide the necessary energy in the response to the crisis, and (3) provide a lawful response that respects other institutions and the written law.

However, some of Lincoln's actions appear unconstitutional. At the very least, expanding the military and disbursing funds were unconstitutional; both powers are reserved explicitly for Congress. Even Lincoln's action to suspend habeas corpus in regions where there was not even the slightest glimpse of insurrection may be considered unconstitutional. But the question to consider here is whether Lincoln considered these actions unconstitutional. In order to answer this, we must consider his contention that necessity justified actions that would otherwise be unlawful. Although this claim of necessity may initially seem to be a maneuver by which to stand above the law when dealing with an emergency, his use of emergency power is more complex. Namely, though his actions were derived from the Constitution, the powers to carry out those actions were not those of the executive. Consequently, to consider his actions constitutional, Lincoln felt that during the war he had the authority to use all the powers enumerated in the Constitution, including those explicitly granted to Congress. Thus, to Lincoln, his actions were constitutional because he was upholding the oath of office that expressly stated that the president has the sole responsibility of preserving and defending the Union.

To begin, we determine whether Lincoln's interpretation of executive emergency power closely associates him with Jefferson's, which itself draws from Locke's concept of "prerogative power." We'll consider first how Jefferson and Lincoln seem to speak to each other, second, how Lincoln speaks to Locke, and, finally, how Lincoln speaks to Alexander Hamilton.

Jefferson stated that a "strict observance of the written laws is doubtless one of the high duties of a good citizen, but it is not the highest."[84] Furthermore, rather than strict adherence to the literal letter of the law, he stated that the "laws of necessity, of self-preservation, of saving our country when in danger, are of higher obligation" because to "lose our country by a scrupulous adherence to written law, would be to lose the law itself, with life, liberty, property and all those who are enjoying them with us; thus absurdly sacrificing the end to the means."[85] Thus, although Jefferson claimed that an executive may have a moral duty to respond to a crisis, he did not insinuate that such action is indemnified. Instead, he, like Lincoln, believed that Congress, the Court, and the people would ultimately judge the legality and constitutionality of the actions taken during the crisis. Therefore, for both Jefferson and Lincoln, the president must go beyond the prescribed law on occasion, but the president's actions are never above the law.

Lincoln pondered the same questions as Jefferson, asking, "are all the laws, but one, to go unexecuted, and the government itself, go to pieces, lest that one be violated? . . . Would not the official oath be broken, if the government should be overthrown, when it was believed that disregarding the single law, would tend to preserve it?" And he provided the same answer as Jefferson did: the executive has a moral duty to respond to the crisis even if such actions go beyond the scope of the law. Lincoln did diverge from Jefferson, however, in that he considered emergency power to be derived from the Constitution; whereas Jefferson suggested that his actions during the Louisiana Purchase were potentially beyond the scope of law. Therefore, although Lincoln appeared to favor Locke's concept of prerogative (which Jefferson supported), that prerogative is cloaked under the shield of Hamilton's suggestion of inherent executive emergency power. Lincoln argued that his powers were constitutional and not conditioned on the test of the people's or Congress's validation. In fact, when he addressed Congress on July 4, 1861, he explained his actions, stating that Congress "would readily ratify them."[86] The question then becomes why Lincoln argued that his actions were constitutional.

Lincoln defended his possibly unconstitutional actions in two ways. First, he argued that his actions, "whether strictly legal or not," responded to the public's demand and were a public necessity, "trusting, then as now, that Congress would readily ratify them." Second, he claimed that his actions—such as suspending habeas corpus, raising an army, and blockading the Southern ports—were consistent with his oath to "preserve and protect the Union" and "take care that the laws be faithfully executed." The Southern rebels violated the law when they declared their secession from the Union and when they fired shots on a federal property, Fort Sumter. In response, Lincoln had to choose between "violating a single law" to a "very limited extent" and risking that every law would fail "of execution, in nearly one third of the States." Therefore, he felt that his oath required him to act, to choose between the lesser of two evils as it related to observing the law. Thus, he answered his question, "Are all the laws, but one, to go unexecuted, and the government itself, go to pieces, lest that one be violated?" Some laws, such as suspending habeas corpus, raising an army, blockading the south, and restricting mail service, were laws that needed to be violated in order to save the Union.[87]

Lincoln's interpretation of executive emergency power is structured on two very important tenets—that emergency power should be used only out of absolute necessity and that the necessity is defined based on the degree of the crisis. In this instance, the Civil War, the degree of the crisis warranted the use of power based on Lincoln's second tenet that emergency power should be used only to preserve the Union. Therefore, Lincoln's interpretation of executive emergency power is a theory of necessity.

Further, evidence strongly suggests that Lincoln supported John Locke's concept of prerogative power. Locke claimed that an executive must have great latitudes to combat a crisis, known as the executive's prerogative. This prerogative power would be broad and, at times, legal, but at other times it might be a prescription against the law. The necessity for prerogative was due to the need for response in the face of factors that could slow that response, such as the possibility that the lawmaking power may not always be in session, that the lawmaking power is too numerous, the laws may not account for the crisis, that the laws may not be flexible enough to deal with the crisis, and accountability. Locke apparently viewed executive emergency powers as occasionally extralegal rather than implicit within a set of laws or constitution.

Lincoln's actions to suspend habeas corpus, raise an army, disperse funds to support the military, blockade the South, and suspend some mail distribution appear unconstitutional when examining the Constitution. In fact, all such actions are reserved to the powers of Congress. However, when we consider the actions in relation to Locke's concept of "prerogative," we see that Lincoln was acting in accordance with Locke's concept, especially considering that Lincoln's own reasons for his actions were to save the Union, a justification that is completely congruent with Locke's assertion that emergency power must be used only for the public's good and with the full intent to preserve the state.

In each of Lincoln's actions, he consistently defended himself as working toward preserving the Union and Constitution. Further, his actions were for the sake of the public good. Additionally, Lincoln's address to Congress on July 4, 1861, marked a deviation from Locke's pure concept of prerogative to Hamilton's concept of prerogative power as an inherent constitutional power. Lincoln was confident that Congress would "readily ratify his actions."[88] Because he seemed to suggest that his power to act was in accordance with the Constitution, we now must investigate where and how he could use his powers. In order to understand this, we may construe that Lincoln supported Hamilton's argument of emergency powers as inherent within Article II of the Constitution, relying on the Oath clause: "I have never understood that the Presidency conferred upon me an unrestricted right to act officially upon this judgment and feeling. It was in the oath I took that I would, to the best of my ability, preserve, protect, and defend the Constitution of the United States."[89] He also cited the Take Care clause—"take care that the laws be faithfully executed, even if I may violate one law"—and the Commander-in-Chief clause—"the Constitution grants me the power to command the army."[90]

Lincoln suggested that these four clauses, taken together, provide an interpretation of executive emergency power that is, in fact, constitutional. This interpretation supports Hamilton's comments in Federalist No 23, which suggests that the Constitution provides for the common defense and preservation of the state, that the power to preserve the state is inherently the executive's discretion. Hamilton wrote,

> Because it is impossible to foresee or define the extent and variety of national exigencies, or the correspondent extent and variety of the means which may be necessary to satisfy them. The circumstances that endanger the safety of nations are infinite, and for this reason no constitutional shackles can wisely be imposed on the power to which the care of it is committed. This power ought to be coextensive with all the possible combinations of such circumstances; and ought to be under the direction of the same councils [executive] which are appointed to preside over the common defense.[91]

Here, Hamilton's assertion that "no constitutional shackles can wisely be imposed on the power [executive emergency power] to which the care of it is committed [the preservation of the state]" is key. Based on this along with Lincoln's interpretation of executive emergency power, it would appear that both Hamilton and Lincoln share the same argument that executive emergency power is an inherent power within Article II of the Constitution. Lincoln asserted that the Oath clause combined with the Commander–in–Chief and Take Care clauses granted him inherent powers to combat the crisis—the clauses Hamilton cited when he argued that the executive must have an inherent power to combat crisis.

However, to state that Lincoln's interpretation of emergency power is strictly a blend of Hamiltonian and Lockean thoughts would be an oversimplification of his thinking. Further analysis of Lincoln's philosophy reveals congruencies with theorists such as Montesquieu, Machiavelli, Plato, and Aristotle.

First, Montesquieu explained that, even though emergency power may rest with the executive during times of emergency, "the presence of federative power" does not allow the executive to ignore or threaten the structure of "separation of powers."[92] Lincoln's address on July 4, 1861, seems to support a respect for separated powers, in which he stated, "I believe the Congress will easily ratify my actions."[93] Thus, Lincoln indicated that he supported the separation of powers when he asked Congress to validate his actions. Rather than ignoring them altogether, he reconvened Congress with the intent of opening the debate regarding the appropriateness of his actions while Congress was in recess. In the end Congress ratified Lincoln's actions, thereby maintaining a balance of power between these two branches of government.

Thus, both Lincoln's words and actions supported Machiavelli's thoughts that executive emergency power must be aimed at preserving the state. Machiavelli asserted that the primary function of government is to preserve itself, and ultimately, this is the sole responsibility of the ruler.[94] Looking at Lincoln's actions, then, we see that he clearly agreed with Machiavelli that a ruler has the obligation to preserve the state.

Further, Lincoln would also support Plato's assertion that the ruling class is obligated to do whatever is necessary to preserve the republic. According to Plato, a just ruler would never let his state collapse into ruin.[95] Again, based on Lincoln's words and actions, we can surmise that he would have agreed with Plato because he believed that allowing the Union to collapse would mean that he had failed to meet his responsibilities and obligations as president.

I also argue that Lincoln's interpretation of executive emergency power is a bit Aristotelian. Lincoln's execution of his power was consistently mindful and reverent of the rule of law and the Constitution. His respect for the law is thus congruent with Aristotle's statement that the law is always supreme, even during a crisis.[96]

Many scholars, such as Clinton Rossiter and Edward Corwin, have debated whether Lincoln was a constitutional dictator. In fact, Corwin suggests that because Lincoln used a great deal of power that was reserved to Congress, his behavior was unconstitutional. However, he also went on to assert that even though Lincoln did things no other president did, he took such sweeping actions because the nation was embroiled in a civil war.[97] In other words, Corwin asserted that Lincoln was clearly the exception, not the rule. Further, Rossiter granted that Lincoln used a lot of power but that the U.S. political system, in contrast to other nations, included restraints that prevented him from becoming a dictator. Rossiter argued that the Constitution, separation of powers, and federalism are all aspects of the U.S. political system, and each in their own way prevent the rise of a constitutional dictator. Rossiter points out that the Constitution clearly does not grant dictatorial powers during emergency and the separation of powers enables the other branches of the U.S. government to restrain power, if necessary. Similarly, federalism may prevent the executive from usurping power.[98]

Consequently, while reviewing both Lincoln's words and actions in order to understand his interpretation of executive emergency power, we can see that he was not a dictator. Although he did use more power and did so more broadly than any previous president, he was responding to a crisis of unprecedented qualification and enormity. The very life of the nation depended on Lincoln. The evidence provided in this chapter helps clarify his interpretation of executive emergency power that combined Lockean principles (prerogative power) with Hamilton's theory of an energetic executive during a crisis so as to create a theory of executive emergency power built on using the power out of necessity and aimed at preserving the Union. Lincoln's ideas are known as the necessity doctrine, which comprises both Locke and Hamilton's theory of executive emergency power. Lincoln was Lockean when he acted alone to preserve the state, even if that meant violating the Constitution, and Lincoln appeared to be Hamiltonian when he urged Congress that his actions were inherent in the Constitution.[99] Lincoln drew heavily on his predecessors' actions and interpretations of emergency power, concluding, as they did, that his constitutional duty to execute the laws, his role as chief executive, and his presidential oath granted him the power to use force, if necessary, against those who opposed the authority of the United States. He correctly understood that preserving the nation was the president's primary and ultimate job responsibility, as seen in Lincoln's understanding of his oath of office: "my oath to preserve the constitution to the best of my ability, imposed upon me the duty of preserving, by every indispensable means, that government, that nation, of which that constitution was the organic law."[100] Lincoln embodies the idea of a cavalier president and clearly, at times, violated the Constitution.

In conclusion, Lincoln was not a dictator. Even as the election of 1864 approached, rather than declaring that an election was unnecessary or might lead to disaster for the nation if he lost, Lincoln instead demanded that a free and fair election must take place, even if the South did not take part. This set of actions is clearly not the behavior of a dictator.

NOTES

1. Edward Corwin, *The President: Office and Powers, 1787–1984: History and Analysis of Practice and Opinion* (New York: New York University Press, 1984), 12.
2. Further readings on the American Civil War should see Don Edward Fehrenbacher, ed., *The Civil War: Rebellion to Reconstruction* (Princeton, NJ: Princeton University Press, 1950).
3. "The Complete Civil War," in Fehrenbacher, *The Civil War*.
4. Ibid.
5. Abraham Lincoln, "Second Inaugural Address 1865," in Abraham Lincoln, *Abraham Lincoln: Speeches and Writings, 1859–1865: Speeches, Letters, and Miscellaneous Writings, Presidential Messages and Proclamations*, edited by Don E. Fehrenbacher, 221–23 (New York: Literary Classics of the United States, 1989).
6. Lincoln, "Second Inaugural Address 1865."
7. Corwin, *The President*, and Clinton Rossiter, *Constitutional Dictatorship: Crisis Government in the Modern Democracies* (Princeton, NJ: Princeton University Press, 1948).
8. Rossiter, *Constitutional Dictatorship*.
9. Congressional Record, General Administrative Office of the Federal Government Registry, July 1861.
10. Abraham Lincoln, Second Inaugural Address 1865, in Lincoln, *Abraham Lincoln: Speeches and Writings, 1859–1865*, 221.
11. Abraham Lincoln, Letter to Albert Hodges, April 4, 1864, in Abraham Lincoln, *Abraham Lincoln: Speeches and Writings, 1832–1858: Speeches, Letters, and Miscellaneous Writings, the Lincoln-Douglas Debates*, edited by Don E. Fehrenbacher, 45–47 (New York: Library of America, 1989).
12. See Rossiter, *Constitutional Dictatorship*, and Corwin, *The President*.

13. Lincoln, Letter to Albert Hodges, April 4, 1864.

14. Rossiter, *Constitutional Dictatorship*, 223.

15. Ibid.

16. "Lincoln's speech at the Springfield Lyceum," in *Collected Works of Abraham Lincoln*, edited by Roy Basler, Abraham Lincoln Association: 2006.

17. Abraham Lincoln, Special Message to Congress, July 4, 1861, in Lincoln, *Abraham Lincoln: Speeches and Writings, 1859–1865*, 247–49.

18. "Letter to Wiliam Herndon," in *Collected Works of Abraham Lincoln*, edited by Roy Basler, Abraha m Lincoln Association: 2006.

19. Abraham Lincoln, Nomination Speech for the Senate, 1858, in *Abraham Lincoln: Speeches and Writings, 1859–1865*, 586–87.

20. Ibid., 585–87.

21. Lincoln, Special Message to Congress, July 4, 1861, in *Abraham Lincoln: Speeches and Writings, 1859–1865*, 247-49.

22. Ibid., 247–50.

23. Ibid., 248–49.

24. Ibid., 249.

25. Ibid., 250.

26. Lincoln, Letter to Albert Hodges, April 4, 1864, 45-47.

27. James D. Richardson, *A Compilation of the Messages and Papers of the Presidents, 1789–1897* (Washington, DC: Government Printing Office, 1896–1899), vol. VI, 78.

28. Ibid.

29. Ibid., 13–14.

30. Rossiter, *Constitutional Dictatorship.*, 223.

31. Abraham Lincoln, "April 19 Proclamation," in Lincoln, *Abraham Lincoln: Speeches and Writings, 1859–1865*, 351–63.

32. Rossiter, *Constitutional Dictatorship.*, 223.

33. Lincoln, "April 19 Proclamation," 351–63.

34. Lincoln, "April 19 Proclamation," 353–65.

35. Abraham Lincoln, "May 3 Proclamation," in Lincoln, *Abraham Lincoln: Speeches and Writings, 1859–1865*, 365–70.

36. Abraham Lincoln, "April 20 Proclamation," in Lincoln, *Abraham Lincoln: Speeches and Writings, 1859–1865*, 366–67.

37. Abraham Lincoln, "April 27 Proclamation," in Lincoln, *Abraham Lincoln: Speeches and Writings, 1859–1865*, 367–69.

38. Ibid.

39. Ibid.

40. Lincoln, Letter to Albert Hodges, April 4, 1864.

41. Richardson, *A Compilation of the Messages and Papers of the Presidents, 1789–1897*, 18–19.

42. Abraham Lincoln, Letter to Attorney General Bates, July 5, 1861, in Lincoln, *Abraham Lincoln: Speeches and Writings, 1859–1865*.

43. S. G. Fisher, "The Suspension of Habeas Corpus During the War of the Rebellion," *Political Science Quarterly* 3, no. 3 (1888): 454–88, 454.

44. Richardson, *A Compilation of the Messages and Papers of the Presidents, 1789–1897*, 102–4.

45. See Rossiter, *Constitutional Dictatorship*, and Corwin, *The President*.

46. Abraham Lincoln, "Special Message to Congress, July 4, 1861," *Abraham Lincoln: Speeches and Writings, 1859–1865*, 252–53.

47. Ibid.

48. Lincoln, "Special Message to Congress, July 4, 1861."

49. Ibid.

50. Ibid.

51. Ibid.

52. Ibid.

53. Ibid.

54. Ibid.

55. Ibid.

56. James Bryce, *The American Commonwealth*, vol. I, *The National Government, the State Government* (Indianapolis, IN: Liberty Fund, 1995), 289.

57. Lincoln, "Special Message to Congress, July 4, 1861."

58. Rossiter, *Constitutional Dictatorship*, 229.

59. Lincoln, "Special Message to Congress, July 4, 1861," and Lincoln, Letter to Albert Hodges, April 4, 1864.

60. Lincoln, "Special Message to Congress, July 4, 1861."

61. This same proposition will confront the George W. Bush presidency, in which the administration would have to determine to what extent the president may act without the accordance of the Constitution in order to preserve the nation from hostilities. Thus, Lincoln's actions clearly shape the doctrine of the Unitary Executive and the necessity for action, setting a precedent for later administrations.

62. Lincoln, Letter to Albert Hodges, April 4, 1864.

63. U.S. Statutory Law, 326, in Federal Registry.

64. *Prize Cases* (67 U.S. 635, 1863).

65. Corwin, *The President*, 20–25.

66. William Whatley Pierson, "The Committee on the Conduct of the Civil War," *The American History Review* 23, no. 3 (April 1918), 550–76, 550, and T. Harry Williams, "The Committee on the Conduct of the War," *The Journal of the American Military Institute* 3, no. 3 (Autumn 1939), 138–56, 139.

67. Williams, "The Committee on the Conduct of the War," 139.

68. Pierson, "The Committee on the Conduct of the Civil War," 550, and Williams, "The Committee on the Conduct of the War," 139.

69. John G. Nicolay, and John Hay, *Abraham Lincoln: A History* (New York: Century Co., 1890), 32–35.

70. Corwin, *The President*, 382–83.

71. Ibid., 383.

72. These acts are, respectively, XII Statutory 319, 589, and 755, in Federal Registry 1863.

73. Lincoln, "Emancipation Proclamation," 424.

74. Ibid.

75. Ibid.

76. Richardson, *A Compilation of the Messages and Papers of the Presidents, 1789–1897*, 96–98, 120, and *Official Records, War of the Rebellion*, vol. 3, Princeton: 1948. On the matter of Reconstruction and the military governments in the rebel territories, Congress refused to seat members of Arkansas under Lincoln's 1864 plan of reconstruction, which was part of the "Ten Percent Plan." Whether Congress or the presidency had the authority to aid people in the rebel areas so as to establish republican and loyal governments is an unsettled question. As such, the period of Reconstruction was contentious between Congress and the presidency. For more, see Allen Harmon Carpenter, "Military Government of Southern Territory, 1861–1865," *Annual Report* 1 (Washington, DC: Government Printing Office, 1900), 465–98.

77. Richardson, *A Compilation of the Messages and Papers of the Presidents, 1789–1897*, 100–101, Executive Orders of the President.

78. Abraham Lincoln, "Proclamation Suspending the Writ of Habeas Corpus, September 24, 1862," in Lincoln, *Abraham Lincoln: Speeches and Writings, 1859–1865*, 365–68.

79. Ibid.

80. *Ex Parte Milligan* (71 U.S. 2 1866).

81. Abraham Lincoln, "Message to Congress in Special Session, July 4, 1861," *Abraham Lincoln: Speeches and Writings, 1859–1865*, 252–53.

82. James Garfield Randall, *Constitutional Problems under Lincoln* (New York, London: Appleton and Co., 1926), chapter 8.

83. Lincoln, Letter to John M. Schofield, in Lincoln, *Abraham Lincoln: Speeches and Writings, 1859–1865*, 592–93.

84. Thomas Jefferson, Letter to John C. Breckenridge, August 12, 1803, in *The Writings of Thomas Jefferson*, edited by Paul Leicester Ford, 1138–39 (New York: G. P. Putnam's Sons, 1892–1899).

85. Lincoln, "Message to Congress in Special Session, July 4, 1861."

86. Ibid.

87. Ibid.

88. Ibid.

89. Lincoln, Letter to Albert Hodges, April 4, 1864, 586.

90. Lincoln, "Message to Congress in Special Session, July 4, 1861."

91. Alexander Hamilton, Federalist No. 23, in Alexander Hamilton, James Madison, and John Jay, *The Federalist Papers*, 135–37 (New York: Bantam Press, 1982), 135–37.

92. Montesquieu, *Spirit of the Laws*, in Michael Morgan, ed., *Classics of Moral and Political Theory* (Indianapolis, IN: Hackett Publishing Co., 1992), 400–403.

93. Lincoln, "Message to Congress in Special Session, July 4, 1861."

94. Machiavelli, *The Prince*, in Morgan, *Classics of Moral and Political Theory*, ch. 1, 454–57.

95. Plato, *The Republic*, Book III, in Morgan, *Classics of Moral and Political Theory*, 235–37.

96. Aristotle, *Politics*, Book II, in Morgan, *Classics of Moral and Political Theory*, 301–10.

97. Corwin, *The President*, 382–84.

98. Rossiter, *Constitutional Dictatorship*, 223–26.

99. Rossiter, *Constitutional Dictatorship*; Corwin, *The President*.

100. Lincoln, Special Message to Congress, July 4, 1861.

Chapter Six

George W. Bush's Interpretation and Application of Executive Emergency Power following the Attacks of September 11, 2001

In this chapter I explore the theory of executive emergency power in modern America, following the attacks of September 11, 2001, to determine (1) President George W. Bush's interpretation of emergency power following the attacks and (2) how Bush's interpretation of executive emergency power either agreed or disagreed philosophically with previous thinkers and presidents.

In order to understand President Bush's interpretation of emergency power, I will examine three key areas of thought: The Unitary Executive Theory; the Office of Legal Counsel Opinions following the attacks of September 11, 2001; and Presidential Signing Statements. An understanding of the Unitary Executive Theory is important because President Bush will support the theory, but offer a nuanced interpretation, favoring a strong presidency and a vigorous use of all presidential power unconstrained by congressional oversight or consultation.[1] Such an interpretation of presidential authority is similar to an imperialist president, and is very critical in times of emergency.

The central questions concerning the Unitary Executive Theory are (1) Is the theory a correct interpretation of Hamilton's words in the *Federalist Papers* and (2) Does the theory suggest that a president may do whatever he wants in times of emergency?

Bush sought advice from his Office of Legal Counsel (OLC) for legal justification of emergency power. In the OLC opinions, Bush advisors relied on Hamilton's interpretation of executive emergency power, drawn from the

Federalist Papers, to define and justify Bush's use of emergency power following the attacks of September 11, 2001.

THE UNITARY EXECUTIVE THEORY

According to the proponents of the Unitary Executive Theory, the concept is rooted in the writings of Alexander Hamilton, particularly the *Federalist Papers*.[2] The *Federalist Papers* were composed and distributed shortly after the Constitutional Convention, during which the founders discussed and ultimately drafted the new constitution. The papers were distributed for the purpose of debating central issues of the convention concerning the federal government. Hamilton, Madison, and Jay wrote the papers with the hope of persuading readers to support the Constitution.

Federalist No. 70 is the primary source of evidence for the Unitary Executive Theory. In Federalist No. 70, Hamilton addressed the question of how the executive branch of government should be conceived, especially the primary debate at the time: how many people would comprise the executive branch. Should there be one person as president, creating a unitary executive, or should multiple people comprise the executive? Unlike the Anti-Federalist opposition, Hamilton was in favor of a singular, that is, unitary, presidency.

In Federalist No. 70 Hamilton's primary reason for a singular presidency is the need for energy in the executive. Hamilton argued that an executive with energy is "a leading character in the definition of good government." He stated that a single "magistrate is essential to the protection of the community against foreign attacks"; and "it is not less essential to the steady administration of the laws; to the protection of property against those irregular and high-handed combinations which sometimes interrupt the ordinary course of justice; to the security of liberty against the enterprises and assaults of ambition, of faction, and of anarchy."[3] Proponents of the Unitary Executive Theory use this short passage from Federalist No. 70 as a primary source to suggest that Hamilton favored a strong, imperial, and independent executive, especially in times of crisis.[4]

Hamilton claimed that unity is essential for sufficient energy in the executive and "that unity is conducive to energy will not be disputed." Unity in the executive will lead to "decision, activity, secrecy, and dispatch" and these actions "will generally characterize the proceedings of one man in a much more eminent degree than the proceedings of any greater number; and in proportion as the number is increased, these qualities will be diminished."[5]

According to Hamilton, "vesting the power in two or more magistrates of equal dignity and authority" destroys unity in the executive. This loss of unity will harm the executive because "wherever two or more persons are engaged in any common enterprise or pursuit, there is always danger of difference of opinion. . . . Whenever these happen, they lessen the respectability, weaken the authority, and distract the plans and operation of those whom they divide." Varying opinions may "assail the supreme executive magistracy of a country, consisting of a plurality of persons, they might impede or frustrate the most important measures of the government, in the most critical emergencies of the state."[6]

In contrast to Hamilton, the Anti-Federalists favored a plural presidency. George Mason of Virginia advocated a plural presidency because he wanted to diffuse presidential power, and feared the rise of an American monarchy. This committee-style presidency would consist of at least two men chosen from the Congress from different sections of the country, who would jointly constitute the executive.[7]

At the Constitutional Convention, the committee on detail was responsible for negotiating the details of the executive branch. James Wilson led the committee and conceded that the pluralist executive would be useless, ineffective, and fail to unify the nation. Wilson suggested that a single authority would be more accountable.[8] After all, who would you impeach if there were several people comprising executive authority?

Hamilton built his argument against a plural presidency upon three distinct and important claims. In Federalist No. 70, Hamilton argued that "the president must be unitary in order to effectively lead, execute the laws, and command the army." Hamilton suggested that a plural president would not be "decisive, would not be swift to respond, and would not be accountable." Dissent and criticism of the presidential office would become problematic; how can you criticize five different heads of one body? Which head is most to blame? Hamilton suggested that a unitary executive would have greater autonomy than a plural leader.[9] According to Hamilton, greater autonomy in the executive would give the public a clear path for expressing their dissatisfaction with the presidency, resulting in greater accountability in the executive.[10]

A straightforward reading of Hamilton's argument indicates that he favored a singular presidency, that is, a unitary executive rather than a committee-style executive. The executive would be responsible to execute the laws, command the army, and respond to emergencies. Hamilton did not suggest in any of his writings that the president will be above "any magistrates" or that the presidency would not coordinate with the other branches of government.[11]

However, supporters of the modern Unitary Executive Theory propose a different interpretation of Federalist No. 70, which posits a strong, unitary executive unconstrained by the supervision of other branches of government. In other words, advocates of the Unitary Executive Theory, especially those who would cite it during the Bush presidency in support of his authority, suggest an interpretation of presidential power similar to an "imperial presidency."[12]

The Unitary Executive Theory claims that the executive has the lawful right to completely control and administer the duties of his office. In administering his duties, the president does not require congressional oversight or consultation.[13] This is especially critical in relation to presidents' execution of laws. Sometimes presidents will object to certain provisions in a law and simply not execute a particular provision of the statute, because they claim a constitutional prerogative or discretion to administer the laws as they see fit.[14] Such logic is congruent with a modern interpretation of the Unitary Executive, and will be explored in the following section.

Steven Calabresi and Christopher Yoo have launched an ambitious project exploring the Unitary Executive Theory in American history, both in practice and rhetoric. They break down the theory into three distinct components: (1) the president's powers to remove subordinate policy-making officials at will; (2) the president's power to direct the manner in which subordinate officials exercise discretionary executive power; and (3) the president's power to veto or nullify such officials' exercises of discretionary executive power.[15]

The first component of the theory, "the president's power to remove subordinate policy making officials at will,"[16] was mostly resolved in 1926 with the Supreme Court decision in *Myers v. U.S.* (272 U.S. 52, 1926). President Andrew Johnson and Congress struggled over the *Tenure in Office Act* of 1867, which required the president to formally receive approval from Congress to remove an official of the executive branch. In *Myers v. U.S.* the Court first considered the original debate of the first Congress in 1789, and held that the power to remove appointed officers is vested in the president alone. According to Chief Justice Taft, to deny the president that power would not allow him to "discharge his own constitutional duty of seeing that the laws be faithfully executed."[17]

Dealing with the two remaining components of the theory—the president's power to direct the manner in which subordinate officials exercise discretionary executive power and the president's power to veto or nullify such officials' exercises of discretionary executive power[18]—scholar Michael Herz, along with Calabresi and Yoo, cited the Take Care clause of the Constitution as evidence to support the president's legal responsibility to oversee the executive branch. Herz argued, "the 'Take Care' clause ensures that the president will not only execute the law personally, but also it obligates him to oversee the executive branch agencies to insure that they are faithfully executing the laws." Herz's interpretation of the Take Care clause explicitly means that the executive agencies are "executing the law according to the president's wishes, as opposed to some independent policy goal."[19]

Justice Elena Kagan reinforced the point that the president has the authority to direct subordinate officials within the executive branch because "when Congress delegates discretionary authority to an agency official, since that official is subordinate of the President, it is so granting discretionary authority (unless otherwise specified) to the President."[20] Here, Kagan suggested that Congress lacks the ability of oversight once it passes a bill, thus leaving the president to ensure the law is faithfully executed.

Calabresi and Yoo offered a general schematic outline that suggests that the "rise of the modern presidency," or the imperial presidency, has resulted in more presidents favoring the Unitary Executive Theory.[21] Calabresi and Yoo conceded that, following the Watergate scandal and the insidious Vietnam era, presidents were "reeled" in by congressional oversight.[22] The War Powers Resolutions are a classic example of congressional oversight.[23]

Following President Jimmy Carter's soft diplomatic approaches and failures in the wake of the Iran hostage crisis and the oil embargos, scholars have suggested a resurrection of the theory.[24] Carter's predecessor Gerald Ford expressed frustration dealing with an overzealous Congress bent on reducing presidential authority as a consequence of Watergate and the Vietnam War. Ford went as far as to state that the presidency was "imperiled."[25]

The Reagan administration is closely associated with the revival of the Unitary Executive Theory. The Reagan administration "created a two-prong strategy of appointing Reagan loyalists and boosting the authority of the Office of Management and Budget to insure the executive branch agency heads made decisions with the president's preferences in mind."[26]

First, Ed Meese, Reagan's attorney general and principal advocate of the Unitary Executive Theory, supervised the hiring process to ensure that Reagan loyalists would comprise the executive branch. Meese stated, "We sought to ensure that all political appointees in the agencies were vetted through the White House personnel process, and to have a series of orientation seminars for all high-ranking officials on the various aspects of the Reagan program . . . we wanted our appointees to be the President's ambassadors to the agencies, not the other way around."[27] Based on this evidence, the Reagan administration appears to have explicitly intended to recruit, employ, and instruct executive branch officials under the president's wishes and orders.

The second strategy involved increasing the Office of Management and Budget's (OMB) role in overseeing the administration of policy orders within the executive branch. The OMB acted as a "gatekeeper to insure that the executive branch was following the president's lead and not, for example, being led astray by external forces such as powerful members of Congress or particularized interest groups."[28]

In order to gain greater oversight of administration officials, Reagan created the Task Force on Regulatory Relief, chaired by Vice President

George H. W. Bush. Reagan instructed this task force to oversee and review the regulatory process. In addition, he issued Executive Order 12.291[29] to create the Office of Information and Regulatory Affairs, which was designed to oversee all regulatory processes within the federal government.[30]

The executive order required "major" rules (defined as those having a projected economic impact in excess of $100 million per year) to be submitted to the OMB's Office of Information and Regulatory Affairs (OIRA) sixty days before the publication of the notice in the Federal Register, and again thirty days before their publication, as a final rule.[31] The second component of the order, which dealt with non-major rules (which cost less than $100 million per year), required their submission to the OMB ten days prior to notice in the Federal Register and ten days prior to final publication.[32] This empowered the OMB "to stay the publication of notice of proposed rule making or the promulgation of a final regulation by requiring that agencies respond to criticisms, and ultimately it may recommend the withdrawal of regulations which cannot be reformulated to meet its objections."[33]

The principle that the president controls the entire executive branch was originally innocuous—based solely on a literal reading of the Article II of the Constitution, but extreme forms of the Unitary Executive Theory have developed. As John Dean stated, "In its most extreme form, unitary executive theory can mean that neither Congress nor the federal courts can tell the President what to do or how to do it, particularly regarding national security matters."[34] Does scholar Dean's interpretation of emergency power mean that the president can do whatever he deems necessary during crisis? In order to answer this question, a review of Hamilton's writings is necessary because it may be possible that modern scholars are exaggerating Hamilton's words in order to favor a more robust interpretation of executive emergency power.

What Hamilton meant by "unity" is plainly not the same as what Yoo and others[35] understood by the "unitary executive." Hamilton wrote that the "unity of the executive" was to be understood as the opposite of a "plurality of magistrates": "the faithful exercise of any delegated power" should rest with one man, the president, not only for the purpose of executing power swiftly and decisively, but also so that the public would know exactly who was accountable for "a series of pernicious measures," and that the right man might be punished for such measures.[36]

Furthermore, Hamilton understood the power of the executive as "any delegated power"—that is, the power delegated to the president by the people, through Congress. Hamilton did not think that the "unitary executive" meant unbridled power, since he wrote that the executive might commit "misconduct," which should lead to "punishment."[37] If the president were above the law, his behavior could not possibly be considered "misconduct." In Federalist No. 77, Hamilton wrote that the executive is to be understood as "faithfully executing the laws . . . of the United States."[38] Hamilton clearly

never intended or supported an interpretation of executive power to go beyond the scope of law, or to exist without oversight from the other branches
of government. The president has the responsibility to command the army,
but commanding the army does not grant the president the power to make
war. Congress must first declare war; the president may command the army
into war only after Congress's declaration.

THE OFFICE OF LEGAL COUNSEL AND
PRESIDENT GEORGE W. BUSH'S INTERPRETATION
OF EXECUTIVE EMERGENCY POWERS

In this section I analyze President Bush's philosophy of executive emergency
powers by examining the OLC and the opinions it drafted following the
attacks of September 11, 2001. While Bush did not offer many comments or
writings on emergency power, since leaving office he has often stated that
the "lawyers" advised him on his constitutional authority regarding emergency power.[39] Therefore, the OLC memos are significant in determining
Bush's interpretation of executive emergency power.

What advice did the OLC give President Bush following the attacks of
September 11, 2001? How did the OLC argue that executive emergency
powers were constitutional? Did the advice support the Unitary Executive
Theory? Did the OLC provide an appropriate interpretation of executive
emergency power? Is the interpretation of Alexander Hamilton's writings
correct, or did John Yoo overstate Hamilton's ideas to zealously promote a
misleading interpretation of the power of the presidency during crisis? To
answer these questions I will first review Yoo's argument in an OLC memo
dated October 23, 2001. Second, I will review the appropriate Federalist
Papers that Yoo cited and examine them carefully to consider the validity of
his argument.

Office of Legal Counsel

The OLC was created in 1953 with the explicit intent to "maintain the constitutional protections of the President."[40] The OLC provides constitutional
legal advice to all the departments within the executive branch and "both
written and oral advice in response to requests from the Counsel of the
President."[41] Over the course of the twentieth century, the OLC "came to
present themselves as agents of the Constitution itself and as guardians of an
office whose significance to our nation far outstrips the petty political dis-
putes that consume the daily life of most of those around the president."[42]

Although the OLC has undertaken the primary responsibility of protecting the president from Congress encroaching upon the constitutional powers
of the office, this does not mean that the OLC is the ultimate authority.

Political expedience has occasionally overruled the opinion of the OLC.[43] For instance, in the late 1980s, the bill to bail out failed savings and loans institutions reached the first President Bush's desk, and the OLC found some constitutional problems regarding the appointment of the director of the Office of Thrift Supervision. The OLC argued that the bill should be vetoed on that defect alone. Many members of Congress and the executive branch found the bill to be too politically important to allow a minor constitutional defect to derail it, and consequently overruled the OLC opinion.[44] In other words, the OLC is not the final say on the constitutionality of a piece of legislation, but as evidenced, it is a clear defender of the president's authority and latitudes of constitutional power.

Furthermore, the president shields his office from encroachments upon his prerogatives by relying upon the Oath clause of the Constitution. As noted, the Department of Justice is the primary protector of the president's prerogatives, particularly the OLC. All enrolled bills that go to the president's desk for signature flow through the OLC, "which reviews them for constitutional problems and makes a recommendation to the President whether to sign or to veto."[45]

The OLC may also play a role in drafting the veto message. If the president chooses to veto a bill, then the OLC may assist in writing the signing statement if constitutional objections need to be made. In addition, if the president is concerned or curious about the latitudes of his power, he may seek legal advice from the OLC to determine the constitutionality of his possible actions in relation to an event, such as the attacks of September 11, 2001.[46]

Office of Legal Counsel Opinions

Table 6.1 outlines all of the OLC memos drafted after September 11, 2001, that were pertinent in addressing the Bush administration's executive emergency power philosophy. The OLC first drafted an advisory memo regarding the president's authority to use emergency powers following the attacks of September 11, 2001, on October 23, 2001. Assistant Attorney Generals John Yoo and Robert Delahunt authored the memo in response to a request from Vice President Cheney, on behalf of President George W. Bush, concerning how to handle the emerging war on terrorism. The president sought advice on the extent of his emergency power in the wake of the attacks. The president desired to know the extent of his authority to respond to the initial attack, and at that time was still concerned about subsequent attacks, even an insurrection or an invasion.[47]

Moreover, the White House needed thorough legal advice on how to respond to the attacks because, according to the OLC, "The situation in which these issues arise is unprecedented in recent American history."[48] The

Table 6.1.   Office of Legal Counsel Opinions, Department of Justice, drafted following the aftermath of the terrorist attacks of September 11, 2001.

OLC Memo	Author	Date
Authority for Use of Military Force to Combat Terrorist Activities within the United States of America	John Yoo, deputy assistant attorney general, and Robert Delahunty, special counsel	October 23, 2001
Authority of the President to Suspend Certain Provisions of the ABM (Anti-Ballistic Missiles) Treaty	John Yoo and Roberty Delahunty	November 15, 2001
Applicability of 18 U.S.C 4001(a) to Military Detention of United States Citizens	Unsigned	June 27, 2002
Determination of Enemy Belligerence and Military Detention	Jay Bybee, assistant attorney general	June 8, 2002
The President's Power as Commander in Chief to transfer captured terrorists to the control and custody of foreign nations	Jay Bybee	March 13, 2002
Constitutionality of Amending Foreign Surveillance Act to Change the Purpose Standard Searches	John Yoo	September 25, 2001
Swift Justice Act	Patrick Philbin	April 8, 2002
Status of Certain OLC Opinions Issued in the Aftermath of the Terrorists Attacks of September 11, 2001	Stephen Bradbury, principal deputy assistant attorney general, President Obama's administration	January 15, 2009

OLC suggested that the attacks of September 11, 2001, were unprecedented because "the attacks took place in rapid succession, aimed at critical American government buildings, on American soil . . . and caused more than five thousand deaths, and thousands more were injured." President Bush agreed that the actions of September 11, 2001, were exceptional when he addressed a joint session of Congress on September 20, 2001, stating, "on September 11th, enemies of freedom committed an act of war against our country."[49]

Yoo claimed it was "vital to grasp that attacks on this scale and with these consequences are more akin to war than terrorism . . . and that the events of September 11, 2001, reach a different scale of destructiveness than earlier terrorist episodes."[50] He stated that "the operatives responsible for the attacks, Al-Qaeda, had a history of attacks aimed at the United States [suicide bombing attack in Yemen on the U.S.S. *Cole* in 2000, the bombings of the United States embassies in Kenya and in Tanzania in 1998, a truck bomb attack on U.S. military housing complexes in Saudi Arabia in 1996, an attempt to destroy the World Trade Center in 1993, and an ambush to kill U.S. servicemen in Somalia in 1993]."[51]

Yoo concluded that this "pattern of terrorist activity of this scale, duration, extent, and intensity . . . can readily be described as a war."[52] As a consequence of the concerns over terrorist activity the OLC drafted a memo to discuss the president's authority to wage war against the terrorists, to discuss the president's constitutional boundaries in taking military action, and his legal authority to combat the possibility of an additional insurrection or invasion.[53]

What advice did the OLC give President Bush following the attacks of September 11, 2001? How did the OLC argue that executive emergency powers were constitutional? Did the advice support the Unitary Executive Theory? The following areas of the OLC memos will be outlined and analyzed: (1) The presence of an emergency, and (2) text and structure of the Constitution that support the power of the executive to combat emergencies.

Did the OLC provide an appropriate interpretation of executive emergency power? Did John Yoo understand Hamilton correctly or overstate his ideas to zealously promote a misleading interpretation of the power of the presidency during crisis? To answer these questions I will review the appropriate Federalist Papers that Yoo cited and examine them carefully to address the validity of his argument.

First, Yoo argued that the attacks of September 11, 2001, were actions of "war against the United States of America," an emergency and a clear danger to the civilian population. He distinguished the attacks from past wars in two ways. Yoo observed that, unlike past wars like Vietnam and the Gulf War, "this conflict may take part on the soil of the United States," and because the war may be "waged on the home front" distinguishing the "appropriate application of civil law and constitutional law" will be difficult. When the war front is "abroad . . . there is a clear distinction between the theatre of war and the homeland . . . making the actions of the military commanders bound only by the laws of war and martial law."[54]

Second, Yoo suggested that the current crisis differed from previous wars because "the belligerent parties in a war are traditionally nation-states . . . however, al-Qaeda is not a nation . . . and its forces do not bear a distinctive uniform, do not carry arms openly, and do not represent the regular or even irregular military personal of a nation." Because al-Qaeda is not a "tradition-al" army, Yoo posited that the "rules of engagement designed for the protec-tion of non-combatant civilian populations come under extreme pressure when an attempt is made to apply them in a conflict with terrorism."[55] He concluded that America is in an "armed conflict with an elusive, clandestine group striking unpredictably at civilian and military targets both inside and outside of the United States." Because al-Qaeda is not a traditional army and is elusive and very dangerous, Yoo suggested that "the scale of violence involved in this conflict removes it from the sphere of operations designed to enforce the criminal laws; legal and constitutional rules regulating law en-forcement activity are *not* applicable."[56]

Yoo suggested that the Constitution grants the executive branch power to deal with the crisis of September 11, 2001, and the battle to be waged against al-Qaeda. Yoo stated, "we [the Office of Legal Counsel] believe that Article II of the Constitution, which vests the President with the power to respond to emergency threats to the national security, directly authorizes use of the Armed Forces in domestic operations against terrorists."[57] He based the ar-gument on the founders' explanation of the federal government's power to respond to an emergency. Yoo also relied on an interpretation of Article II of the Constitution to support executive emergency power.

First, Yoo suggested that the framers were aware of the possibilities of emergencies, invasions and insurrections, and this led the framers to under-stand that "some cases such emergencies could only be met by the use of the federal military force."[58] Although Yoo used the word *framers*, he referred only to Alexander Hamilton in the memo, constructing his entire argument solely on Hamilton's remarks. Yoo suggested that the framers (i.e., Hamil-ton) understood the Constitution to "amply provide the federal government with the authority to respond to such exigencies."[59]

Yoo relied on Hamilton's writings in the *Federalist Papers* to support and develop his argument for a strong response to combat the crisis by any means necessary. Yoo cited Federalist No. 36 to evidence the government's power to combat a crisis: "there are certain emergencies of nations in which expe-dients that in the ordinary state of things ought to be forborne become essen-tial to the public weal." Yoo continued, citing Hamilton from Federalist No. 23 to argue that the framers afforded the federal government with broad power to combat an emergency: "the circumstances which may affect the public safety are not reducible within certain determinate limits . . . as a necessary consequence that there can be no limitation of that authority which is to provide for the defense and protection of the community."[60]

Yoo's interpretation of Hamilton's words in Federalist No. 23 is a bit concerning because he construed from Hamilton's last point "that there can be no limitation of that authority which is to provide for the defense and protection of the community" to mean that the executive can do whatever he

deems necessary during a crisis. However, as I will discuss during an examination of each Federalist Paper that Yoo cited, Yoo's interpretation of Federalist No. 23 is simply exaggerated. Hamilton was not making the argument
that an executive can act alone, with indefinite powers to defend the country;
instead, as will be discussed shortly, Hamilton was asserting that the
branches of government "coextensively" will combat the crisis and do whatever is necessary to combat the crisis.

Yoo cited Federalist No. 34 to claim that the federal government possess-
es "an indefinite power of providing for emergencies as they might arise."
According to Yoo, this power "includes the authority to use force to protect
the nation, whether at home, or abroad."[61] Yoo defended his advice that the
president may do whatever is necessary within the president's discretion to
combat the crisis, with Hamilton's words from Federalist No. 28: "there may
happen cases in which the national government may be necessitated to use
force . . . and insurrections are unhappily, maladies as inseparable from the
body politic as tumors and eruptions from the natural body . . . should such
emergencies at any time happen under the national government, there could
be no remedy but force."[62]

Yoo argued that, in order to address the concerns of dealing with emergencies, the framers granted that "Article II vests in the President the Chief
Executive and Commander-in-Chief Powers. The framers' understanding of
the meaning of executive power confirms that by vesting that power in the
President, they granted him the broad powers necessary to the proper functioning of the government and to the security of the nation."[63] The distinguishing feature between Article I and Article II's vesting clauses is Article
II's lack of the word "herein." Yoo suggested that the framers "intentionally"
left out the "herein" wording in Article II's Vesting clause because they
wanted the executive to have more power than what the Article explicitly
states.[64]

Yoo concluded that "an executive power, such as the power to use force
in response to attacks upon the nation, not specifically detailed in Article II,
section II must remain with the President."[65] Hence, Yoo argued that executive emergency power is an un-enumerated power.[66] Yoo cited Hamilton's
comment that Article II "ought . . . to be considered as intended by way of
greater caution to specify and regulate the principal articles implied in the
definition of Executive power; leaving the rest to flow from the general grant
of that power."[67]

Furthermore, Yoo claimed that "such enumerated power [commander in
chief] includes the authority to use military force, whether at home or abroad,
in response to a direct attack upon the United States. There can be little doubt
that the decision to deploy military force is executive in nature, and was
traditionally regarded as so." Citing Hamilton's argument in Federalist No.
70 that an executive must have energy to respond to a crisis, Yoo agreed with

Hamilton that "using the military to defend the nation requires action and execution, rather than deliberative formulation of rules to govern private conduct."[68] As Hamilton posited, "the direction of war implies the direction of the common strength . . . and the power of directing and employing the common strength forms a usual and essential part in the definition of the executive authority."[69]

According to Yoo, "Congress has the authority to raise and support an army, Article I, section 8, clauses 12–13, and once Congress has provided the President with armed forces, he has the discretion to deploy them both defensively and offensively to protect the nation's security." Yoo's argument that the president has discretion to use the armed forces, "both defensively and offensively to protect the nation's security," is based on Yoo's interpretation of the Commander-in-Chief clause of Article II. Yoo asserted that the president has sole discretion to command the army in time of crisis because the Commander-in-Chief clause names the president as the sole commander of the army, and according to Yoo the Congress provides the army to the commander in chief who then has the sole responsibility of carrying out the actions to combat the crisis.[70]

Furthermore Yoo cited Hamilton's words as evidence to support Yoo's interpretation of the Commander-in-Chief clause. Yoo claimed that, without a strong federal force, the United States would be "a nation incapacitated by its Constitution to prepare for defense before it was actually invaded . . . we must receive the blow before we could even prepare for it." Yoo's argument that the framers envisioned the Federal government being capable and prepared to combat a crisis is drawn from Hamilton's remarks in Federalist No. 26 as Hamilton argued for a standing army because "a certain number of troops for guards and garrisons were indispensable; that no precise bounds could be set to the national exigencies; that a power equal to every possible emergency must exist somewhere in the government." According to Yoo, "the power equal to every possible emergency [that] must exist somewhere in the government," is the executive.[71]

Yoo drew from Hamilton's argument to claim that " a fundamental purpose of a standing army and a permanent navy was that they be used in such emergencies . . . and by creating such forces and placing them under the president's command, Congress is necessarily authorizing him to deploy those forces." Yoo understood the president's power as commander in chief to "necessarily possess ample direction to decide how to deploy the forces committed to him. He could decide it was safer to preempt an imminent attack rather than to wait for a hostile power to strike first."[72]

Based on Yoo's assessment of Hamilton's argument, this book argues that Yoo overemphasized Hamilton's words and therefore overestimated Hamilton's relevance to executive emergency power.

Yoo cited Federalist Nos. 23, 24, 25, and 26 to support his argument that in times of emergency a president may combat the crisis by using the executive powers explicitly and implicitly outlined in Article II of the Constitution. These Federalist Papers do not fully support Yoo's argument, however. Just looking at the titles shows evidence of how Yoo selectively chose passages from unrelated papers to construct an interpretation of Hamilton's words to favor Yoo's argument that the executive is all powerful during a crisis. Here are the titles of the papers Yoo used to construct his argument based on Hamilton's remarks: Federalist No. 23 is entitled, "The Necessity of a Government as Energetic as the One Proposed to the Preservation of the Union," and Federalist No. 24 is entitled, "The Powers Necessary to the Common Defense Reconsidered Further." Federalist No. 25 is entitled, "The Powers Necessary to the Common Defense Further Considered (continued)," and Federalist No. 26 is entitled, "Idea of Restraining the Legislative Authority in Regard to the Common Defense Reconsidered."

In Federalist No. 23 Hamilton argued for a standing army: "the Union ought to be invested with full power to levy troops; to build and equip fleets; and to raise the revenues which will be required for the formation and support of an army and navy, in the customary and ordinary modes practiced in other governments." Hamilton claimed that an army is necessary so that the government may respond to crises as needed: "there can be no limitation of that authority which is to provide for the defense and protection of the community, in any matter essential to its efficacy that is, in any matter essential to the *formation*, *direction*, or *support* of the NATIONAL FORCES."[73] He did not assert that the president may use the army unilaterally to preemptively deal with crisis, as Yoo suggested.

Rather, Hamilton stated that an army is crucial to the longevity and preservation of the Union and that "These powers [emergency powers as the military uses them] ought to exist without limitation, *because it is impossible to foresee or define the extent and variety of national exigencies, or the correspondent extent and variety of the means which may be necessary to satisfy them*, both of which is necessary to preserve the Union."[74] Hamilton was simply stating that a military presence is necessary for the preservation of the Union from potential threats or national emergencies. He did not make clear in Federalist No. 23 that the executive, simply because he commands the army (as Yoo asserted), has expanded authority (unstated constitutional powers), during a crisis.

Yoo incorrectly read Hamilton as suggesting "that there can be no limitation of that authority which is to provide for the defense and protection of the community" and that power rests solely with the executive. Hamilton never made such a proposition in Federalist No. 23. Instead, Hamilton wrote, "This power ought to be *coextensive* with all the possible combinations of such circumstances; and ought to be under the direction of the same councils which are appointed to preside over the common defense."[75] According to the Constitution both Congress and the presidency are responsible for the oversight and administration of war. Hamilton did not explicitly state that a president may use the army without prior consent from Congress. Such a reading of an inherent power to use the army in time of crisis,[76] is possible, but Hamilton never suggested that executive emergency power is absolutely unilateral or that other branches of government may not constrain this power.

In Federalist No. 24 Hamilton argued for a standing army even during peacetime. He warned of potential enemies: "Though a wide ocean separates the United States from Europe, yet there are various considerations that warn us against an excess of confidence or security." He identified the Indian tribes as threats to the nation: "Previous to the Revolution, and ever since the peace, there has been a constant necessity for keeping small garrisons on our Western frontier. No person can doubt that these will continue to be indispensable, if it should only be against the ravages and depredations of the Indians."[77]

In examining Federalist No. 24 this book suggests that Yoo exaggerated the purpose of Federalist No. 24. The primary purpose Hamilton outlined in this Federalist Paper was to explain why the country needs a standing army. According to Hamilton the need is to protect the nation from external enemies because the nation will never know the time, nor place of a sudden attack. Yoo construed Hamilton's reasons for a standing army to mean that Hamilton favored an aggressive executive in times of emergency; however, nothing in Federalist No. 24 addresses the executive's role in commanding the army, or combating an external threat. The paper does not address an interpretation of executive emergency power, only the need for a standing army.

Hamilton continued to argue for a standing army in peacetime in Federalist No. 25, claiming that the United States would be foolish not to have a standing army: "If, to obviate this consequence, it should be resolved to extend the prohibition to the *raising* of armies in time of peace, the United States would then exhibit the most extraordinary spectacle which the world has yet seen, that of a nation incapacitated by its Constitution to prepare for defense, before it was actually invaded."[78]

Yoo cited Federalist No. 25 to suggest that the framers favored an executive able to combat an insurrection and that the Constitution grants him such power.[79] However, Hamilton never referred to the executive in the paper, only the government. In fact, Hamilton's statement, "We must receive the blow, before we could even prepare to return it," simply supports an inherent power to combat emergency. Yoo, however, cited this line most frequently to support his argument that an executive may combat an insurrection or invasion without cooperation or consent from Congress. Federalist No. 25 never asserts that an inherent power to combat emergency is the executive's providence alone. Rather, Hamilton suggested that such power may rest with all rulers, "because we are afraid that *rulers*, created by our choice, dependent on our will, might endanger that liberty, by an abuse of the means necessary to its preservation."[80] Again, Hamilton's remarks seem to suggest he had a grave concern over the power of the executive, as it related to the military, hence he supported a shared venture between the executive and the legislature when using the military.

In Federalist No. 26 Hamilton argued that the legislature will have the power to raise and support a military: "The legislature of the United States will be *obliged*, by this provision, once at least in every two years, to deliberate upon the propriety of keeping a military force on foot; to come to a new resolution on the point; and to declare their sense of the matter, by a formal vote in the face of their constituents."[81] He even went on to state that the legislature is not at "*liberty* to vest in the executive department permanent funds for the support of an army, if they were even incautious enough to be willing to repose in it so improper a confidence." Hamilton apparently supported a coordinated venture between the executive and legislature on matters pertaining to the military. He went on to state that any "subversion of liberty" that may arise due to the size of a standing army may occur "not merely as a temporary combination between the legislature and executive, but a continued conspiracy for a series of time."[82] Hamilton appeared to assert that the use of an army over time should be a grave concern to Congress, because with a prolonged use of the military the chances of subverting liberty will increase. Yoo seemed to read Federalist No. 26 as evidence of Hamilton urging an executive to deal solely with crisis and ignores Hamilton's specific comments showing Hamilton's support for sharing the power of the military between the executive and Congress. I wish to convey here that Hamilton did consistently speak to the shared venture between the Congress and the executive when using the military.

Yoo's interpretation of Hamilton is peculiar. I think Yoo drew broad conclusions from Hamilton's remarks to support his theory of executive emergency power. Did Hamilton advocate emergency power as an inherent power? Possibly, but Hamilton's writings do not support such a reading beyond a doubt. Hamilton's only writing in the Federalist Paper that shows evidence of him supporting executive emergency power as an inherent power is availed in Federalist No. 70. In this Federalist Paper one may infer from Hamilton's words that he would assert that emergency power may rest with the executive because the executive will be sufficiently strong, decisive, and, as a singular entity, energetic to respond to the emergency swiftly. Hamilton's energetic executive theory was used early in the republic as Washington combated the Whiskey Rebellion; however, Yoo never cited the rebellion or Federalist No. 70 to support his argument.

I would agree with Yoo that Hamilton made the case that an executive should have emergency power, but I would suggest that the evidence to discern Hamilton's theory for executive emergency power is in Federalist No. 70 and the advice Hamilton gave Washington during the Whiskey Rebellion. In both pieces Hamilton did argue for a swift, energetic response to the crisis and asserted that the executive may act boldly and singularly to the crisis because the power to do so is inherent in Article II of the Constitution.

Furthermore, in an OLC memo dated October 6, 2008, Stephen Bradbury issued a reversal of opinion against Yoo's interpretation of emergency power as stated in the October 23, 2001, memo: "The October 23, 2001 memo should not be treated as authoritative for any purpose . . . the context of the memo was the product of extraordinary, indeed we hope, a unique period in the history of the Nation . . . the memo did not address specific and concrete policy proposals; rather it addressed in general terms and broad contours of hypothetical scenarios involving possible domestic military contingencies."[83]

Bradbury concluded that "the October 23, 2001, memo represented a departure from the preferred practice of the OLC to render formal opinions only with respect to specific and concrete policy proposals, not to undertake a general survey of a broad area of the law or to address general or amorphous hypothetical scenarios that implicate difficult questions of law."[84] Bradbury's comments, which suggest that Yoo has broadly interpreted emergency power, support this book's argument. Bradbury clearly scolded Yoo for using the OLC in a way that created hypotheticals and undertook broad theories of law, which goes against the intent and purpose of the OLC. Furthermore, and most important, Bradbury made clear in the October 6, 2008, memo that Yoo was creating theories not expressly based on law or related to "concrete policy proposals." Bradbury's comment reinforces my concern over Yoo's interpretation of executive emergency power, which was exaggerating Hamilton's words and arguments throughout specified Federalist Papers.

In the October 23, 2001, memo, Yoo reasoned that the president has broadened authority due to an emergency. Based on the declassified OLC memos produced following the attacks of September 11, 2001, the following actions were advised to be constitutional in order to respond to the crisis of the war against al-Qaeda: military tribunals, suspending habeas corpus for enemy combatants, extraordinary rendition, warrantless surveillance of citizens' homes, abrogation of the Geneva Conventions, unilateral dispensation from treaties, and interrogation methods.

A memo from the OLC, dated November 6, 2001, advised the president that he may use military commissions to try enemy combatants (terrorists). The OLC concluded that the president has such authority because of "his inherent powers as Commander in Chief, the President may establish military commissions to try and punish terrorists apprehended as part of the investigation into, or the military and intelligence operations in response to, the September 11 attacks."[85] The OLC stated that "The Uniform Code of Military Justice (UCMJ) expressly addresses the use of military commissions in article 21. 10 U.S.C. § 821, supported the president's authority to detain and try enemy combatants in military tribunals."[86]

Regarding the detainment, arrest of enemy combatants, abrogation of Geneva Convention treaties, and extraordinary rendition, the OLC in a memo drafted March 13, 2002, advised that the president "has full discretion to transfer al-Qaeda and Taliban prisoners captured overseas and detained outside of the United States to third countries."[87] The memo went on to state that the president is not restrained by the "Geneva Convention Relative to the Treatment of Prisoners of War," because "the President has determined that the al-Qaeda detainees are not legally entitled prisoner of war status within the meaning of the Conventions."[88] The OLC concluded that as part of the "President's power as Commander-in-Chief he may dispose of the liberty of prisoners captured during military engagements . . . treaties regarding the transfer or detainment of enemy combatants do not restrict the president's commander in chief power . . . the president since the founding of the country has had an unfettered control over the disposition of enemy soldiers captured during a time of war"[89]

In a memo dated August 1, 2002, the OLC advised that "certain interrogation methods" are not prohibited by Section 2340A of Title 18. The memo advised the CIA to continue interrogation because the al-Qaeda operative "is withholding information regarding terrorist attacks in the United States and information regarding plans to conduct attacks within the United States."[90]

In a memo dated September 25, 2001, the OLC advised that "amending the Foreign Surveillance Act to include the collection of foreign information as a purpose of the search would not violate the 4th Amendment warrant requirements . . . the amendment would simply allow the department to apply FISA warrants up to the limit permitted by the Constitution."[91]

The OLC advice partly comprised a response to the potential threat of continued terrorist attacks on the country. Fortunately, such attacks did not occur. Therefore, the armed forces were never deployed domestically, and the suspension of *Posse Comitatus* did not occur. In light of the OLC advice, what actions did President George W. Bush deploy to combat the emergency? In this section I review the use of executive emergency power following the attacks of September 11, 2001.

I will explore the actions President Bush took following the September 11 attacks, which exhibited his use and interpretation of executive emergency power. The nation was in shock after the attacks. News agencies began nonstop coverage of the horrific event as it unfolded. Early reports assumed that the plane crashes were a major accident, only to learn shortly thereafter that the event was terrorism—coordinated hatred against the United States.

War power is possibly the most immediate and obvious example of executive emergency power. Following the attacks of September 11, 2001, many Americans wanted some sort of retribution against the terrorists responsible for the violence.[92] President Bush had to act in response to these demands. Like presidents before him, Bush claimed the authority to use force to defend the nation's security.[93] In the wake of the September 11, 2001, attacks, President Bush sought and received an Authorization to Use Military Force (AUMF) from Congress on September 18, 2001.[94] Scholars have suggested the AUMF was "sweeping," perhaps the "broadest" grant of war power by Congress since World War II.[95] The AUMF formally authorized the president "to use all necessary and appropriate force against those nations, organizations, or persons he determines planned, authorized, committed, or aided the terrorist attack."[96] Therefore, the AUMF constitutes the statutory permission for President Bush to launch war in Afghanistan, where the administration deemed al-Qaeda was located. The administration relied on legal advice from OLC and from the Congressional statute to assert that it would "deal with terrorism wherever it is being harbored."[97]

In addition the AUMF recognized that the "President has the authority under the Constitution to take action to deter and prevent acts of international terrorism against the United States."[98] As a consequence of the legislation, some scholars suggest the power granted was "unlimited as to time and to geography."[99]

This book suggests that Bush espoused three distinct applications of executive emergency powers: (1) military campaign in Afghanistan, (2) interning enemy combatants, and (3) broadening the military use of Rendition against enemy combatants.

Afghanistan War

At Camp David on September 16, 2001, President George W. Bush used the phrase "war on terror" for the first time: "This crusade—this war on terrorism—is going to take a while. . . . And the American people must be patient. I'm going to be patient. But I can assure the American people I am determined."[100] On September 20, 2001, Bush launched the war on terror during a televised address to a joint session of Congress, stating, "Our 'war on terror' begins with al-Qaeda, but it does not end there. It will not end until every terrorist group of global reach has been found, stopped and defeated."[101]

As Bush announced a war on terror to the public, his operatives began pursuing authorizations from Congress to combat the enemies. Some scholars suggest that Bush's ability to obtain authorizations easily from Congress was due to Congress's "acquiescent" nature.[102] Bush's argument that the

United States of America was in a "constant and under continuing threats from the enemies" and that "the war the nation faced was unprecedented and of uncertain duration,"[103] aided him in his pursuit of authorizations.

On September 18, 2001, Congress passed a joint resolution without any substantive input into the drafting of the legislation. The resolution, known as the Authorization for Use of Military Force (hereafter AUMF), Public Law 107-40, was drafted by the White House and granted Bush the broadest authority to combat any nation, organization, or person "determined to have been involved in the 9/11 terrorist attacks against the United States."[104] Section 2(a) of the AUMF stated, "In general, that the President is authorized to use all necessary and appropriate force against those nations, organizations, or persons he determines planned, authorized, committed, or aided the terrorist attacks that occurred on September 11, 2001 or harbored such organizations or persons, in order to prevent any future acts of international terrorism against the United States by such nations, organizations, or persons."[105] Scholars agree that the AUMF granted unprecedented authority to the president.[106] In particular, David Currie suggested that the president was granted "all necessary and appropriate force against nations harboring or aiding terrorists" and that "the president may use force in order to prevent any future acts of international terrorism."[107] Armed with the AUMF, President Bush initiated what later would be known as the Bush Doctrine, which argued for a worldwide pursuit of terrorism aimed at the United States. President Bush sought the authority to invade Afghanistan from Congress.

Operation Enduring Freedom

On September 20, 2001, George W. Bush delivered an ultimatum to the Taliban government of Afghanistan to turn over Osama bin Laden and al-Qaeda leaders operating in the country, or else face attack.[108] The Taliban demanded evidence of bin Laden's link to the September 11 attacks and, if such evidence warranted a trial, they offered to try him in an Islamic court.[109] The United States refused to provide any evidence.

Subsequently, in October 2001 United States forces (with United Kingdom and coalition allies) invaded Afghanistan to topple the Taliban regime. The official invasion began on October 7, 2001, with air strike campaigns from British and American forces.

Waging war in Afghanistan had been of a lower priority than the war in Iraq for the U.S. government. Admiral Mike Mullen, staff chairman of the Joint Chiefs of Staff, said that while the situation in Afghanistan was "precarious and urgent," the ten thousand additional troops needed there would be unavailable "in any significant manner" without withdrawals from Iraq. Mullen stated that "my priorities . . . given to me by the commander in chief are:

Focus on Iraq first. It's been that way for some time. Focus on Afghanistan second."[110]

Patriot Act

The Patriot Act is another example of Bush's use of emergency power. Led by Attorney General Ashcroft (MO) and Dep. Attorney General Dinh, the Bush administration pursued legislation from Congress to empower the federal government in responding to potential threats within the homeland. The government sought a measure to protect citizens from potential terrorist attacks. The 2001 Patriot Act was 342 pages of legislation drafted by the White House and pushed through Congress without any formal drafts from congressional leadership.[111] There were no hearings on the legislation in the House of Representatives and only about one legislative day of debate in the Senate before it was passed.[112] In typical Washington legislative fashion, the bill was submitted the morning of the vote, replaying a common scenario in which possibly many members of Congress never read the entirety of the bill before voting.

The Patriot Act (Public Law 107-56) gave the executive branch extensive and secret power, especially the administration's intelligence-gathering agencies—the Federal Bureau of Investigation (FBI), the National Security Administration (NSA), the Central Intelligence Agency (CIA), and the Defense Intelligence Agency (DIA)—to fight terrorists worldwide. Some scholars suggest that the Patriot Act's broad powers of gathering foreign information made the agencies "too powerful" and endowed them with "unchecked powers."[113]

This act clearly follows the precedent of earlier legislation, the Foreign Intelligence Surveillance Act of 1978 (Public Law 95-511). FISA originally authorized federal agencies to gather intelligence on foreign entities or persons suspected of criminal activities with the Soviet Union or conspiring against the United States. FISA authorized federal agents to pursue "the collection of foreign intelligence in furtherance of U.S. counterintelligence."[114] FISA made clear that authorities had to acquire a warrant before wire-tapping a suspected perpetrator. However, under the Patriot Act, Bush officials secured provisions enabling the federal agents to act without warrants in the pursuit of terrorist counterintelligence.[115]

Title II of the Act, "Enhanced Surveillance Procedures," grants the executive another emergency power. It authorizes federal agencies to intercept wire, oral, and electronic communications relating to terrorism or computer fraud and abuse. Scholars suggest that this provision allows law enforcement and counterintelligence agencies to share "information and to conduct sneak-and-peek searches."[116]

Within days of the September 11, 2001, attacks, FBI and Immigration and Naturalization Service (INS) agents began a secret roundup and "unprecedented" detention of thousands of people across the United States. The people who garnered the interest of the FBI and INS were "mostly of Muslim or bearing Arabic names."[117] According to Kate Martin, contributing scholar from the Center for National Security Studies, the "gathering of individuals was a perpetrated effort by the government to arrest people in secret. We have 200 years of law and tradition saying that arrests are public. . . . We do not have secret arrests."[118]

Critics have observed that, following the passage of the Patriot Act, a "domestic reign of terror visited the U.S. immigrant community because the Act authorized the INS to detain immigrants without charge for up to seven days. But as a belated report by the Justice Department's inspector general revealed, many captives were in fact held illegally without charge for as long as eight months, denied access to attorneys, and then, after secret hearings, deported."[119]

According to a Department of Justice's own report by the Office of the Inspector General, released in June 2003, only one person was ultimately convicted of "supporting" terrorism out of the thousands of immigrants detained. The report criticized the Department of Justice and the INS for using "the Patriot Act and federal immigration statutes to detain, in the federal detention center in New York City more than 1,100 aliens for months without their families knowing where they were and what crimes they may have committed. . . . It was not until the second half of 2002 that the detainees were investigated and released."[120]

Extraordinary Rendition

Following the attacks of September 11, 2001, rendition, or the outsourcing of high-value detainees to third party states, such as Egypt or Syria, that use torture for "aggressive interrogation," occurred regularly.[121] Formally, "rendition transfers individuals from one country to another, by means that bypass all judicial and administrative due process . . . in order to have these high level valued detainees questioned by the intelligence and military communities of the receiving nation."[122]

Egypt, Syria, Thailand, Morocco, Saudi Arabia, South Africa, Jordan, and Pakistan receive detainees from the Central Intelligence Agency for questioning. These nations, among others, use torture as one of the mechanisms to gather intelligence information.[123] After the attacks of September 11, 2001, the CIA secretly began sending high-valued detainees to their home nations for further questioning, that is, according to some, for "torture heavy" interrogations.[124]

President George W. Bush's Signing Statements

The signing statement provides additional evidence of President Bush's support for the Unitary Executive Theory and his theory of executive emergency power. A signing statement is the president's acknowledgment of supporting or disagreeing with all or parts of a piece of congressional legislation that while the president may disagree in part, still signs the bill into law. Furthermore, presidential signing statements are official pronouncements issued by the president contemporaneously with signing a bill into law. These pronouncements have been used to forward the president's interpretation of the statutory language. In the presidential signing statement, a president may assert constitutional objections to the provisions contained therein, and concordantly, to announce that the provisions of the law will be administered in a manner that concurs with the administration's conception of presidential prerogatives.[125]

While the history of presidential issuance of signing statements dates to the early nineteenth century, the practice has become a source of significant controversy in the modern era as presidents have increasingly asserted constitutional objections to congressional enactments in the statements.[126] Presidents also provide evidence of their particular philosophies towards executive power in their use of signing statements.

To assess whether President Bush supported the Unitary Executive Theory and to evidence his interpretation of executive emergency powers, I examine the signing statements issued during his presidency. The signing statements might shed light on President Bush's interpretation of his executive power during a crisis and may evidence his support for the Unitary Executive Theory. If so, then I can examine his use of presidential prerogative following the attacks of September 11, 2001. Later I will explore in greater detail the president's use of emergency powers.

Like his predecessors, George W. Bush has employed the signing statement to voice constitutional objections to and concerns with congressional enactments, and, more importantly, to enunciate a particular interpretation of an ambiguous enactment. While the nature and scope of the objections raised during the Bush presidency are similar to prior administrations, they differ in the sheer number of constitutional challenges contained in the signing statements, which reflect a strong executive prerogative in relation to Congress and the judiciary.

The quantity of presidential signing statements has strayed approximately 50 percent during the Bush presidency versus previous administrations. President Bush issued 152 signing statements, compared to 382 during the Clinton administration. However, the qualitative difference in Bush's approach becomes apparent upon consideration of the number of individual challenges or objections to statutory provisions contained in the statements.[127] Of President Bush's 152 signing statements, 118 (78 percent) contain some type of constitutional challenge or objection, compared to only 70 (18 percent) during the Clinton administration. [128]

Which of President Bush's signing statements corroborate his support for a unitary executive and illuminate his interpretation of emergency power? According to scholars Charles Savage, Garry Wills, and a study conducted by the Congressional Research Service, of his 152 signing statements, Bush "cited the unitary executive theory eighty-two times to explain reasons for rejecting some aspect of a bill . . . he rejected aspects of a bill based on his role as Commander in Chief, thirty-seven times." [129]

The following examples from the 152 signing statements clearly indicate the president's support for the Unitary Executive Theory and his interpretation of emergency power. In the signing statement accompanying the USA Patriot Improvement and Reauthorization Act of 2005, President Bush declared that the provisions requiring the executive branch to submit reports and audits to Congress would be constructed "in a manner consistent with the President's constitutional authority to supervise the unitary executive branch and to withhold information which, if disclosed, could impair foreign relations, national security, the deliberative processes of the Executive, or the performance of the Executive's constitutional duties." [130] He demonstrated an interpretation of his emergency power, stating that "Congress is limited in intervening with the President's handling of 'national security' matters." The national security matter in 2001 was the "war on terror," a significant national emergency, according to President Bush. [131]

Similarly, in the signing statement accompanying the law that contained the McCain Amendment (as part of the Detainee Treatment Act), prohibiting the use of torture, or cruel, inhuman, or degrading treatment of prisoners, the president declared that the executive branch would construe that provision "in a manner consistent with the constitutional authority of the President to supervise the unitary executive branch and as Commander-In-Chief . . . [in order to protect] the American people from further terrorist attacks." [132]

Recent scholars also acknowledge that Bush's signing statements provide evidence of his interpretation of executive emergency power. [133] Scholars have organized Bush's constitutional objections into several categories. Most importantly, they suggest that the objections assert presidential authority to supervise the "unitary executive branch" and to assert command over the army as it relates to emergency. [134] Scholars go on to state that the Bush administration was "particularly prolific in issuing signing statements that object to provisions that it claims infringe on the President's power over foreign affairs, provisions that require the submission of proposals or recommendations to Congress; provisions imposing disclosure or reporting requirements; conditions and qualifications on executive appointments; and legislative veto provisions." [135]

In a signing statement attached to P.L. 107-77, Department of Commerce, Justice, State, Judiciary, and Related Agencies Act, President Bush clearly endorsed the unitary executive theory: "I note that Section 612 of the bill sets forth certain requirements regarding the organization of the Department of Justice's efforts to combat terrorism. This provision raises separation of powers concerns by improperly and unnecessarily *impinging upon my authority as President to direct the actions of the Executive Branch and its employees.* I therefore will construe the provision to avoid constitutional difficulties and preserve the separation of powers required by the Constitution."[136]

In a signing statement attached to the Enhanced Border Security and Visa Entry Reform Act of 2002, Bush again asserted executive autonomy, and rejected legislative mandates for coordination or consultation from Congress. He stated that such provisions would be treated as advisory only:

> Several actions of the Act raise constitutional concerns. Sections 2(6), 201 (c), and 202 (a) (3) purport to require the President to act through a specified assistant to the President in coordination or consultation with specified officers of the United States, agencies, or congressional committees. *The President's constitutional authority to supervise the unitary executive branch and take care that the laws be faithfully executed cannot be made by law subject to requirements to exercise those constitutional authorities through a particular member of the President's staff or in coordination or consultation with specified officers or elements of the Government.* Accordingly, the executive branch shall treat the purported requirements as precatory.[137]

In a signing statement attached to the Military Construction Appropriation Act of 2002, Bush asserted his constitutional authority to use emergency power:

> The U.S. Supreme Court has stated that the *President's authority to classify and control access to information bearing on national security flows from the Constitution and does not depend upon a legislative grant of authority.* Although the notice can be provided to Congress in most situations as a matter of comity, *situations arise, especially in wartime, in which the President must act promptly under his constitutional grants of executive power and authority as Commander in Chief while protecting sensitive national security information.* The executive branch shall construe these sections in a manner consistent with the President's constitutional authority.[138]

Bush's use of signing statements diverged from the historical precedent in the nature and sheer number of provisions challenged or objected to.[139] The key qualitative difference was President Bush's use of the signing statement to "emphatically endorse the unitariness of the executive branch."[140] He took very clear steps to assert sole presidential authority over the executive branch and the administration of policy initiatives, in particular, to assert his constitutional authority to prosecute the War on Terror.

The following signing statements further evidence Bush's logic regarding his constitutional authority to prosecute the war on terror and his support for the unitary executive theory. In a statement attached to the Homeland Security Act, Bush stated,

> The executive branch shall construe and carry out these provisions, as well as other provisions of the Act, including those in title II of the Act, in a manner consistent with the President's constitutional and statutory authorities to control access to and protect classified information, intelligence sources and methods, sensitive law enforcement information, and information the disclosure of which could otherwise harm the foreign relations or national security of the United States. [141]

In a signing statement attached to the Intelligence Reform and Terrorism Prevention Act of 2004, Bush objected to provisions requiring the executive branch to consult congressional committees prior to executing the provision:

> Many provisions of the Act deal with the conduct of United States intelligence activities and the defense of the Nation, which are two of the most important functions of the Presidency. The executive branch shall construe the Act, including amendments made by the Act, in a manner consistent with the constitutional authority of the President to conduct the Nation's foreign relations, as Commander in Chief of the Armed Forces, and to supervise the unitary executive branch, which encompasses the authority to conduct intelligence operations. [142]

As suggested earlier, foreign affairs and points of executive emergency power are two of the primary areas in which President Bush has repeatedly raised constitutional objections and or challenges. For example, Bush remarked on provisions of the Syria accountability and Lebanese Sovereignty Restoration Act of 2003, which required the imposition of sanctions against Syria absent a presidential determination and certification that Syria had met certain conditions or that a determination of national security concerns justified a waiver of sanctions. The president declared,

> A law cannot burden or infringe the President's exercise of a core constitutional power by attaching conditions precedent to the use of that power. The executive branch shall construe and implement in a manner consistent with the President's constitutional authority to conduct the Nation's foreign affairs as the Commander in Chief, in particular with respect to the conduct of foreign diplomats in the United States, the conduct of United States diplomats abroad, and the exportation of items and provisions of services necessary to the performance of official functions by United States government personnel abroad. [143]

Bush advocated the president's unilateral control over powers under Article II of the Constitution, in which he declared, "a law cannot burden or infringe upon the President's exercise of a core constitutional power." This constitutional power includes executive emergency power. Second, Bush advocated unilateral control over the execution of combating the emergency. He stated, "the executive branch shall construe and implement in a manner consistent with the President's constitutional authority to conduct the Nation's foreign affairs as the Commander in Chief."[144]

These signing statements imply that President Bush advocated both the Unitary Executive Theory and an interpretation of emergency power that suggests that a president may take any necessary actions to combat and dispel the crisis. Apparently, the president endorsed a theory of emergency power that suggests his powers during crisis were strong, swift, aggressive and necessary when dealing with the crisis. Furthermore the president seemed to suggest he was not bound solely by the Constitution, but was instead emboldened to protect, defend and use all the power granted in the Constitution to deal with the crisis.

DISCUSSION

Indubitably, the attacks of September 11, 2001, were an unprecedented emergency, and as such, President Bush bore the responsibility to respond to the crisis. He was confronted with determining the scope and magnitude of his authority to combat the crisis. I suggest President Bush fashioned Hamilton's theory of emergency power and Lincoln's necessity theory of executive power in times of crisis—making a new theory, a theory of a cavalier presidency during times of crisis.

I think the most surprising conclusion about President Bush's actions and interpretation of executive emergency power is that they were limited, and consistent with the precedent of emergency power. Moreover, most of the anger or disagreement with Bush's use of such power is overstated primarily because it had been so long since a president had used emergency powers. Would the same critics of President Bush's use of emergency power, who declared Bush was an "American Monarch," have made the same insinuation about Abraham Lincoln during the Civil War?[145]

Contemporary Americans are so far removed from the observation of emergency power, that we forget the potency and vigor of emergency power. The question remains, however; did President Bush have legal justification to use emergency power? A reassessment of the OLC's advice to the president will answer this question. According to the OLC, the lawyers concluded that President Bush had authority to act and repel the crisis based on an interpretation of Hamilton's writings. The OLC suggested that executive emergency powers are un-enumerated, derived from an interpretation of clauses within Article II of the Constitution.

The evidence suggests that Bush's interpretation of emergency power favored a strong, decisive executive, responsible for preserving the nation, and doing whatever was necessary to combat any threat posed towards the nation. Is this theory congruent with Hamilton's argument for executive emergency power as implicit within Article II of the Constitution?

In Federalist No. 70, Hamilton argued for swift, energetic, singular responses to crisis. He asserted that an executive must have the power to repel insurrection and invasions. Hamilton further suggested that an executive may have to act with "secrecy" and with "appropriate dispatch" to deal with the "insurrection."[146] With regard to responsiveness to the crisis, Bush advocated Hamilton's arguments in Federalist No. 70. Bush acted swiftly; the invasion of Afghanistan took place on September 23, 2001, just twelve days after the attacks. Bush authorized "secretive" investigations into potential terrorist activity both at home and abroad through the use of the Patriot Act and the detainment of enemy combatants at Guantanamo Bay. Both actions took effect by October 26, 2001, just forty-five days after the September 11, 2001, attacks.

However, as evidenced through the analysis of the Federalist documents presented in this chapter, Hamilton never suggested that a president may act in discordance with Congress and never advocated presidential authority to necessarily make war, or further still, to not seek consultation or oversight from Congress while he was using executive emergency power.

The OLC argued that the attacks of September 11, 2001, constituted an invasion, hence warranting an executive response to the attack. The OLC argument further promoted that an executive may do whatever is necessary to deal with the crisis; implicitly, the executive may act without receiving Congressional approval.[147] The OLC further argued that the executive may act without seeking any Congressional consultation, or oversight in responding to the crisis.[148] This level of prerogative was not congruent with Hamilton's ideas. Hamilton was consistent in his argument that, even though an executive may have "broadened" power and responsibility during a crisis, the executive was not above any "magistrate" within the shared system of powers that is the federal government.[149]

Analysis of President Bush's signing statements produces a clear picture of his theory of emergency power, which asserted presidential dominance over dealing with the crisis. Furthermore, Bush objected to any congressional restraint or requirements placed on his actions, prior to his acting. Bush's assertion to act singularly, was consistent with Hamilton, but as evidenced in the signing statements Bush exceeded Hamilton's argument to suggest a complete disregard for congressional consultation or oversight. Bush apparently believed he was "above magistrates" during a time of crisis, and was thus not consistent with Hamilton's argument.

The theorists detailed in this book I provide a solid framework to understand the intellectual history and theory of executive emergency power. Although the OLC concluded that Bush had authority to take actions after the terrorist attacks, the question becomes whether his interpretation was congruent with political thinkers on the subject.

How did Bush's lawyers' theory of executive emergency powers align with political philosophers? In light of the OLC opinions it would appear that Bush supported Locke's prerogative, cloaked in the implicit power argument of Hamilton. This is similar to Lincoln's interpretation of emergency power. Bush supported the idea that the president, while acting as commander in chief, must protect, defend, and preserve the Constitution, or what Bush called the "homeland." This logic recalls Locke's argument that emergency power, or prerogative, must be aimed at preserving the public good.

Bush strayed from the intellectual history of executive emergency power, and I think strayed from Lincoln, on the matter of separation of powers. According to the OLC opinions, the Bush administration advocated a Unitary Executive argument, that is, that the executive has unilateral control over the executive branch. This means the other branches have no oversight over the executive's prerogatives, and so support for a unitary executive makes the executive, in times of emergency, nothing less of an imperial president.

The OLC opinion argued for an interpretation of emergency power which supported a strong president in times of emergency. The power of commander in chief is the most critical. Accordingly, the OLC argued that in times of emergency, the president may respond to the crisis with whatever strength necessary because he has the power to command the army.[150] The president may conduct his actions without consultation or oversight from Congress because he alone is responsible for protecting, preserving, and defending the Union. This logic is congruent with modern interpretation of the Unitary Executive Theory, which suggests that presidents are inherently powerful, especially in times of emergency, and are not subject to other branches of government's constraints or limitations on presidential prerogative. This advice supports a theory of executive emergency power favoring a centralization of power during a crisis—an imperial presidency based on the Hamiltonian American model. Therefore, Bush appears to have adopted an interpretation of executive emergency power very close to Lincoln's interpretation—of course outlined in Yoo's OLC argument, suggesting a president is imperialistic during a crisis.

Such an assertion conflicts with Montesquieu's theory of separation of powers, even during an emergency. Montesquieu suggested that an executive may have to use emergency power, but still must respect the boundaries of separated powers.[151] Even in times of emergency the executive should respect the other branches of government.

Was the "war on terror" as much of a crisis as the Civil War? In terms of magnitude, the answer is obviously no. However, the OLC suggested that the potential "insurrection" of enemy combatants was unquantifiable, and therefore led the OLC to conclude that Bush's power was similar to Lincoln's necessary actions of emergency power during the Civil War.[152] But was the landscape similar enough to the Civil War circumstances to warrant broad authority, at least philosophically, after the attacks of September 11, 2001?

Unlike the early days of the Civil War, Congress was in session during the attacks. Bush initially sought congressional authority for his actions, unlike Lincoln,[153] and received congressional approval for his actions. The Military Authorization Act was passed in late September 2001, along with the Patriot Act. Did Bush use any power comparable to Lincoln's? The extraordinary renditions, and the detainment of enemy combatants at Guantanamo Bay may constitute a kind of habeas corpus suspension; the detainees are enemies of the state, however. The more important point to consider is that the OLC advised the president that he had broad authority if an "insurrection" actually occurred or intensified.[154]

However, the insurrection did not happen, which prevented broader use of power during the Bush presidency. If a greater insurrection had occurred, then I do think Bush would have embarked on a broader use of power that probably would have appeared similar to Lincoln's actions during the Civil War. Luckily that is not the case, though the unlucky ones are the enemy combatants.

NOTES

1. Steven G. Calabresi and Christopher S. Yoo, *The Unitary Executive: Presidential Power from Washington to Bush* (New Haven, CT: Yale University Press, 2008). By reviewing the history of the republic and its corresponding theory, we find that modern interpretations have become more "extreme"; hence, previous presidents adopted a more nuanced interpretation.

2. Calabresi and Yoo, *The Unitary Executive*, 3–7.

3. Alexander Hamilton, Federalist No. 70, in Alexander Hamilton, James Madison, and John Jay, *The Federalist Papers*, 354–62 (New York: Bantam Press, 1982).

4. See especially John C. Yoo, Memorandum Re: Authority for Use of Military Force to Combat Terrorist Activities *Within the United States*, October 23, 2001, U.S. Department of Justice, Office of Legal Counsel.

5. Hamilton, Federalist No. 70.

6. Ibid.

7. Max Farrand, ed. *The Records of the Federal Convention of 1787* (New Haven, CT: Yale University Press, 1911), vol. 2, 537.

8. Ibid.

9. Hamilton, Federalist No. 70.

10. All of Hamilton's claims are drawn from Federalist No. 70. For an Anti-Federalist response, see George Clinton, Anti-Federalist No. 69, in Herbert J. Storing, and Murray Dry, *The Complete Anti-Federalist*, 115–17 (Chicago: University of Chicago Press, 1981).

11. Hamilton, Federalist No. 70.

12. Edwin Meese, *With Reagan: The Inside Story* (Washington, DC: Regnery Gateway, 1992); J. Yoo, Memorandum Re: Authority for Use of Military Force to Combat Terrorist Activities *Within the United States*, October 23, 2001.

13. Calabresi and Yoo, *The Unitary Executive*, 3–5.

14. I will explore constitutional objections to laws when I review presidential signing statements.

15. Calabresi and Yoo, *The Unitary Executive*, 3–5.

16. Ibid.

17. *Myers v. United States* (272 U.S. 52, 1926).

18. Calabresi and Yoo, *The Unitary Executive*, 3–5.

19. Michael Herz, "Imposing Unified Executive Branch Statutory Interpretation," *Cardozo Law Review* 15, no. 1–2 (October 1993): 219–72, 252–53.

20. Elena Kagan, "Presidential Administration," *Harvard Law Review* 114, no. 8 (June 2001): 2245–2385, 2327.

21. Calabresi and Yoo, *The Unitary Executive*, 4–6.

22. Ibid., 5–8.

23. War Powers Resolution of 1973 (50 U.S.C. 1541–48).

24. Ibid.

25. Thomas Cronin, "An Imperiled Presidency," in *The Post-Imperial Presidency*, edited by Vincent Davis (New Brunswick, NJ: Transaction Books: 1980), 137–39.

26. Christopher Kelley, *Executing the Constitution: Putting the President Back into the Constitution* (Albany: State University of New York Press, 2006), 45–46.

27. Meese, *With Reagan*, 77.

28. Kelley, *Executing the Constitution*, 45–46.

29. Executive Order, signed March 13, 1937 , 2 FR 619, March 16, 1937, revoked by Public Land Order 5887, May 18, 1981 (46 FR 28414), 46 Federal Register 131937, February 1981.

30. John Gattuso, *Washington D.C.: Know the City Like a Native* (Singapore: APA Publications, 2008).

31. Ibid.

32. Executive Order, signed March 13, 1937.

33. Joseph Cooper and William F. West, "Presidential Power and Republican Government: The Theory and Practice of OMB Review of Agency Rules," *The Journal of Politics* 50, no. 4 (November 1988): 864–95, 873–75.

34. John Dean, "George W. Bush as the New Richard Nixon: Both Wiretapped Illegally, and Impeachably; Both Claimed That a President May Violate Congress' Laws to Protect National Security," FindLaw, December 30, 2005, http://writ.lp.findlaw.com/dean/20051230.html.

35. Meese, *With Reagan*; Calabresi and Yoo, *The Unitary Executive*; J. Yoo, Memorandum Re: Authority for Use of Military Force to Combat Terrorist Activities *Within the United States*, October 23, 2001.

36. Hamilton, Federalist No. 70.

37. Ibid.

38. Alexander Hamilton, Federalist No. 77, in Hamilton, Madison, and Jay, *The Federalist Papers*, 388–92.

39. George W. Bush Interview, *60 Minutes*, CBS, November 17, 2010.

40. Nancy V. Baker, "The Attorney General as a Legal Policy Maker: Conflicting Loyalties," in *Government Lawyers: The Federal Legal Bureaucracy and Presidential Politics*, edited by Cornell W. Clayton (Lawrence: University of Kansas Press, 1995), 31–59.

41. Obtained from the U.S.DOJ OLC index.

42. Nelson Lund, "Guardians of the Presidency: The Office of the Counsel to the President and the Office of Legal Counsel," in Clayton, *Government Lawyers*, 209–57.

43. This is in addition to the Court overturning, in short, some of the OLC opinions regarding the removal and detainment of enemy combatants. See *Hamdi v. Rumsfeld* (542 U.S. 507 2004), and *Hamdan v. Rumsfeld 2006* (548 U.S. 557, 2006), (542 U.S. 507, 2004).

44. William P. Barr, Testimony of William Barr, Hearing of the Commission on the Roles and Capabilities of the United States Intelligence Community, Room SD-106, Dirksen Senate Office Building, Washington, DC, Friday, January 19, 1996, transcript, 38.

45. Those bills that the administration advances are circulated to all interested agencies for comment. The OLC will get a bill only if the Office of Legislative Affairs seeks a legal review. Statement of Robert B. Shanks, Deputy Assistant Attorney General, Office of Legal Counsel, before the Committee on Energy and Natural Resources, Subcommittee on Energy Conservation and Supply, U.S. Senate, Concerning Revised Constitution of American Samoa on May 8, 1984, 1–43.

46. Department of Justice, Office of Legal Counsel, www.justice.gov/olc/index.html.

47. Ibid.

48. J. Yoo, Memorandum Re: Authority for Use of Military Force to Combat Terrorist Activities *Within the United States*, October 23, 2001.

49. Ibid., 2.

50. Ibid.

51. Ibid.

52. Ibid., 3.

53. Ibid., 2.

54. Ibid., 3.

55. Ibid.

56. Ibid., 4.

57. Ibid.

58. Ibid., 3.

59. Alexander Hamilton, Federalist No. 23, in Hamilton, Madison, and Jay, *The Federalist Papers*, 111–15.

60. J. Yoo, Memorandum Re: Authority for Use of Military Force to Combat Terrorist Activities *Within the United States*, October 23, 2001, 5.

61. Ibid.

62. Ibid., 6.

63. Ibid.

64. John Yoo, *Crisis and Command: The History of Executive Power from George Washington to George W. Bush* (New York: Kaplan, 2009), ch. 1.

65. J. Yoo, Memorandum Re: Authority for Use of Military Force to Combat Terrorist Activities *Within the United States*, October 23, 2001, 6.

66. Ibid., 5.

67. Pacificus, "No. 1," in *The Complete Anti-Federalist*, edited by Herbert J. Storing, and Murray Dry, 23–27 (Chicago: University of Chicago Press, 1981).

68. J. Yoo, Memorandum Re: Authority for Use of Military Force to Combat Terrorist Activities *Within the United States*, October 23, 2001, 7.

69. Alexander Hamilton, Federalist Paper No. 74, in Hamilton, Madison, and Jay, *The Federalist Papers*, 374–76.

70. J. Yoo, Memorandum Re: Authority for Use of Military Force to Combat Terrorist Activities *Within the United States*, October 23, 2001, 9.

71. Ibid.

72. Ibid.

73. Hamilton, Federalist No. 23.

74. Ibid.

75. Ibid.

76. This is demonstrated most notably in Hamilton, Federalist No. 70.

77. Alexander Hamilton, Federalist No. 24, in Hamilton, Madison, and Jay, *The Federalist Papers*, 116–20.

78. Alexander Hamilton, Federalist No. 25, in Hamilton, Madison, and Jay, *The Federalist Papers*, 120–25.

79. J. Yoo, Memorandum Re: Authority for Use of Military Force to Combat Terrorist Activities *Within the United States*, October 23, 2001, 7.

80. Hamilton, Federalist No. 25.

81. Ibid.

82. Alexander Hamilton, Federalist No. 26, Hamilton, Madison, and Jay, *The Federalist Papers*, 125–30.

83. Stephen G. Bradbury, Memorandum for the Files Re: October 23, 2001 OLC Opinion Addressing the Domestic Use of Military Force to Combat Terrorist Activities, October 6, 2008, U.S. Department of Justice, 1–2.

84. Ibid., 2.

85. Patrick F. Philbin, Legality of the Use of Military Commissions to Try Terrorists, November 6, 2001, U.S. Department of Justice.

86. Ibid., 7.

87. Jay S. Bybee, Memorandum Re: the President's Power as Commander in Chief to Transfer Captured Terrorists to the Control and Custody of Foreign Nations, March 13, 2002, U.S. Department of Justice.

88. Jay S. Bybee, Memorandum for John Rizzo, Acting General Counsel of the Central Intelligence Agency, Interrogation of al-Qaeda Operative, August 1, 2002, U.S. Department of Justice, 2–3.

89. Ibid., 2–4.

90. Ibid., 2–3.

91. John Yoo, Memorandum Re; Constitutionality of Amending Foreign Intelligence Surveillance Act to Change the "Purpose" Standard for Searches, September 25, 2001, 2–4.

92. NBC/Washington Post Poll, *Wall Street Journal*, September 17, 2001.

93. J. Yoo, Memorandum Re: Authority for Use of Military Force to Combat Terrorist Activities *Within the United States*, October 23, 2001.

94. Authorization for Use of Military Force, September 18, 2001, Public Law 107-40 (S. J. RES. 23) 107th Congress.

95. See Louis Fisher, *Presidential War Power*, 2nd ed. (Lawrence: University Press of Kansas, 1995); Garry Wills, *Bomb Power: The Modern Presidency and the National Security State* (New York: Penguin Press, 2010).

96. Authorization for Use of Military Force, September 18, 2001.

97. J. Yoo, Memorandum Re: Authority for Use of Military Force to Combat Terrorist Activities *Within the United States*, October 23, 2001.

98. Authorization for Use of Military Force, September 18, 2001, 5.

99. Ibid.

100. George W. Bush, Remarks on Arrival at the White House and an Exchange with Reporters, September 16, 2001, www.presidency.ucsb.edu/mediaplay.php?id=63346&admin=43.

101. Ibid.

102. Some also suggest that this can possibly be attributed to the continuation of Congress's willingness to allow the president to "make war." See Fisher, *Presidential War Power* and Wills, *Bomb Power*.

103. George W. Bush, Address before a Joint Session of the Congress on the United States Response to the Terrorist Attacks of September 11, September 20, 2001, www.presidency.ucsb.edu/mediaplay.php?id=64731&admin=43.

104. Authorization for Use of Military Force, September 18, 2001.

105. Ibid.

106. See Fisher, *Presidential War Power* and Wills, *Bomb Power*.

107. David Currie, "Rumors of War: Presidential and Congressional War Powers," *University of Chicago Law Review* 67, no. 1 (2000): 1–40.

108. Bob Woodward, *Bush at War* (New York: Simon and Shuster, 2002), 15–30.

109. Ibid., 23–35.

110. Ibid., 15–30.

111. Howard Ball, *The USA Patriot Act of 2001: Balancing Civil Liberties and National Security: A Reference Handbook* (Santa Barbara, CA: ABC-CLIO, 2004).

112. Fred Barbash, "Justices Reject Appeal Over the Secret 9-11 Detainees," *Washington Post*, January 12, 2004.

113. Timothy Lynch, *Breaking the Vicious Cycle: Preserving Our Liberties while Fighting Terrorism* (Washington, DC: CATO Institute, June 26, 2002), Policy Analysis 443.

114. James Risen, *State of War: The Secret History of the CIA and the Bush Administration* (New York: Free Press, 2006), 42–44.

115. Ibid., 37, 43. See Patriot Act, Title II, Section 215, under "sneak and peek" and "roving wiretaps" provisions, both of which allow federal agents to secure the gathering of terrorist information without first requesting a specified warrant.

116. J. Yoo, Memorandum Re: Authority for Use of Military Force to Combat Terrorist Activities *Within the United States*, October 23, 2001, 6.

117. Kate Martin, "Legal Detainment?," Center for National Security Studies, 2004, in *SAIS Review* 29, no. 1 (Winter–Spring 2004), 6–7.

118. J. Yoo, Memorandum Re: Authority for Use of Military Force to Combat Terrorist Activities *Within the United States*, October 23, 2001, 6.

119. U.S. Department of Justice, Department of Justice Inspector General Issues Report on Treatment of Aliens Held on Immigration Charges in Connection with the Investigation of the September 11 Terrorist Attacks, June 2, 2003, www.justice.gov/oig/special/0306/press.pdf.

120. Ibid.

121. John Mayer, "Outsourcing Torture: The Secret History of America's Extraordinary Rendition Program," *New Yorker*, February 14, 2005.

122. *Amnesty International,* "Below the Radar," 2008.

123. Mayer, "Outsourcing Torture."

124. Risen, *State of War*, 28.

125. Phillip J. Cooper, "George W. Bush, Edgar Allen Poe, and the Use and Abuse of Presidential Signing Statements," *Presidential Studies Quarterly* 35, no. 3 (September 2005): 515–32, 517.

126. Christopher May, "Presidential Defiance of Unconstitutional Laws: Reviving the Royal Prerogative," *Hastings Constitutional Legislative Quarterly* 21 (1994): 932. President Jackson was the first to issue a signing statement, and John Tyler was first to use the statement to question the constitutionality of the statute submitted to him. Letter from John Tyler to the House of Representatives, June 25, 1842, in *A Compilation of the Messages and Papers of the Presidents*, edited by James D. Richardon, 2012 (Washington, DC: Government Printing Office, 1897).

127. T. J. Halstead, Congressional Research Service, "Presidential Signing Statements: Constitutional and Institutional Implications" (Washington, DC: Congressional Research Service, Library of Congress, 2007).

128. Neil Kinkopf, "Index of Presidential Signing Statements, 2001–2007," American Constitution Society of Law and Policy, August 2007.

129. Wills, *Bomb Power*, 219; Charlie Savage, *Takeover: The Return of the Imperial Presidency and the Subversion of American Democracy* (New York: Little, Brown, 2007), 35; Halstead, Congressional Research Service, "Presidential Signing Statements."

130. USA Patriot Improvement and Reauthorization Act of 2005, P/L 109-177; George W. Bush, Statement upon Signing H.R. 3199, March 9, 2006.

131. George W. Bush, Address to the Nation, September 21, 2001, President Bush's Library Archives, Arlington Texas.

132. J. Yoo, Memorandum Re: Authority for Use of Military Force to Combat Terrorist Activities *Within the United States*, October 23, 2001, 6.

133. Cooper, "George W. Bush, Edgar Allen Poe, and the Use and Abuse of Presidential Signing Statements," 517.

134. Curtis A. Bradley, Eric A. Posner, "Presidential Signing Statements and Executive Power," *Constitutional Commentary* 23 (2006), 307, 323.

135. Cooper, "George W. Bush, Edgar Allen Poe, and the Use and Abuse of Presidential Signing Statements," 522.

136. Presidential Signing Statement, P.L. 107-77, *Weekly Compilation of Presidential Documents* 37 (2001), 1724.

137. Enhanced Border Security and Visa Entry Form Act of 2002, P.L. 107-173, signed June 2002, *Weekly Compilation of Presidential Documents* 38 (2002), 822.

138. Military Construction Appropriation Act of 2002, P.L. 106-52, *Weekly Compilation of Presidential Documents* 38 (2002), 1836.

Bush's Interpretation and Application following September 11, 2001 159

139. Cooper, "George W. Bush, Edgar Allen Poe and the Use and Abuse of Presidential Signing Statements"; Christopher Yoo, Steven G. Calabresi, and Anthony J. Colangelo, "The Unitary Executive in the Modern Era, 1945–2004," *Iowa Law Review* 90, no. 2 (2005): 601, 722.
140. Yoo, Calabresi, and Colangelo, "The Unitary Executive in the Modern Era," 722.
141. Homeland Security Act, P.L. 107-296, *Weekly Compilation of Presidential Documents* (2002), 2093.
142. Intelligence Reform and Terrorism Prevention Act of 2004, P.L. 108-458, *Weekly Compilation of Presidential Documents* (2004), 2993.
143. George W. Bush, Statement upon Signing the Syria Accountability and Lebanese Sovereignty Restoration Act of 2003, December 12, 2003.
144. George W. Bush, Statement upon Signing USA Patriot Improvement and Reauthorization Act of 2005, P/L. 109-177, H.R. 3199, March 9, 2006.
145. Wills, *Bomb Power*, 145–63.
146. Hamilton, Federalist No. 70.
147. J. Yoo, Memorandum Re: Authority for Use of Military Force to Combat Terrorist Activities *Within the United States*, October 23, 2001, 4–7.
148. Ibid., 6.
149. Alexander Hamilton, Federalist No. 76, in Hamilton, Madison, and Jay, *The Federalist Papers*.
150. J. Yoo, Memorandum Re: Authority for Use of Military Force to Combat Terrorist Activities *Within the United States*, October 23, 2001.
151. Montesquieu, *Spirit of the Laws*, in Michael Morgan, ed., *Classics of Moral and Political Theory* (Indianapolis, IN: Hackett Publishing Co., 1992), 431–40.
152. J. Yoo, Memorandum Re: Authority for Use of Military Force to Combat Terrorist Activities *Within the United States*, October 23, 2001, 13.
153. Initially Lincoln could not seek congressional authority because Congress was out of session. However, in his message to Congress on July 4, 1861, he made clear that he felt that Congress would support all his actions, which they did.
154. J. Yoo, Memorandum Re: Authority for Use of Military Force to Combat Terrorist Activities *Within the United States*, October 23, 2001.

Chapter Seven

Conclusion

Emergencies are as old as the historical record, as no states are immune from internal insurrections, environmental crises, or foreign invasions that threaten the fabric of the nation's character as well as its very survival. In this book I examined a wide trajectory of intellectual thought on executive emergency power, demonstrating that state crises and the resultant need to consolidate power appropriately is an issue that dates back to the beginning of ancient civilizations' written record. Through my examination of many key theorists, I sought to address a central question, why is emergency power vested in the executive, and to understand why there are different theoretical approaches to executive emergency power.

Throughout both the theoretical and historical research, I revealed a wide philosophical development regarding executive emergency power that, although presenting many strands of agreement on reasons why this expanded power must rest with the executive, also brought to light many nuances of the dynamic of this power. The nuances were whether the power should be implied or explicit with a government's founding documents, whether it should be constrained by the rule of law or free from it, or whether any other governmental agents or agencies may have the power to intervene in, pass judgment on, counteract, or cut the executive's access to and/or use of such power, and if so, under what circumstances and how.

In order to understand the theories of executive emergency powers and how they relate to the normal precepts of the rule of law in a constitutional state, I first examined the intellectual history of the ideas surrounding the need for, as well as the justification and legal limits of, executive-branch power during a crisis. The intellectual history of executive emergency power led me to explore the thoughts of Greek theorists Plato and Aristotle; Renaissance thinkers Rousseau, Locke, Hobbes, Montesquieu, and Machiavelli; and finally, American thought on the matter, particularly the debate between Anti-Federalists and Federalists Alexander Hamilton, Thomas Paine, James Madison, Richard Henry Lee, Patrick Henry, and George C. Clinton as well as the rhetoric of American presidents during emergencies, namely George Washington, Thomas Jefferson, James Madison, Andrew Jackson, Abraham Lincoln, and George W. Bush.

By examining both the theory and practice of executive emergency power from ancient to recent history, I was able to delineate, among other issues, how the balance of power during a crisis can or should be negotiated, as well as the effect of emergency power on the law both during and following said crisis.

In this chapter, after reviewing the intellectual history of executive emergency power, I will re-examine presidential rhetoric and interpretations of executive emergency power that expressed reasons and justifications for emergency power in early and modern America. In the United States assessing presidential interpretations of executive emergency power is useful because executives inevitably combat crises and are expected to do so legally. According to precedent, executive emergency power is an inherent, or un-enumerated, power within Article II of the Constitution,[1] although the word "emergency" never itself appears in the Constitution. Presidents have combated emergencies, and in doing so they, in a way, have defined what emergency power is and what it is not in the United States. Therefore, it is important to conclude this book by synthesizing and analyzing what theories of executive emergency power the presidents subscribed to when determining the scope and use of their emergency power. In sum, this book explored the intellectual ideas on and arguments for executive emergency power, the main points and contributions to which this conclusion will now analyze.

Understanding the implications of presidential interpretations of executive emergency powers on the effects of executive power is important because, as the power is centralized—causing the denial of normal processes of U.S. constitutional democracy that otherwise diffuses, balances, and decentralizes power—it becomes an unlimited and thus undemocratic power. Therefore, a major focus of this research considers the consequences of the two main approaches to incorporating executive emergency power into a constitutional democracy. As stated throughout this book, the two competing schemas of executive emergency power are explicit versus implicit. In an explicit schema the power is overtly stated or enumerated within a constitution, whereas in an implicit schema executive emergency power is implied, or inherent, within the constitution.

The following analysis will review the theory of executive emergency powers, outlining the chosen theorists' main theoretical contributions.[2] After outlining the main theorists' thoughts on executive emergency power, I will examine the major agreements and differences among the thinkers' suppositions as well as the relative feasibility of critiquing their contributions to the current theory of executive emergency power. For example, let's suppose a theorist suggested that during an emergency the law is subject to the prerogative or discretion of the executive; would limiting such power be feasible, or would expanding that be the only solution to combat the crisis? Further, I will examine the theorists' thoughts on whether executive emergency *ought* to be limited. To do so I construct a scale in which I measure each theorists' approach to executive emergency power from limited to unlimited, placing emphasis on the measured degree of executive emergency power.

After reviewing the theorists, I then turn to presidential thoughts and rhetoric on executive emergency power. I consider whether presidents in early and modern America favored a particular theory of executive emergency power and whether they favored centralizing power during a crisis. To do so I present a table summarizing the presidential thoughts, which were discussed thoroughly throughout this book.

In table 7.1 I summarize, title, and gather each chosen theorist's substantive contribution to the debate surrounding executive emergency power. I then summarize the main points of each theory. The theorists all agree that executive emergency power is an extraordinary executive power used solely to preserve and protect the state in the event of extraordinary emergency or crisis. In the following summary I will review the theorists' major themes or contributions around the following key points regarding executive emergency power: the constitutional schema authorizing executive emergency power, the resetting of executive emergency power, and limitations on executive emergency power.

The constitutional schema for executive emergency power could be one that explicitly authorizes executive emergency power with formal written provisions in the constitution or one that is potentially beyond the scope of the law, with no written provisions and relies solely on the executive's prerogative to act according to his own discretion to do whatever is necessary to combat a crisis. Formally, we may think of the differences among the schemas, in light of crisis, as one of the following two approaches to exercising executive emergency power:

Table 7.1. Theories of executive emergency power.

a. Locke, "Of Prerogative Power"

b. Hamilton, "Energy in the Executive"

c. Lincoln, "Necessity Doctrine"

d. Machiavelli, "Rule of Law"—Constitutionalists

e. Rossiter, "Constitutional Dictatorship"

f. Yoo, "Imperialist Presidency"

1. An unfettered, unlimited prerogative, whereby executive prerogative determines how an executive exercises emergency power, with no legal provision guiding his rubric (per Locke and Hamilton).[3]
2. Explicitly written constitutional provisions, in which the executive's authorization to exercise executive emergency power is provided for through express rules for the use of that power, thereby an executive does not use his prerogative in determining how to exercise emergency power. The Constitution both authorizes the exercise of executive emergency power and places limits on the use of that power (per Machiavelli and Rossiter).[4] (Examples of the provisions will be examined in the following section.)

THEORISTS SUPPORTING THE CONSTITUTIONAL MODEL TO EXECUTIVE EMERGENCY POWER

This model seeks to control or limit the executive prerogative by creating written rules authorizing how and when to exercise executive emergency powers. A major difference among the theorists concerns the formal constitutional schema that provides for the creation and limitation on executive emergency power. Rossiter and Machiavelli agree that explicit provisions should exist in a constitution to authorize the expansion of executive power during a crisis, such as the creation of a constitutional dictator, or rather, a person who is constitutionally authorized to exercise emergency power. Machiavelli and Rossiter do not provide exact examples of nations where such constitutional provisions would exist; instead, they theorize potential constitutional provisions, proscribed as follows:

1. The legislature will appoint the dictator.
2. The legislature will declare the emergency.
3. The legislature establishes the dictator's powers to combat the crisis.
4. The legislature will establish how long the dictator will have to combat the crisis, therefore placing a clear duration of time in which the emergency powers will be in effect.
5. The legislature will declare when the emergency is over.[5]

The theorists' previously mentioned provisions (not exact in language), in light of an emergency, would authorize a constitutional dictatorship, which is an expansion of power to combat the crisis, whereby the constitutional provisions also limit the power to the specific provisions enumerated. The provisions mentioned previously authorize a constitutional dictator to exercise executive emergency power to combat a crisis—expanding power—whereby the constitution also limits the power to the specific provisions enumerated.

THEORISTS SUPPORTING THE UNFETTERED
EXECUTIVE PREROGATIVE MODEL

In this model the law does not place limitations on an executive's prerogative to determine how to exercise emergency power. Locke, Hamilton, Lincoln, and Yoo suggest that no formal constitutional schema or provision should exist authorizing the exercise of executive power during crisis. Instead, they argue that during a crisis the executive should have full latitude to act according to his own prerogative, which may or may not be in accordance with the written law.[6] Therefore, there would be no formal written constitutional provision that would limit the executive's authority to exercise emergency power during a crisis. These theorists never define precisely their meaning of the word prerogative, which today leaves the courts to determine whether or not prerogative power has any boundaries or limitations. Further, these theorists agree that the reasons an executive would exercise emergency power according to his own prerogative are because:

1. the law cannot foresee the magnitude of any crisis, thereby the actions necessary to combat the crisis cannot be prescribed;
2. the legislature is too cumbersome, too delayed to act swiftly enough to determine how to combat the crisis;
3. the courts are passive institutions and therefore cannot adjudicate until well after the events have happened; and
4. the executive will declare an emergency and will do whatever is necessary to combat the crisis.[7]

Regarding the matter of whether to reset the executive emergency powers following an emergency, there is no variation among the theorists; they all agree that executives' must relinquish emergency powers when the crisis is over. Locke and Hamilton, the most forceful proponents of the prerogative model, differ regarding a nuance related to the constitutional schema of the model. The nuance in Locke prescribes that an executive may act in way that might violate existing law or going beyond the scope of the law, whereas Hamilton argues that the American model presumes an inherent constitutional executive emergency power that is lawfully granted to the president under the authority that is given to him under Article II of the Constitution—thus, executive emergency power does not go beyond the scope of law.

Moreover, a thorough discussion and analysis follows in the remainder of this conclusion that will address the constitutional schema for executive emergency power and limitations on executive emergency power.

IS THE EXECUTIVE THE BEST OR THE ONLY ONE
SUITED TO HANDLE CRISIS?

The theorists I reviewed in this book suggested that during a crisis it is the executive who should be vested with emergency power. They believed this because the legislature would be too disparate, possibly not in session, and/or too slow to act, and the judiciary does not have the authority to create law or act without someone petitioning it and would therefore also be too slow to adjudicate a response to a crisis.[8] In particular, Locke was wary of a legislature's ability to produce an appropriate law to combat a crisis because it is too numerous, diverse, and cumbersome.[9] Hamilton would agree; for instance, he offered sharp criticisms of the Anti-Federalists, who thought the presidency could be a plurality, and he concluded that a plural presidency would lead to a feeble government and execution of the law.[10] He felt that any delayed response to a crisis, which a plural presidency could produce, would lead to a weak response or feeble actions, either of which would be detrimental to the viability of the state.[11] According to Hamilton, such a feebleness of government, especially during crisis, would make the republic inept and jeopardize the health of the state, the maintenance of which, he argued like others, was the executive's primary responsibility.[12]

In sum, the theorists agree that during a crisis, centralizing power and placing it in the hands of the executive is best, even though doing so creates an undemocratic power, hence a power of crisis—a power in time of crisis that is possibly unlimited and contradicts the very fabric of the republic, the fundamental design to decentralize power via a system of separate powers and checks and balances. During crisis, however, democracies suspend the normal procedures that limit, balance, and separate powers, instead favoring centralizing power.

This centralization of power, then, is the most critical moment in a republic's history to analyze because it is the moment when power is being used counter to all of the republic's written laws and rules, which were designed to prevent usurping of power and, as a result, tyranny. A republic may choose different ways to centralize power during a crisis, such as attempting to maintain some balance of power among the branches of government and the written law, or allowing the emergency power to be unchecked and absolute during the crisis. As such, the fact that all the theorists reviewed in this book argued that power should be consolidated in the executive and that most of the theorists supported giving the executive full discretion with his new power is worth a brief discussion here.

We have repeatedly seen the supposition asserted that only an executive could handle a crisis because he would then have the power necessary to combat the crisis (presumably) successfully. This claim, however, although seemingly logical, that executive power is the only solution is not entirely convincing. Although Locke asserted that the legislature would be too cumbersome and slow to act, the historical record does not support that all crises require such swift—and, possibly, knee-jerk—reactions. For instance, following the attacks of September 11, 2001, only ten days or so after the attacks Congress passed a resolution granting military force to combat the terrorist cells in Afghanistan. In fact, because another attack did not follow, presumably the United States could have taken as long as it needed to debate how best to respond to these attacks. Although we know this now in hindsight, many such crises exist that, arguably, would be better served if the response given to them was based on deliberate and calm dialogue that allowed for a fuller assessment of the facts available and possible approaches to that crisis. Locke's assertion that the legislature would be too cumbersome and slow to act is predicated solely on the assumption that all crises are of the nature that require an immediate response.

Further, Hamilton argued the same Lockean claim—that swiftness to act is critical in chaos; however, swiftness could lead to hasty or even bad decisions, such as violating the Constitution. Concerns such as these are exactly why Rossiter and Machiavelli argued for explicit parameters of power during crisis. They were concerned that an executive with no limitations could be harmful to the republic, and this is why they suggested the creation of some boundary of power, legally created and explicitly stated in a nation's constitution.[13] I will expand this point further when I discuss constitutional executive emergency power versus extra-constitutional executive emergency power.

By taking stock of both the historical record and our current list of national as well as global crises, we can see that only a handful of emergencies are best served with a swift and singular response; today, because most crises are ongoing issues, such as financial crises or long wars against terrorist cells, longstanding conceptions regarding how emergencies should be handled on a national scale may be increasingly inappropriate. Because many crises have the potential to be decades long, allowing an executive broadened implied power may not be suitable, especially in a democracy and especially because the longer he holds that power, chances increase that he could abuse it or harm the essence of the republic—the protection of civil liberties.

This means that Rossiter's and Machiavelli's suggestions for parameters to executive emergency power during a crisis may be more relevant when examining the nature of emergency power in the modern era; perhaps Rossiter's concerns in particular are rooted in his observation and experience with the demise of republics in Western Europe in the 1930s, Germany especially. Future research in executive emergency powers should more deeply address the nature of an emergency, the length of the emergency, and the power used to combat the emergency so as to determine just what effect executive power had on a nation during and after a crisis.

LIMITATIONS ON EXECUTIVE EMERGENCY POWER

Although many of the theorists argue that the executive should have full discretionary power in order to combat the crisis, this practice is not only undemocratic but also very dangerous to the rule of law, particularly during a crisis. As above, the reason for this store of power rests on the assumption that the emergency warrants a potent response. Locke and Hamilton argued for an immediate, swift response and even suggested that the executive may act beyond the scope of law or even take action counter to the written law.[14] Lincoln, in his actions, speeches, and writings, agreed with this. Clearly, all three men held a strong assumption regarding the nature of the ruler: that he would be benevolent and could be entrusted with this expanded power and not harm the republic. However, history tells us that such an assumption is foolish; rarely, if ever, are rulers wholeheartedly kind or benevolent, so casting a blanket trust over any executive and endowing him with such power could lead to harmful consequences.

Machiavelli and Rossiter understood this when they suggested that a state create constitutional dictators. They demonstrated their distrust for the purity of the executive during crisis by arguing very clearly that a ruler (1) could not declare an emergency (this would be done by another part of government) and (2) the newly formed constitutional dictator would not be the current executive (the classic example is Rome, where during crisis the Roman councilors could not become the constitutional dictator).[15] Clearly, both Machiavelli and Rossiter sought to create distinctions and separations between the normal government and crisis government, with the intent of reducing or even eliminating the chances of the executive abusing his expanded power during a crisis.

Whereas Locke, Hamilton, and Yoo created executive dictators—although they are not named such but rather fit the title in both theory and application—the general consensus among these three theorists appears to be that only a single person can act with enough might and latitude to combat a crisis successfully. What is of note about the latter argument is that all three theorists placed no limitation on the executive's expanded power during the crisis. Locke asserted that if there are concerns about the executive abusing his power, the people will easily be able to tell and will act out against the ruler.[16] Locke assumed, therefore, that the public will be aware of their rights as well as the actions of the ruler; however, this assumption is idealistic at best, and basing the executive's limitations on the public's ability to collectively understand and act against the executive in a manner that is effective as well as respected by the state does not offer a reassuring check on that power. Further, Hamilton and Yoo argued that an executive, as Locke suggested, would do only what was necessary to combat the crisis and save the state, but as stated above, assuming such benevolence in the face of contrary history is naïve at best.

Machiavelli and Rossiter would not support a system in which the constitution would not bind a ruler to explicit constitutional provisions that would prescribe and impose formal parameters on the executive's exercise of executive emergency power during a crisis. If in time of crisis expansive power is needed, then why not just create an explicit parameter of law to guide the actions of a ruler? Conversely, Locke, Hamilton, and Yoo would create unlimited power; then a republic, by default is creating some form of a mechanical constitutional dictator. In so doing, why not err toward the latter so the republic would then be able to exercise some control over the agent as he combats the crisis, therefore maintaining some essence of a rule of law even during an extreme crisis. However, understanding all this—that not all crises are the same, and thus, response strategies should be appropriate to the nature of the crisis at hand—prompts a fecund trajectory of research and theory worthy of examination at a future time.

In figure 7.1 executive emergency power is scaled from unchecked, or unlimited, to a checked, limited power. In so doing each theorist is placed on the scale, respective to his own conditions for checking or unlimiting executive emergency power during a crisis, then the placement of the theorist is relative to the other theorists' conditions, reflecting their respective theories.

The scale reports executive emergency power as a linear function, in which emergency power is measured by degree. Power to the left is limiting, or reducing the degree of power, and moving to the right indicates reducing limitations on power, with no limitation to the furthest right, and increasing the degree of power. Note that Locke, the classic liberal, is aligned on the right end of the spectrum and, conversely, Machiavelli here is the restrainer. The figure measures the exercise of executive emergency power from (left to right) either a constitution explicitly authorizing how and when an executive may exercise emergency power, thereby granting the expansion of power while also limiting that power, or, at the very far right end, an executive's prerogative determines how and when to exercise emergency power, with no formal written constitutional provision either authorizing the power or limiting that power.

Further, one end is unilateral, prerogative power, with the law placing no limitation, and on the other end, power is expanded though constrained by the provisions given in the constitution. Therefore, in either direction power is expanded: either it is expanded as the executive uses his prerogative to determine how to exercise emergency power or by the constitution through explicit provisions formally expanding executive power and determining how an executive will exercise that power.

The most important factor of executive emergency theory is to determine whether executive emergency power is limited or unlimited, or in other

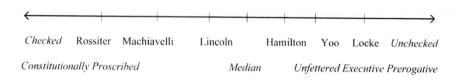

Figure 7.1.   Magnitude and degree determining how to exercise executive emergency power from a checked/explicit constitutional power to an unchecked/unfettered power, according to a median.

words, whether the emergency power is a checked or unchecked power, in which exercising emergency power is either an unfettered executive prerogative determining how to exercise that power or it is an authorized constitutional power, thereby creating the expanded power while also limiting that power. There is a degree of executive emergency power, ranging from an unchecked power, meaning it could be an unfettered prerogative or unconstitutional, to the opposite extreme—a fully checked, legal power created through a constitutional provision that both expands executive authority while also explicitly limiting or prescribing that authority within the rule of law—the constitution—during crisis. Therefore, the magnitude of the power changes depending on whether the power is constitutional or not. Thus, beginning at the left of the scale, the power is unfettered executive prerogative with a full magnitude of power, and, as we move right, the power is decreased but increases in constitutionality, in which constitutional provisions authorize the exercise of emergency power, thereby expanding power (though not as much as an unfettered prerogative) but also places limitation on that power. Furthermore, measuring the limitation—or lack thereof—of executive emergency power also suggests the degree or magnitude of executive emergency power. As emergency power becomes less limited, the power increases in degree, and vice versa. In figure 7.1 I created an index of emergency power by creating a scale that measures the power from unlimited to limited, by theorist. In so doing the figure indicates the magnitude of executive emergency power within a constitutional democracy, as each theorist prescribed that power. As the scaling of executive emergency power moves from a limited power to an unlimited one, we can observe the change in the degree or magnitude of the power—either increasing or decreasing in degree by theorist.

   The critical observation in the scaling of executive emergency power is the directional movement of emergency power as it moves toward being unlimited. This is critical because an unlimited power in a constitutional democracy is paradoxical, as it is juxtaposed to the design and to the foundational principles of a constitutional democracy. In other words, during a crisis the rule of law is suspended or even rendered irrelevant. With this risk in mind, I now examine each theorist's reasons for either completely discarding the written law and, thus, authorizing an unfettered executive prerogative in determining the exercise of emergency power, or supporting a constitutional schema in which constitutional provisions authorize and may determine how and when an executive exercises emergency power as it also limits that power.

Figure 7.1 indicates that Locke favored an unlimited, unchecked executive power during crisis. This finding, indicating that Locke favored an executive prerogative that would determine how and when to exercise emergency power and in which that power is unlimited during an emergency, is unusual because Locke is historically known as a classic liberal, defending the decentralization of power towards the people throughout his writing. However, in light of crisis Locke asserted the absolute need for an executive to use his prerogative when determining how to exercise emergency power. His "prerogative power" is an unlimited power because no law can "account for every possible crisis"[17] ; therefore, the power must be flexible enough and not limited in order to challenge and defeat whatever the causes of crisis may be. Locke assumes that written law is unable to account for all possible causes of crisis, and because of this, the executive needs latitude or "prerogative" to do what is necessary to defeat the causes of any crisis.[18]

Locke prescribed a remedy to combat the magnitude of crisis: a prerogative power, reserved only for the executive to act according to his own discretion "to save the state." He asserted that the power may "go beyond the scope of the law" and must be aimed "at the public's good."[19] Therefore, he believed that executive emergency power must be unlimited because it is the only power left to combat a crisis and thus is the only power strong enough to ensure the state is preserved.

Is Locke completely, unequivocally asserting that emergency power be unchecked? He did argue that although executive emergency power is unlimited, it is not a "power of choice, but a power of necessity."[20] He suggested that the people present a slight limitation, though, as quoted in chapter 1, he conceded that "the people have no other remedy in this, as in all other cases where they have no judge on earth, but to appeal to Heaven."[21] Thus, Locke, though he understood the inherent flaws of human nature, on this issue believed that the executive should be constrained only by his own motives, his own respect for the law, and by God. He suggested that the people present a slight limitation on executive emergency power but never stated exactly how they could place a check on executive emergency power.[22] If we take Locke's assertion that if any limitation may exist on executive emergency power, it must rest with the people, and apply it to modern America, then we may assert that elections provide a means to control emergency power. However, as Locke prescribed it, because the executive would always be the one to assert the use of emergency power initially—not requiring any other popular or institutional consent—the power would be made unlimited at the onset, although the popular or institutional will may possibly limit it thereafter.

In summary Locke asserted that executive emergency powers are necessarily "beyond the scope of law" because it is not possible for the "law to foresee or proscribe for all future emergencies."[23] Therefore, he argued that it is essential to allow the executive "discretion" to combat an emergency as he sees fit, which may entail going beyond the scope of the written law, and this is what Locke called "prerogative power."[24] Hence, during crisis Locke would prescribe—in a democracy—a ruler who has unlimited power, making the ruler akin to a dictator except that, according to the idealistic Locke, he would be a benevolent ruler.

Conversely, Clinton Rossiter suggested constraining or checking the executive's emergency power, most commonly with what he called a constitutional dictatorship—giving a person expanded legal power during a crisis. He believed that in constitutional democracies the written law must always be protected and never jeopardized. However, the law is most vulnerable during crisis because people are willing to surrender liberty for security. As Rossiter correctly asserted, surrendering liberty to executive discretion to combat a crisis is unwise, if not even foolish, because there is little to stop the executive from usurping power and then never giving it back, thereby making the executive a dictator without a constitution or any means to control his actions.[25]

Thus, Rossiter favored placing limitations on determining how and when an executive exercises emergency powers. This could be done by writing explicit provisions in a constitution, thereby creating an emergency regime, or a constitutional dictator who received his power as proscribed by the constitution during a crisis. Once the emergency was over, so too were the powers of the constitutional dictator. Therefore, according to Rossiter, the written law is always the absolute check on power in a constitutional state, even during crisis. As opposed to leaving executive authority as an implicit or inherent power, Rossiter endorsed an explicit schema of executive emergency power, and in so doing he placed explicit constraints on executive emergency power. He asserted that governments can combat emergencies legally within the boundaries of the law, therefore suggesting an institutional answer to executive emergency power.

However, Rossiter's schema for explicit executive emergency power is not feasible. Not only is it impossible to foresee emergencies and, hence, be able to preemptively legislate to deal with them, but also the creation of a legal limitation on executive emergency power seems counterintuitive to what the necessary requirements of executive emergency power are—broad power to combat the crisis.

Below I list Rossiter's provisions for a constitutional dictatorship. He likely formulated the constitutional dictatorship theory out of real-life concerns about executives becoming too powerful during crisis, in particular in reaction to World War II Europe.[26] Rossiter argued that if more exact provisions were in place before a crisis to enact a constitutional dictator during a crisis, then fewer abuses of power would occur, thus preserving the republic from the rise of a dictator.[27] He insisted that the law must be preserved, though he acknowledged that during a crisis power must be centralized and expanded to address that crisis; he asserted that the republic *can* be preserved during crisis while also preserving the law of that republic, hence the creation of a legal, constitutional dictator.[28]

Rossiter's main constitutional provisions for a constitutional dictatorship are:

- An executive may not declare an emergency and, hence, cannot declare himself a constitutional dictator.
- The powers conferred during a crisis to the constitutional dictator may not last indefinitely.
- The laws creating constitutional dictatorship powers must be in place prior to a crisis.
- The other branches of government will confer and create the constitutional dictatorship.[29]

In order to analyze or assess the feasibility of Rossiter's constitutional dictatorship provisions, I will engage in a hypothetical discussion, reducing the theory into a simple proposition. According to Rossiter, laws exist prior to the crisis happening, and these laws are sufficient enough to resolve any crisis. Therefore, assuming a severity of the crisis—on a scale of 1 to 10, say 5—the breadth of the laws would be equal to the severity of the crisis. Thus, a simple equation would appear as follows: crisis = laws. The breadth and effectiveness of the law would change based on the magnitude or the severity of the crisis.

However, within the modern scientific paradigm we are often confounded with such deductive theoretical frameworks; they become ineffective or, at minimum, reductive, so much so that modern science has moved toward explaining phenomena after the event, not before. Therefore, in modern scientific models knowing the severity of the crisis is critical in order to explore and advance a theory. Thus, going back to our discussion, knowing the severity of the crisis before writing the law is critically important—and necessary so as to apply the correct remedy or solution—because only after knowing the conditions of the crisis can we prescribe appropriate variables to explore the best remedies to analyze and address the event. Hence, the law is always theorized after the crisis has occurred.

Imagine trying to enact some of Rossiter's constitutional dictator provisions without knowing the nature of the crisis. First, he suggested that definite time limitations be placed on the executive's power; thus, the powers given by the law can be used only during a prescribed amount of time—perhaps a month, a year, and so forth—to deal with the crisis. This assumes that the prescribed power could combat the crisis in a set amount of time, but as above, without knowing the nature of the crisis, we cannot begin to estimate how much time is necessary for the constitutional dictator to address and alleviate the emergency. Further, even if the law limits the executive emergency power to a terminate amount of time, this does not necessarily mean that the crisis is likewise terminate; in other words, the crisis could expand or change, which may mean that more time would be needed to combat the crisis. This also means that the necessary laws needed to combat the crisis would need to change as well so that the constitutional dictator could combat the crisis with enough force and have enough time to do so.

This is a limitation in Rossiter's theory. Returning to our simple equation, he asserted that the breadth of the laws is fixed because it is prescribed regardless of the magnitude of the crisis, and is done so explicitly in the constitution—thus, it is not to be changed after the crisis occurs. However, because crises change as they progress, the breadth of the law would not sufficiently address the crisis. In other words, say the magnitude of the crisis started at 5, but over the course of the crisis it progressed to 6; however, the breadth of the law would remain at 5, and this means that the laws would no longer be able to combat or contain the crisis.

Second, the idea of prescribing laws before a crisis is known or understood is likely to be unfeasible. It is akin to prescribing medicine to a patient before we know the diagnosis—and then refusing to adapt or alter the treatment as more is known about the illness or after it progresses or reacts to treatments. Laws simply cannot foresee or prescribe all possible remedies for all possible crises because no one can say with exact precision or certainty the magnitude of the next crisis. As the magnitude or dynamic of a crisis changes, the law would need to change in response. Flexibility is necessary in the law to combat the ever-changing magnitude of any given crisis. Thus, creating explicit constitutional provisions—laws that maintain or possibly even limit legal executive emergency powers—could harm or render the republic incapable of combating the crisis with enough force to defeat it, and this could seriously jeopardize the survival of the republic.

Like Locke, discussed above, Alexander Hamilton argued that executive emergency power should be unfettered, differing from Locke only in claiming that the executive, while wielding emergency power, is not "above any other magistrate" within government.[30] Although Hamilton did state that emergency power is an inherent constitutional power lawfully granted to an executive under authority given to him in Article II of the Constitution—meaning that the power is solely the domain of the executive (implicitly so)—he did not argue that other branches of government could not limit or constrain the exercise of executive emergency power through challenging the chosen exercise of that power in a court of law (likely long after the fact). However, because he does assert that executive prerogative determines how and when to exercise emergency power, this is why I scale Hamilton's theory of executive emergency power closest to Locke. But Hamilton's argument that exercising emergency power is an inherent constitutional power lawfully granted to an executive under authority given to him in the Constitution accounts for the distance between the two theorists on the scale.

Although Hamilton agreed with Locke that the nature of particular emergencies will most likely be unprecedented or hard to foresee, he did not agree that the power should reside outside the scope of law. Rather, he suggested that the power should be implicit within Article II of the Constitution.[31] However, it is hard to glean any real difference between Hamilton's thought that executive emergency power is implied and Locke's theory of prerogative power; the two theories both make clear that executive powers during crisis are prerogative. Therefore, whether or not the power is inherent within the Constitution, the logic of these two theories diverges very little; implicit power and power outside the Constitution could be argued as being one and the same. Consequently, the theoretical difference between Locke and Hamilton may just be semiotics.

Hamilton's theory rested on the notion that energy in the executive is "the leading characteristic of good government" and is needed because it is "essential to the protection of the community against foreign attacks . . . to the protection of property against those irregular and high handed combinations, which sometimes interrupt the ordinary course of justice, to the security of liberty against the enterprise and assaults of ambition, of faction and of anarchy." "Unity" is the main ingredient to constitute energy and the executive may have to be "secretive and swift" when responding to a crisis. Hamilton and his supporters argued that the executive must have the energy to respond to a crisis, and as commander in chief, he will respond to the crisis first, sometimes with "secrecy," but always with "energy" and "dispatch."[32] From his writings, executive emergency power has been construed as an unenumerated constitutional power.[33] Thus, the president may do whatever he deems reasonable to combat the crisis, and all actions he takes in response to the crisis is, according to Hamiltonian logic, a constitutional, implicit power of Article II. As discussed in chapters 2, 5, and 6, Hamilton argued that executive emergency power is inherent or implicit within Article II of the Constitution. Hamilton asserted that the following constitutional clauses, when taken together, suggest that an executive has inherent power to exercise emergency power: the Vesting clause, the Oath clause, the Commander-in-Chief clause, and the Take Care clause. Coupled all together, this constructs the American model for exercising executive emergency power, in which executive prerogative determines how and when to exercise emergency power and is an inherent constitutional power lawfully granted to an executive under authority inherently granted to him in Article II of the Constitution.

Toward the other end of the scale, toward limited executive emergency power, we have Machiavelli (again, see figure 7.1). According to Machiavelli, a republic should account for all the actions of the state by drafting law to declare the actions of the state legal. His assertion is that laws must exist for all actions, and this also applies to emergencies. Accordingly, Machiavelli argued that law must exist to combat crisis, and not prescribing law to do so would be the greatest failure and weakness of any republic. Therefore, he asserted that even during an emergency the rule of law must limit and check executive power. Machiavelli favored a model of emergency power enumerated within a constitution. He used the Roman model as his preferred example to explain how having a constitutional dictator to be used only during a crisis was a wise and prudent measure to have within a constitution.[34]

In summary, Machiavelli agreed with all three theorists that an executive must have the power to combat emergency; however, he would not agree that the power should go beyond the scope of law, as Locke asserted, or that the power should be inherent or implicit within a constitution, as Hamilton and Lincoln suggested. Instead, Machiavelli claimed that executive emergency power should be explicit, or stated within the constitution. Machiavelli thought that laws should be written, as was the case in ancient Rome, and should clearly outline and direct the powers of an executive during an emergency, stating, "and in a Republic, it should never happen that it be governed by extraordinary methods [not governed by laws]. For although the extraordinary method would do well at the time, none the less the example does evil . . . republics must provide remedy for every incident, and fix the method of governing it."[35] Thus, according to Machiavelli, the executive should "never be above the law" but rather be a constitutional dictator during an emergency. There never should exist a time—even in crisis—when the law does not rule the agents of government.

While leading the nation through the Civil War, Abraham Lincoln adopted an American model for exercising executive emergency power that combined the elements of Lockean "prerogative" and Hamilton's assertions of emergency power as an inherent power within the Constitution. Lincoln argued that his actions to wage war against the South without prior congressional approval were completely necessary to save and preserve the Constitution and the Union. He asserted that his power was unlimited in that, while acting to preserve the Union he must do things that otherwise would be unconstitutional—that is, suspend habeas corpus, raise an army, appropriate funds, and prohibit the correspondence of mail through the post office.[36] His argument favoring a strong, imperial response to the Southern rebels is difficult to place accordingly on a scale of emergency power because, although Lincoln acted assertively, he also remarked that his actions would be adopted by Congress, therefore, according to Lincoln, rendering his actions constitutional. His doctrine of necessity is Locke's theory of prerogative power cloaked in Hamilton's implicit executive emergency power theory.

Thus, based on Lincoln's actions, he appears to have favored Locke's argument that executive emergency power is unlimited and may "go beyond the scope of law"; however, when applying his actions to his rhetoric, he then appears more like Hamilton in that executive emergency power is inherent in the Constitution because "the president must uphold and defend the Constitution and preserve the Union," making him responsible to act during crisis.[37] Consequently, I scale Lincoln to the left of Hamilton, as Hamilton favored implicit emergency powers, suggesting that the president's use of power is discretionary during crisis and an inherent power in Article II of the Constitution. Further, I place Lincoln far left from Locke, who favored no check on emergency power, and that power could go beyond the written law. I place him here only because Lincoln did argue that his power is within the Constitution, and during crisis the executive may call upon all the powers—any enumerated power in the Constitution, not just reserved to Article II, that is, powers reserved to Congress—of the Constitution to preserve the Union. Unlike Locke, Lincoln clearly asserted that emergency power is not intended to go beyond the scope of the Constitution, and his actions demonstrated this position, as the powers he used were powers reserved to Congress, as written in the Constitution.

Furthermore, Lincoln always asserted that Congress would have the final say on whether his actions were constitutional. And on July 4, 1861, Congress did approve all of Lincoln's actions, supporting his claim that his actions were constitutional. Therefore, his theory of necessary executive emergency power is checked and limited by the Constitution, and his emergency power did not go beyond the scope of the Constitution; instead, Lincoln's theory of executive emergency power used all the prescribed powers in the Constitution to combat the crisis.

In addition, Lincoln agreed with Hamilton that the executive must act during an emergency. He expanded Hamilton's argument for energy in the executive to combat the crisis by asserting that the executive must do whatever is necessary to combat the crisis. Lincoln argued that during an emergency the president may need to take some actions that may be unconstitutional, stating, "Was it possible to lose the nation, and yet preserve the Constitution? By general law, life and limb must be protected, yet often a limb must be amputated to save a life; but a life is never wisely given to save a limb." Thus, to act beyond the Constitution is to act with the objective to preserve the Union and the Constitution. Therefore, Lincoln believed that executive emergency powers are inherent within Article II of the Constitution because the executive takes an oath to "preserve, protect, and defend the Constitution."[38]

Lincoln postulated that the oath of office meant, "I should do to the best of my ability, to preserve, protect and defend the Constitution. . . . I did understand that my oath to preserve the Constitution to the best of my ability imposed upon me the duty of preserving, by ever indispensable means, that government, that nation, of which that Constitution was the organic law." He believed that preserving the nation was his top priority and that measures "otherwise unconstitutional, might become lawful, by becoming indispensable to the preservation of the Constitution, through the preservation of the nation."[39] His logic became known as the necessity doctrine, as, during an emergency, the executive should do whatever is necessary to preserve the Union.[40]

More recently, John Yoo, the leading attorney at the Office of Legal Counsel (OLC) during the George W. Bush presidency and principal author of the OLC documents advising the president on what legal actions he could take to combat the crisis following the attacks of September 11, 2001, posited a theory of executive emergency power that is Hamiltonian. As such, I place him closest to Hamilton on the scale (figure 7.1). Yoo asserted that the president may take any necessary action to combat future insurrections or crises caused by al-Qaeda because he has an inherent power to act with swiftness and energy to command the army and dispel the crisis.[41]

Yoo argued that executive emergency power is inherent within Article II because the president must carry out the function of the enumerated powers in Article II to command the army, defend and preserve the Constitution and Union, and execute the laws faithfully. According to him, the president, while adhering to the previously stated clauses, has constitutional authority during crisis to do whatever is needed to dispel the causes of the crisis in order to preserve the Union and execute the law. Yoo's interpretation of executive emergency power does not suggest any limitation on the power other than the Constitution, but because this power is inherent, it is the court's responsibility to interpret the constitutionality of the power after it is used.[42] In a sense Yoo's argument favors an imperial presidency or an implied constitutional dictator, though this dictator is not bound by any explicit laws, unlike Machiavelli's suggestions favoring the Roman model.

Contemporary scholars who disagree with Yoo and, in general, attack the Bush administration's use of emergency power are Adler, Ackerman, Pfiffner, and Matheson.[43] They all agree that presidential emergency power is a power balanced and constrained by republicanism. In other words, these scholars agree with Hamilton that presidents have expanded power during crisis but that the tenets of republicanism—separated powers, oversight, consultation, and the rule of law—oversees and limits this power. Although these scholars make a case to support Hamilton's argument, as shown in this book, there is little substantive evidence to support this conclusion. Of the presidents examined in this book, only Madison's thoughts and actions support a precise Hamiltonian view; all other presidents supported a Lockean prerogative model not constrained by the rule of law or republicanism. This supports this book's claim that presidents are dictatorial during crisis—not men of law nor men constrained by the rule of law.

Adler and Ackerman argue explicitly that even though presidents use a great deal of power during crisis, they do so to protect the nation and thus do not harm the rule of law because, they argue, presidents are doing everything in their means to save the republic from demise—very Lincolnian logic.

These scholars support the broad violation of the Fourth Amendment as the government uses the NSA program to surveil Americans. They argue that because the president is protecting the people and the nation from terrorism, he is, therefore, maintaining the essence of both his oath and the rule of law because congressional and judicial oversight constrain his actions. However, the president is clearly violating the law.

The major agreement in all the theorists' conceptualizations in the degree and magnitude of executive emergency power is quite simple: they all agree that a growth or centralization of power is needed in time of crisis. They agree that emergency power must be in the hands of the executive so he may respond to the crisis with energy, force, and swiftness in order to combat and defeat the crisis. Therefore, during crisis the normal constitutional democratic procedures to diffuse, separate, and balance power become silenced and the opposite occurs: there is mammoth growth and usurpation of power toward the executive, thereby making the executive emergency power an authoritarian—or totalitarian—power, even in constitutional democracies. Further, all the theorists also agree that the growth of power should always be limited in its aim—preserving the state: the growth of executive power in time of crisis is to maintain and preserve the state, not to create a despot. Where they differ is that the emergency power is not necessarily constrained in terms of what the action may be or whether the action is legal.

Consequently, the primary difference among the theorists' conceptualizations of executive emergency power regards the limitations or checks on the power—whether the emergency power, as it is being used, has any meaningful constitutional provisions limiting it, or if the power is purely an executive's prerogative. Therefore, the difference is gleaning whether or not the executive's will is bound to exact legal provisions when exercising emergency power. Locke, Hamilton, and Lincoln agreed that the power may violate the Constitution, thus making a dictator, but they never called the executive such. Conversely, Rossiter and Machiavelli asserted that risking the state to a president who has all the power of a dictator but is never called one is foolish. Therefore, according to them, laws should be written so that they authorize a dictator during an emergency and try to prescribe some rules limiting those dictatorial powers, thereby creating formal written legal limitations on emergency power.

PRESERVATION OF THE STATE

All six theorists agreed that the executive must be responsible for preserving the nation during an emergency. According to the theorists, preserving the state is a paramount concern for any ruler because, as the analysis offered here suggests, the main responsibility of any ruler is the health of the republic, which can be gauged by assessing the state's self-sustenance over time. Lincoln wisely suggested that the most important role of a president is to uphold his oath of office. This, according to Lincoln, above all else meant preserving the Constitution and inherently meant preserving the Union. [44] Likewise, Machiavelli argued that the primary responsibility of government is to protect and secure the people; hence, the government's utmost concern is preserving the state, and thus, the government must act accordingly so as to do what is necessary to overcome any crisis. [45] Rossiter also claimed that the state must act—and act with vigor—to defend and preserve itself. [46]

However, regarding the concerns outlined in the previous two sections, Is the Executive the Best or the Only One Suited to Handle Crisis? and Limitations on Executive Emergency Power, can the executive emergency power itself jeopardize the state? If an executive usurps and abuses power, the essence of the state—the principles on which it thrives—is at risk. However, if limitations to that power are put in place, although the rule of law (i.e., the Constitution) is protected, in certain crises, the state could be jeopardized. Machiavelli and Rossiter would argue the state would survive because the powers granted legally to the ruler would suffice, aiding him to combat and defeat the crisis, after which the law of the state is not harmed in any way. Conversely, according to Locke, Hamilton, and Lincoln, a republic changes after any given crisis; we can see through history how the United States changed notably after the Civil War. Thus, presidents reinforce each other's interpretation of executive emergency power, favoring an executive prerogative.

However, another way to approach and understand these changes is to see them through the spectrum of how the rule of law was altered and diminished during each crisis, when the executive had free rein to combat the crisis with whatever means necessary; as a result, after the changes that occurred during that executive-power expansion, the political and legal landscape may possibly never return to what it was before.

CONSTITUTIONAL AND LEGAL BASIS FOR GRANTING EXECUTIVE EMERGENCY POWER

As discussed above, the theorists do not agree about the source of the legal authority from which executive emergency power will be derived or substantiated in a republic's model of government. Locke, who, surprisingly, is the most extreme, argued that executive prerogative determines how and when to exercise executive emergency power and the prerogative may be derived from outside the boundaries of the prescribed law, claiming that the power could be considered beyond the scope of the law. He does condition emergency power to be exercised only to protect and preserve the state and that an executive should not abuse that power at the expense of the people.[47] Although both Hamilton and Lincoln agreed with Locke—that the aim of the power is to preserve the state—they advocate an American model for exercising executive emergency power, in which executive prerogative determines how and when to exercise emergency power and is an inherent constitutional power lawfully granted to an executive under authority given to him in Article II of the Constitution.

Conversely, Machiavelli and Rossiter disagreed with the previous thinkers on this point; they argued that constitutional provisions ought to authorize how and when to exercise emergency powers. Thus, they believed that during a crisis constitutional provisions will authorize how and when to exercise emergency power, thereby creating constitutionally an expansion of executive authority, that which Rossiter and Machiavelli called a constitutional dictator. A more in-depth discussion of Rossiter's theory of a constitutional dictator is discussed in more detail below.

PRESIDENTIAL INTERPRETATIONS OF
EXECUTIVE EMERGENCY POWER

A critical part of the research of this book was the examination of presidential interpretations of executive emergency powers, demonstrated through writings, so as to determine whether those theories are congruent with any of the major intellectual theorists' thoughts on executive emergency power. To do so, it was imperative to examine key presidential cases in which presidents used emergency power and demonstrated a particular theory of executive emergency power. This section will focus on presidential interpretations of executive emergency power, establishing which theorist each executive would most closely favor and providing evidence of the executive's interpretation regarding the centralization of power. I then outline the evolving presidential interpretations of executive emergency powers as examined in this book, with a focus only toward the president's reasons and justifications for executive emergency power (see chapters 3 through 6 for more in-depth analyses).

To summarize, the presidents all agreed that an executive should exercise his emergency power to preserve and protect the state. Clearly, they did not all face the same magnitude of crisis; Lincoln's crisis was much more serious than Jackson's, for example, though hindsight gives us a larger context in which to judge the severity of any given crisis; therefore, hindsight makes evident that Jackson's crisis was more akin to a national interest, not an emergency. However, it is important to note that each president certainly believed that his crisis was of a significant magnitude that warranted the term "emergency." The presidents, similar to the theorists analyzed, do not delineate how one could measure the magnitude of a crisis—that is, how one would determine to what extent a crisis truly threatens the state.

The following will reexamine American presidential interpretation of the theory of executive emergency power. The presidents' words and rhetoric indicated support for the Lockean/Hamiltonian model of executive emergency power, thereby creating an American model of executive emergency power. Executive prerogative may go beyond the scope of law (Lockean) or may be an inherent constitutional power lawfully granted to the president under constitutional authority given to him in Article II of the Constitution (Hamilton).

In the remaining body of the conclusion I will reexamine presidential writing and rhetoric, further demonstrating how the presidential rhetoric and writings subscribe to the Lockean and Hamiltonian conceptualizations of constitutional schemas for executive emergency power. The evidence suggests that although the presidents supported an unfettered executive prerogative for determining how to exercise emergency power, they agreed that their emergency power should not go beyond the scope of law; rather, the presidents agreed that emergency power was an inherent constitutional power lawfully granted to the president.

George Washington

George Washington combated the "whiskey rebels" in Western Pennsylvania without congressional approval. As he heard news of the violence in the Pittsburgh area he told Hamilton that he would use all power necessary to combat the crisis: "I have no hesitation in declaring, if the evidence is clear and unequivocal, that I shall, however reluctantly I exercise them [emergency powers], exert all the legal powers with which the executive is invested to check so daring and unwarrantable a spirit."[48] In order to respond to the crisis Washington centralized power when he called up the militias and rode into battle in Western Pennsylvania. Thus, he advocated Hamilton's theory of executive emergency power in which executive prerogative determines when and how to exercise emergency power and that power is an inherent constitutional power lawfully granted to an executive under authority given to him in Article II of the Constitution. Further, during crisis it is necessary for government to assume more power so as to uphold and protect the state from grave harm or injury.

Thomas Jefferson

Thomas Jefferson both purchased the largest U.S. territory without consulting Congress and fired upon the *Chesapeake* naval ship without congressional approval.[49] He did, however, struggle with the decision to act without congressional approval when acquiring the Louisiana territory:[50] "Our confederation is certainly confined to the limits established by the revolution. The general government has no powers but such as the Constitution has given it; and it has not given it a power of holding foreign territory, and still less incorporating it into the Union."[51] He went on to confess that "an amendment to the Constitution seems necessary for this acquisition."[52]

Although Jefferson decided to act alone, he believed that the people would determine the legitimacy of his actions by either reelecting him or voting him out of office.[53] This view was consistent with Locke's principles of "prerogative power," in which executive prerogative determines when and how emergency powers are exercised and that power may or may not be an inherent constitutional power lawfully granted to the executive under authority given to him in Article II of the Constitution. Jefferson, like Locke, believed that through elections, the American people would determine whether or not the president's emergency actions were constitutional. He stated, "We shall not be disavowed by the nation . . . the people's act of indemnity will confirm and not weaken the Constitution, by more strongly marking out its lines."[54] In the end Jefferson won an easy reelection in 1804.[55] For philosophical reasons he was reluctant when he purchased the Louisiana Territory and when he exacerbated hostilities with Britain by responding to attacks on the *Chesapeake* naval ship, leading to the War of 1812. Even though he agreed philosophically with Locke's theory of "prerogative power" (that a ruler should use emergency power only for the public good and that at times the emergency power may go beyond the scope of law), Jefferson had difficulty acting alone and against the Constitution.[56] Nevertheless, he did so for both of these issues of critical national interest. Consequently, during an emergency concentrating power toward the executive is necessary, even for Jefferson, who despised the very idea of a strong, imperial presidency.

James Madison

James Madison decided to seek congressional approval while deliberating on how to handle the hostilities of the British Navy in U.S. waterways. He believed that the president must act only with congressional approval because "the tasks of foreign policy, declaring war, making treaties, and concluding peace, were among the highest acts of sovereignty of which the legislative power must at least be an integral and preeminent part of."[57] His handling of the War of 1812—his decision to act only with congressional consent—proved to be disastrous. Based on these statements, concluding whether Madison advocated for an American model for exercising emergency power is unclear; rather, his words indicate a possible departure from other presidents advocating the American model. Instead, Madison might be advocating a model in which determining the how and when to exercise emergency power might be a shared power among the branches of government and only within the boundaries of explicit written constitutional provisions authorizing the how and when to exercise that power.

However, Madison is significant here because he is the lone constitutionalist in this study. As we saw during the more in-depth discussion in chapter 4 on his presidency and his approach to handling the belligerent British forces, Madison observed the literal rule of law—he obeyed his constitutional authority to act during a crisis and did not act on his prerogative. Before acting, he consulted the Constitution and Congress to determine how and when to exercise emergency power. He argued that emergency power must be shared between the presidency and Congress.[58] Unlike earlier presidents, Madison did not agree that during a crisis the centralization of power toward the executive was absolute; therefore, he maintained his belief and supported shared power during the war.[59]

Andrew Jackson

Andrew Jackson bullied and provoked the Native Americans into submission by using the U.S. military without congressional approval.[60] His generals relayed the president's announcement that "the Federal Government could and would protect them fully in the possession of the soil [which was described as 'fertile and abundant country'] and their right of self government."[61] Jackson made it very clear, however, that if they refused to move, "they must necessarily entail destruction upon their race."[62] His mobilization of the military to address the Cherokee Indians in Georgia without congressional approval appears to support Hamilton's executive emergency power theory that executive prerogative determined how to exercise that power and that emergency power was an inherent constitutional power lawfully granted to him under his authority in Article II of the Constitution.

Abraham Lincoln

Abraham Lincoln fought a war without congressional approval. He believed he must act immediately, basing this on his understanding that the oath of office meant, "to preserve the Constitution to the best of my ability imposed upon me the duty of preserving, by every indispensable means, that government, that nation, of which that Constitution was the organic law."[63] Therefore, he believed he must do whatever was necessary to preserve the Union, including the pursuit of actions that "otherwise unconstitutional, might become lawful, by becoming indispensable to the preservation of the Constitution, through the preservation of the nation."[64] Lincoln's ideas are known as the necessity doctrine, which comprises both Locke and Hamilton's theory of executive emergency power. Lincoln is Lockean when he acted alone to preserve the state, even if that meant violating the Constitution, and he appeared to be Hamiltonian when he urged Congress that his actions were inherent in the Constitution.[65] Lincoln supported the centralization of power during the crisis as a necessary function of government if the only intent for doing so was to preserve the Union.

George W. Bush

Finally, in a memo drafted shortly after the attacks of September 11, 2001, the OLC advised President George W. Bush that "because the scale of violence involved in this conflict removes it from the sphere of operations designed to enforce the criminal laws; legal and constitutional rules regulating law enforcement activity are *not* applicable."[66] The OLC went on to state that the president may act alone to pursue military actions against the terrorists: "We [the Office of Legal Counsel] believe that Article II of the Constitution, which vests the President with the power to respond to emergency threats to the national security, directly authorizes use of the Armed Forces in domestic operations against terrorists . . . such enumerated power [Commander in Chief] includes the authority to use military force, whether at home or abroad, in response to a direct attack upon the United States."[67] Based on this OLC recommendation, we can infer that Bush's lawyers supported Hamilton's theory of energy in the executive and that executive emergency powers are inherent in Article II of the Constitution. Of course, most of the advice Bush received was related to the potential threat of a future attack, regarding which the advice stated the president may do whatever is necessary to preserve the state. This advice supports a theory of executive emergency power favoring a centralization of power during a crisis—an imperial presidency based on the Hamiltonian American model. Therefore, Bush appeared to adopt an interpretation of executive emergency power very close to Lincoln's interpretation, of course, outlined in Yoo's OLC argument, suggesting that a president is imperialistic during a crisis.

SUMMARY

In each instance U.S. presidents determined the parameters of their power based on their own interpretation of presidential power during crisis. In no instance did the president appeal to the people for their input for dealing with the crisis.

All of the discussed presidents, with the exception of Madison, favored centralizing power so as to preserve or to protect the state from grave injury and to end the crisis. Based on this study, the centralization of power appears to be a common behavior during crisis, and the theory conforms with a long history of intellectual thoughts supporting the importance of centralized power during a national emergency. The presidents studied here indicate support for the Lockean prerogative model, in which executive prerogative will determine how and when to exercise emergency power and is an inherent constitutional power lawfully granted to an executive under authority given to him in Article II of the Constitution. The American Hamiltonian model does not support explicitly writing constitutional provisions authorizing the how and when an executive will exercise emergency power; thus, the American model does not explicitly authorize executive emergency power nor does it explicitly limit that power.

Furthermore, preserving the state is the paramount concern, and in order to do so, more and focused power is needed to combat any crisis, regardless of the crisis's dynamic, and the magnitude of force is dependent on the magnitude of the crisis (below I discuss different kinds of crises), hence the need to centralize power towards the executive. Therefore, even in constitutional democracies the rule of law may be superseded during crisis, thereby creating an undemocratic, totalitarian power that runs counter to all of the normal functions of the constitutional democracy. Consequently, in a time of crisis all those who have written on the topic of emergency power, even constitutional democratic thinkers, agree that the executive must concentrate his power. Rather, as discussed, the main difference in the intellectual conceptualizations of executive emergency power is whether or not to place explicit limitations on that power, thereby writing explicit constitutional provisions determining how and when an executive exercises emergency power or not placing limitations on emergency power in which executive prerogative determines how and when to exercise emergency power.

THE NATURE OF THE THREAT: HOW TO QUALIFY AN EMERGENCY

Qualifying emergencies—that is, understanding the nature of emergency and determining the different kinds of emergencies that may confront liberal democratic orders like the United States—is a crucial topic of consideration. The thinkers do not shed light on understanding the magnitude of crisis and judging when they are indeed facing a bona fide crisis; in this area they do not provide guidance, so we in modern times are left to parse out this question on our own. Emergency may be defined as a situation that produces a grave disturbance of the political system or order, threatening the survival of the state. The emergency can have either exogenous or endogenous origins. A war or an invasion is the most obvious case of an exogenous threat; the enemy's objective is to destroy, occupy, or otherwise take control of the country. Special measures to protect the integrity of the territory and the very nature of the liberal democratic order are justifiable, and an executive is warranted to protect the nation and combat the crisis without explicit legislation or authorization to act. The key question, though, is to what extent or end is executive emergency power limited? Either a provision in a constitution for a constitutional dictator during a crisis needs to be created or the executive must be given discretion to act without direct authorization, thereby establishing some inherent or implied executive emergency power.

Endogenous emergencies are more problematic. Possible cases comprising an endogenous emergency are terrorism, insurrections, and civil war. Civil war arises from internal political actors' attempts to destroy the constitutional order. The American Civil War, with the secession of Southern rebel states, is the classic example in our history. Terrorism, especially when it is internal, bears a resemblance to civil war: internal political actors wish to destroy the constitutional order of the state. International terrorism, such as the attacks of September 11, 2001, is more complicated and ambiguous, falling closer to the classification of war because the actors wishing to destroy the state are external, though they may begin recruit and use domestic actors.

In any event the political order must confront enemies who want to destroy or dramatically alter the nature of the state. The writers agreed that an executive in the United States may take necessary actions that the executive deems important and is necessary to render the enemies incapable of threatening the status quo. However, this becomes more problematic when, in order to prosecute the conflict, the government suspends citizens' rights. This happens when Congress writes laws at the request of the executive, who deems the laws necessary to combat the crisis, regardless of how those laws may strain citizens' civil liberties. A perfect example of this is the Patriot Act, which granted the president expansive authority to pursue enemy combatants and people suspected of aiding or facilitating the terrorist activities.[68] This authority may have consequences on citizens' civil liberties because the government can target innocent people who have been mistakenly associated with terrorism because of profiling practices based on characteristics consistent with past terrorist demographics.

Furthermore, the government may need to be secretive about information in order to pursue terrorists. A government struggling with enemies has good reason to keep information secret that could affect the public's safety if made public. Secrecy, however, may be an instrument to protect the government from criticism. Excessive secrecy hinders citizens' abilities to evaluate the government's performance in combating the terrorists; as such, it moves the government closer toward a despotic regime because it evades accountability. Additionally, the citizenry, the Congress, and even the courts may find it hard to obtain all the necessary information to prosecute or hold accountable the culpable elements of government during the crisis. If government cannot be held accountable during a time of emergency, the system of separated powers has been lost, at least during crises. More generally, when a government is in crisis mode and uses executive emergency powers, it could use its powers to delegitimize its competition. The party in power could use the fear resulting from the crisis as a weapon against the opposition party by making claims that if the opposition party were in power, it would be unable to combat the crisis or would even cause another emergency. In the United States this phenomenon can be seen in the high percentage of reelected wartime presidents.[69]

FINAL THOUGHTS

This research project began in response to George W. Bush's legal reasoning for his expansive power in response to the attacks of September 11, 2001. I set out to understand the theory of executive emergency power in order to discern whether the current American interpretation of expansive power was in fact congruent with the longstanding intellectual history regarding the concept. The reason I felt this exploration was vitally important is because the very nature and essence of executive emergency power is to counter to the normal procedures of a constitutional democracy and is, therefore, very critical to understand. Crisis yields more centralized power, which although it appears undemocratic, may in fact be necessary so as to preserve the state and, thus, the democracy.

Despite the emergencies that have imperiled the United States, the republic still stands. The current model for combating emergencies is a robust executive centric model—that is, executives with wide-ranging emergency power. The Constitution does not explicitly state that an executive may combat emergencies; however, the historical precedent of U.S. presidential rhetoric and behavior suggests that emergency power is an un-enumerated power inherent within the powers of the presidency as outlined in Article II of the Constitution. If the United States continues to employ an implicit model of emergency power rather than one that is explicit—conforming to written constitutional provisions authorizing and limiting emergency power—would this implicit model endanger the republic and civil liberties?

Implicit power seems dubious and undemocratic. When emergency power is implicit, as is the case in the United States, the power is exercised at the discretion of the executive, who decides what actions are best to combat the emergency. The executive is even responsible for declaring that an emergency exists. With implicit emergency power, the executive alone sets the parameters of that power, thereby increasing the possibility of the presidency devolving into despotism. Obviously the chances that the executive will usurp power may be greater during an emergency, as people are scared and may be willing to surrender liberty in return for security. We should be most wary and mindful of executives during times of crisis.

However, inherent executive emergency power provides a distinct advantage. If emergency power is an un-enumerated power, inherent within Article II of the Constitution, then executives are able to have the necessary flexibility with the law during a crisis that would otherwise not be possible with explicit emergency laws. Inherent power, or power not delineated in writing, enables the executive to combat the crisis with no hesitation or delay and with the full force and latitude of power necessary to combat the crisis. Theoretically, explicit executive emergency power—or power enumerated in constitutional provisions—which would cause an executive to adhere to explicit written law, may handicap the executive in his ability to combat a crisis, therefore possibly causing hesitation or delays and weakening the executive's response to the crisis.

Also, implicit or inherent power is easily open to interpretation—and not only by the executive. Interpreting emergency power would be a clear limitation on such power. This is true because interpreting the power would allow the courts to strike down an action an executive took while exercising emergency power, thereby deeming that action not to be an inherent power and thus ruling it an unconstitutional action. The other branches of government, in particular, the legislature, have just as much a right to offer their interpretation of emergency power and could challenge the executive's interpretation, possibly calling for impeachment if the executive went too far in exercising emergency power. Therefore, the other branches, especially the courts, may have the chance to strike down executive actions that they decide were outside the boundaries of the president's inherent power. Although this may not be a restraint during the crisis, it may cause the executive to be cautious because the emergency will invariably subside, after which lawsuits may emerge that challenge his authority and actions during the emergency (e.g., *Hamdi v. Rumsfeld* [542 U.S. 504, 2004], *Hamdan v. Rumsfeld* [548 U.S 55, 2006], or *Ex parte Milligan* [75, U.S. 2, 1866]).[70]

The American model, in which executive prerogative determines when and how emergency power is exercised and is an inherent constitutional power lawfully granted to an executive under authority granted to him in Article II of the Constitution, is unique in that executives who have used emergency power share the belief that their power is to be used to preserve the nation, not usurp power. Classic examples of such rhetoric supporting the executive's actions only to preserve the nation are Presidents Abraham Lincoln and George W. Bush. Both men repeatedly asserted that their broadened power was not to undermine the civil liberties of Americans but rather to preserve the nation so that liberties may live on long after the crisis subsides. Both presidents strongly supported a robust interpretation of the Oath clause of the Constitution, by which they believed that their affirmation to uphold and defend the Constitution meant that, during crisis, they may do whatever is necessary to combat the emergency—the executive has a greater obligation to uphold and defend the Constitution and preserve the nation than he does to his own aspirations and vanity.

Our republic is vulnerable during emergencies; such is the case with all nations. However, the United States is possibly unique in its concept of the executive's use of emergency power to protect its citizenry from the natural vulnerability emergencies cause because of its emphasis on *trust*—reminding us of Locke's assertion that the executive must be trusted to act accordingly and justly because during crisis he is the law.[71] Therefore, the onus is placed on the key factor of trust between the citizenry and executive's relationship: an executive should never betray that trust by doing something unjust against the citizenry.

The trust between the executive and the citizenry that assures the people that the executive will act only to preserve and defend the nation and not take advantage of the citizenry's vulnerability caused by the crisis may be the genius of the American model of executive emergency power. This might explain why Americans "rally around the flag" in times of crisis. When the towers fell after the attacks of September 11, 2001, George W. Bush's approval ratings soared to 91 percent.[72] It seems that in times of great peril Americans trust that their presidents are going to do the right thing. The executive may or may not act appropriately, but if there is a factor of trust between them, then perhaps the citizenry does not have to worry so much about the executive's power during the crisis. The peoples' trust in the executive will be ascertained by the president's reelection—or lack thereof. Trust is the unspoken, tacit assumption that allows for the preservation of a state, even though the ruler has unmatched authority.

In conclusion, the evidence offered, in this book, outlines and supports that presidents are becoming more powerful, in light of crisis. Presidents are supporting a general doctrine that, in time of crisis, they can do whatever is necessary to save the Republic. Whereby, presidents are becoming cavalier in determining what and how to exercise emergency power. In fact, presidents are violating, abusing, and disregarding the law, in times of crisis—all further evidence of the rise of a cavalier presidency. In times of crisis, American presidents behave, and appear more like kings, then presidents of a constitutional, constrained power, Republic. Finally, I evidence that presidents are unconstitutional, legitimated by an apathetic populace, and a misguided legal community. The fall of the Republic will likely happen during the time of a cavalier president, masking legitimate power, to save the Republic, whereby the power destroys the Republic.

NOTES

1. In chapter 2 I outlined the Anti-Federalist and Federalist debate regarding executive emergency power as well as the particular clauses of Article II that scholars provide when arguing for an interpretation that supports inherent executive emergency power, thereby making executive emergency power an un-enumerated constitutional power.

2. By "chosen theorists," I mean those theorists who provided the most substantive contributions to the theory of executive emergency power. As evidenced in chapter 1, many theorists contribute to the dialogue, but the amount of substance varies, with many of the theorists' contributions being very small and not providing enough for thorough analysis. Therefore, those were not included in this discussion.

3. John Locke, *Second Treatise on Civil Government*, in Michael Morgan, ed., *Classics of Moral and Political Theory* (Indianapolis, IN: Hackett Publishing Co., 1992), 702–704; Alexander Hamilton, Federalist No. 74, in Alexander Hamilton, James Madison, and John Jay, *The Federalist Papers*, 376–78 (New York: Bantam Press, 1982).

4. Clinton Rossiter, *Constitutional Dictatorship: Crisis Government in the Modern Democracies* (Princeton, NJ: Princeton University Press, 1948), 75 and 300–305; Niccolò Machiavelli, *The Discourses*, in Morgan, *Classics of Moral and Political Theory*, 1321–24.

5. Rossiter, *Constitutional Dictatorship*, 75 and 300–305; Machiavelli, *The Discourses*, 1321–24.

6. Locke, *Second Treatise on Civil Government*, 702–704.

7. Ibid.

8. Ibid.

9. Ibid.

10. Alexander Hamilton, Federalist No. 74, in Alexander Hamilton, James Madison, and John Jay, *The Federalist Papers*, 376–78 (New York: Bantam Press, 1982).

11. Ibid.

12. Ibid.

13. Clinton Rossiter, *Constitutional Dictatorship: Crisis Government in the Modern Democracies* (Princeton: Princeton University Press, 1948), 75 and 300–305.

14. Locke, *Second Treatise on Civil Government*, 702–704; Hamilton, Federalist No. 74.

15. Rossiter, *Constitutional Dictatorship*, 75 and 300–305; Niccolò Machiavelli, *The Discourses*, in Michael Morgan, *Classics of Moral and Political Philosophy* (Indianapolis, IN: Hackett Publishing Co., 1992), 1321–24.

16. Locke, *Second Treatise on Civil Government*, 702–704.

17. Ibid.

18. Ibid., 705

19. Ibid., 701–705.

20. Ibid.

21. John Locke, *Of Civil Government*, in Morgan, *Classics of Moral and Political Theory*, Book II, ch. 14.

22. Locke, *Second Treatise on Civil Government*, 702–704.

23. Ibid., 703.

24. Ibid., 1123.

25. Rossiter, *Constitutional Dictatorship*, 75 and 300–305.

26. Ibid., 1–3.

27. Ibid., 554–65.

28. Ibid.

29. Ibid.

30. Hamilton, Federalist No. 74.

31. As mentioned in chapters 1 and 2, for Locke, implicit, or prerogative, power means that the executive will decide what they deem most suitable or necessary to combat the crisis, and this may go beyond the written law.

32. Alexander Hamilton, Federalist No. 70, in Hamilton, Madison, and Jay, *The Federalist Papers*, 355–56.

33. John C. Yoo, Memorandum Re: Authority for Use of Military Force to Combat Terrorist Activities *Within the United States*, October 23, 2001, U.S. Department of Justice, Office of Legal Counsel.

34. Machiavelli, *The Discourses*, 1321–24.

35. Ibid.

36. Abraham Lincoln, Special Message to Congress, July 4, 1861, in Abraham Lincoln, *Abraham Lincoln: Speeches and Writings, 1859–1865: Speeches, Letters, and Miscellaneous Writings, Presidential Messages and Proclamations*, vol. 2, edited by Don E. Fehrenbacher (New York: Literary Classics of the United States, 1989), 250.

37. Abraham Lincoln, Letter to Albert Hodges, April 4, 1864, in Lincoln, *Abraham Lincoln: Speeches and Writings, 1859–1865*, 235.

38. Ibid.

39. Ibid.

40. Edward Corwin, *The President: Office and Powers, 1787–1984: History and Analysis of Practice and Opinion* (New York: New York University Press, 1984); Rossiter, *Constitutional Dictatorship*.

41. Yoo, Memorandum Re: Authority for Use of Military Force to Combat Terrorist Activities *Within the United States*, October 23, 2001, 2–12.

42. Ibid.

43. David Gray Adler, "Presidential Power and Foreign Affairs in the Bush Administration: The Use and Abuse of Alexander Hamilton," *Presidential Studies Quarterly* 40, no. 3. (September 2010): 531–44; Scott M. Matheson Jr., *Presidential Constitutionalism in Perilous Times* (Cambridge, MA: Harvard University Press, 2009); James P. Pfiffner, *Power Play: The Bush Presidency and the Constitution* (Washington, DC: Brookings Institution, 2008).

44. Lincoln, Letter to Albert Hodges, April 4, 1864.

45. Machiavelli, *The Discourses*, 1321–24.

46. Rossiter, *Constitutional Dictatorship*, 75 and 300–305.

47. Locke, *Second Treatise on Civil Government*, 702–704.

48. Richard Kohn, "The Washington Administration's Decision to Crush the Whiskey Rebellion," *Journal of American History* 59, no. 3 (December 1972), 567–84; Leland D. Baldwin, *Whiskey Rebels: The Story of a Frontier Uprising* (Pittsburgh: University of Pittsburgh Press, 1939), 185; Alexander Hamilton, Letter to George Washington, September 1, 1792, and Hamilton, Letter to John Jay, September 3, 1792, in Harold Coffin Syrett, ed., *The Papers of Alexander Hamilton* (New York: Columbia University Press, 1961), 316–17.

49. As stated above, though we may be able to judge, in hindsight, that these events were not truly threats to the nation and perhaps should be classified here as "emergencies," Jefferson considered both to be crucial issues of national interest, especially as the nation was still burgeoning, and its growth and security were particularly critical for its survival. In this way, Jefferson believed that they constituted acting with what we call emergency powers.

50. In chapter 3 I further detail how Jefferson framed the purchase of the Louisiana Territory as a matter of critical national interest because of the persistent violence on the frontier, which Jefferson concluded was a national emergency.

51. Thomas Jefferson, Letter to John Dickinson, August 9, 1803, in Thomas Jefferson, *The Writings of Thomas Jefferson*, edited by Paul Leicester Ford, vol. 140 (New York: G. P. Putnam's Sons, 1892–1899), 54–55.

52. Ibid.

53. Locke, *Second Treatise on Civil Government*, 701–704.

54. Thomas Jefferson, Letter to John Breckenridge, August 18, 1803, in Jefferson, *The Writings of Thomas Jefferson*, 55.

55. Jefferson defeated Charles Pinckney with a popular vote margin of 72 to 28 percent and an electoral vote margin of 162 to 14.

56. Thomas Jefferson, f38, p55, in Jefferson, *The Writings of Thomas Jefferson.*

57. James Madison, "Letters of Pacificus and Helvidius," in Hamilton, Madison and Jay, *The Federalist Papers*, 53–64. Again, in these letters Madison advocates the diffusion of executive power, in direct opposition to the monarchist Hamilton, who seems to be advocating for a constitutional monarchy, at least in Madison's opinion.

58. James Madison, "Proclamation on Anglo-American Affairs," June 1, 1812, in *The Writings of James Madison*, 34, and 146-47

59. Gaillard Hunt, *The Life of James Madison* (New York: Russell & Russell, 1968); James Madison, *Writings*, edited by Jack N. Rakove (New York: Library of America, 1999), 34 and 146–47.

60. As above, we classify these events as "emergency" for the purpose of this discussion because Jackson classified them as such and, therefore, used executive emergency powers in response. Though we may not see them as emergencies when we look at them through the lens of history, when analyzing how presidents justified and asserted executive emergency powers, the perspective afforded by hindsight is best left to another discussion.

61. Robert Remini, *Andrew Jackson and the Course of American Freedom* (Baltimore, MD: Johns Hopkins University Press, 1998), and Remini, *Andrew Jackson and His Indian Wars* (New York: Viking, 2001), 371–73.

62. Daniel Walker Howe, *What Hath God Wrought: The Transformation of America 1815–1848* (New York: Oxford University Press, 2007), 414–21.

63. Lincoln, Letter to Albert Hodges, April 4, 1864.

64. Ibid.

65. Rossiter, *Constitutional Dictatorship*; Corwin, *The President.*

66. Yoo, Memorandum Re: Authority for Use of Military Force to Combat Terrorist Activities *Within the United States*, October 23, 2001, 4.

67. Ibid.

68. USA Patriot Improvement and Reauthorization Act of 2005, P/L 109-177, Title II, specifically "lone wolf provisions" and "sneak and peak" provisions, sections 14–17.

69. Consider President George W. Bush, who had historically low approval ratings at the time of his reelection. According to 2004 NBC/Wall Street polls, they were in the fortieth percentile, yet he was still reelected. Obviously there are many factors that contribute to the reelection of a president, though it is interesting to consider for a moment how crises may or may not aid in the reelection and the campaigning that precedes it.

70. Note that each case cited in the oral arguments here is not in close proximity to the beginning of the crisis. The Hamdi cases are 2004 and 2006, which is still during the crisis of fighting terrorism, but are at minimum three years removed from the original cause of the crisis. The Milligan case is in 1866, a year after the end of the Civil War and five years after Lincoln first suspended habeas corpus in 1861.

71. Locke, *Second Treatise on Civil Government*, 702–704.

72. Gallup/CNN poll, October 1, 2001.

Afterword

Prior to Barack Obama's election to presidential office he consistently chastised his predecessor, President George W. Bush, for overusing executive prerogative when determining to what extent and how to exercise emergency power. In January 2009, shortly after taking office, President Obama's Office of Legal Counsel issued a scathing memo calling for an immediate "halt" and "repudiation" of all former presidential legal opinions regarding emergency powers authored during the Bush administration.[1] Further, the Obama administration campaigned on reconsidering Bush's handling of the War on Terror, and this included reevaluating surveillance, interrogation, drone use, and the prison at Guantanamo Bay.

In December 2009 President Obama was awarded the Nobel Peace Prize, and in his acceptance speech he continued to chastise world leaders who did not adhere to a strict rule of law when determining how to handle terrorism. He went on to support "just war" theories that maintained a "restrained" approach, his speech reinforcing the general precepts that war is at times necessary to protect the innocent but this does not include doing whatever is necessary to combat a crisis.[2] Further, President Obama gave an international address in Cairo, Egypt, in July 2009 in which he again committed a pledge to the world that the United States was no longer pursuing its aggressive, hostile and combative approach to handling terrorism; rather, America would pursue a legal, tempered approach.[3]

In this research I concluded that when confronted with national emergencies, presidents tend to support an unfettered approach when determining to what extent and how to exercise emergency powers, thus transforming such presidents into cavalier leaders. Contrary to his rhetoric, President Obama is no exception. As the following facts demonstrate, he has maintained and continues to support a cavalier approach when invoking his prerogative to exercise executive emergency powers.

- In Executive Order 13618 President Obama declared that the U.S. government may spy on American citizens through the National Security Agency "PRISM" program. This program collects meta-data on all Americans, provided by warrant, from all major telecommunications and social media networks in the United States. Although its intent is not to violate the privacy of law-abiding citizens, it nonetheless sweeps data on all law-abiding citizens, essentially rendering all Americans as potential suspects in the War on Terror.
- The Obama administration continues to use drone strikes against enemy combatants of the state, and the executive branch is still the sole branch of government authorized to determine not only whether a foreigner or American citizen is an enemy combatant but also when, where, and how the U.S. government attacks an enemy combatant, all with no congressional oversight.
- The Obama administration's Department of Justice issued warrants to seize journalist records in an investigation pursuing a "mole" in the Associated Press. The warrant was unprecedented, and the president supports the action in the name of national security.
- President Obama has left Guantanamo Bay open and operating.

In the end President Obama's actions support the general thesis of this book: presidents will do whatever is necessary to protect the nation during a crisis and will use their own prerogative to determine to what extent and how to exercise emergency power. Further, President Obama confirms, yet again, that emergency power is beyond partisanship. Regardless that he is a Democrat, spoke and voted against the Iraq War, and won the Nobel Peace Prize, his actions as president contradict his prior peace rhetoric. Emergency power is nonpartisan and antithetical to the reverence and process of law as well as the spirit of republicanism. If anything, the years since President George W. Bush left office have demonstrated that the republic is changing quickly, increasingly becoming unmatched as a centralized, powerful federal government. The fate of the American experiment lay in our ability to balance a reverence for the rule of law with the occasional state-sanctioned, temporary violation of that law in the name of national security. And although we hope the rule of law prevails, power is a forbidden fruit of which people in power tend to crave more, not less.

NOTES

1. Office of Legal Counsel, "Re: Status of Certain OLC Opinion Issued in the Aftermath of the Terrorist Attacks of September 11, 2001," U.S. Department of Justice, January 15, 2009, www.justice.gov/opa/documents/memostatusolcopinions01152009.pdf.

2. "Remarks by the President at the Acceptance of the Nobel Peace Prize," The White House, December 10, 2009, www.whitehouse.gov/the-press-office/remarks-president-acceptance-nobel-peace-prize.

3. "Remarks by the President on a New Beginning," The White House, June 4, 2009, www.whitehouse.gov/the_press_office/Remarks-by-the-President-at-Cairo-University-6-04-09.

References

Adler, David Gray. "Presidential Power and Foreign Affairs in the Bush Administration: The Use and Abuse of Alexander Hamilton." *Presidential Studies Quarterly* 40, no. 3. (September 2010): 531–44.

Amnesty International. "USA: Below the Radar: Secret Flights to Torture and 'Disappearance.'" April 2006. www.amnesty.org/en/library/info/AMR51/051/2006.

Aristotle. *Politics*. In Morgan, *Classics of Moral and Political Theory*.

———. *Treatise on Government*. In Morgan, *Classics of Moral and Political Theory*.

Bailey, Jeremy. *Thomas Jefferson and Executive Power*. Cambridge, New York: Cambridge University Press, 2007.

Baker, Nancy V. "The Attorney General as a Legal Policy Maker: Conflicting Loyalties." In Clayton, *Government Lawyers*.

Baldwin, Leland D. *Whiskey Rebels: The Story of a Frontier Uprising*. Pittsburgh, PA: University of Pittsburgh Press, 1939.

Ball, Howard. *The USA Patriot Act of 2001: Balancing Civil Liberties and National Security: A Reference Handbook*. Santa Barbara, CA: ABC-CLIO, 2004.

Barbash, Fred. "Justices Reject Appeal Over the Secret 9-11 Detainees." *Washington Post*. January 12, 2004.

Boyd, Steven R. *The Whiskey Rebellion: Past and Present Perspectives*. Westport, CT: Greenwood Press, 1985.

Brackenridge, Henry M. *History of the Western Insurrection, 1794*. New York: Arno Press, 1969.

Bradbury, Stephen G. Memorandum for the Files Re: October 23, 2001 OLC Opinion Addressing the Domestic Use of Military Force to Combat Terrorist Activities. October 6, 2008. U.S. Department of Justice.

Bradley, Curtis A., and Eric A. Posner. "Presidential Signing Statements and Executive Power." *Constitutional Commentary* 23 (2006): 307–64.

Brands, H. W. *Andrew Jackson: His Life and Times*. New York: Doubleday, 2005.

Bryant, Irving. "Madison Encouraged the War Movement." In *The Causes of the War of 1812: National Honor or National Interest?* edited by Bradford Perkins, 104–7. New York: Holt, Rinehart and Winston, 1962.

Bryce, James. *The American Commonwealth*, vol. I, *The National Government, the State Government*. Indianapolis, IN: Liberty Fund, 1995.

Bush, George W. Address before a Joint Session of the Congress on the United States Response to the Terrorist Attacks of September 11. September 20, 2001. www.presidency.ucsb.edu/mediaplay.php?id=64731&admin=43.

———. Interview, *60 Minutes*, CBS, November 17, 2010.

————. Remarks on Arrival at the White House and an Exchange with Reporters. September 16, 2001. www.presidency.ucsb.edu/mediaplay.php?id=63346&admin=43.

Bybee, Jay S. Memorandum for John Rizzo, Acting General Counsel of the Central Intelligence Agency, Interrogation of al-Qaeda Operative. August 1, 2002. U.S. Department of Justice.

————. Memorandum Re: the President's Power as Commander in Chief to Transfer Captured Terrorists to the Control and Custody of Foreign Nations. March 13, 2002. U.S. Department of Justice.

Calabresi, Steven. "Advice to the Next Conservative President of the United States." *Harvard Journal of Law and Public Policy* 24, pt. 2 (Spring 2001): 369–80.

Calabresi, Steven G., and Christopher S. Yoo. *The Unitary Executive: Presidential Power from Washington to Bush.* New Haven, CT: Yale University Press, 2008.

Carpenter, Allen Harmon. "Military Government of Southern Territory, 1861–1865." *Annual Report.* Washington, DC: Government Printing Office, 1900.

Clayton, Cornell W., ed. *Government Lawyers: The Federal Legal Bureaucracy and Presidential Politics.* Lawrence: University of Kansas Press, 1995.

Cooper, Joseph, and William F. West. "Presidential Power and Republican Government: The Theory and Practice of OMB Review of Agency Rules." *The Journal of Politics* 50, no. 4 (November 1988): 864–95.

Cooper, Phillip J. "George W. Bush, Edgar Allen Poe, and the Use and Abuse of Presidential Signing Statements." *Presidential Studies Quarterly* 35, no. 3 (September 2005): 515–32.

Corwin, Edward Samuel, Randall Walton Bland, Theodore T. Hindson, and J. W. Peltason, *The President: Office and Powers, 1787–1984: History and Analysis of Practice and Opinion.* New York: New York University Press, 1984.

Cronin, Thomas. "An Imperiled Presidency." In *The Post-Imperial Presidency*, edited by Vincent Davis. New Brunswick, NJ: Transaction Books, 1980.

Cunningham, Noble E. *The Process of Government under Jefferson.* Princeton, NJ: Princeton University Press, 1978.

Currie, David. "Rumors of War: Presidential and Congressional War Powers." *University of Chicago Law Review* 67, no. 1 (2000): 1–40.

Dean, John. "George W. Bush as the New Richard Nixon: Both Wiretapped Illegally, and Impeachably; Both Claimed That a President May Violate Congress' Laws to Protect National Security." FindLaw. December 30, 2005. writ.lp.findlaw.com/dean/20051230.html.

Ehrenberg, Victor. *From Solon to Socrates: Greek History and Civilization During the 6th and 5th Centuries B.C.* London: Routledge, 1996.

Farrand, Max, ed. *The Records of the Federal Convention of 1787.* New Haven, CT: Yale University Press, 1911.

Fehrenbacher, Don Edward. *The Civil War: Rebellion to Reconstruction.* Princeton, NJ: Princeton University Press, 1950.

Fisher, Louis. *Presidential War Power*, 2nd ed. Lawrence: University Press of Kansas, 2004.

Fisher, S. G. "The Suspension of Habeas Corpus During the War of the Rebellion." *Political Science Quarterly* 3, no. 3 (1888): 454–88.

Fitzpatrick, John C., ed. *The Writings of George Washington from the Original Manuscript Sources, 1745–1799*, 39 vols. Washington, DC, 1944.

Ford, Paul Leicester, ed. *The Writings of Thomas Jefferson.* New York: G. P. Putnam's Sons, 1892–1899.

Friedrich, Carl. *Constitutional Government and Democracy: Theory and Practice in Europe and America.* Boston: Ginn & Co, 1950.

————. "The Problem of Constitutional Dictatorship." In *Public Policy: A Yearbook of the Graduate School of Public Administration, Harvard University*, edited by C. J. Friedrich and Edward S. Mason. Cambridge, MA: Harvard University Press, 1940.

Gattuso, John. *Washington D.C.: Know the City Like a Native.* Singapore: APA Publications, 2008.

Halstead, T. J., and Congressional Research Service. "Presidential Signing Statements: Constitutional and Institutional Implications." Washington, DC: Congressional Research Service, Library of Congress, 2007.

Hamilton, Alexander, James Madison, and John Jay. *The Federalist Papers*. New York: Bantam Press, 1982.

Harrington, James. *Commonwealth of Oceana*. In Morgan, *Classics of Moral and Political Theory*.

Heidler, David S., and Jeanne T. Heidler. *The War of 1812*. Westport, CT: Greenwood Press, 2002.

Herodotus. *Writings on Athenian Democracy*. In Morgan, *Classics of Moral and Political Theory*.

Herz, Michael. "Imposing Unified Executive Branch Statutory Interpretation." *Cardozo Law Review* 15, no. 1–2 (October 1993): 219–72.

Hickey, Donald. *The War of 1812: A Forgotten Conflict*. Urbana: University of Illinois Press, 1989.

Hobbes, Thomas. *The Leviathan*. In Morgan, *Classics of Moral and Political Theory*.

Howe, Daniel Walker. *What Hath God Wrought: The Transformation of America 1815–1848*. New York: Oxford University Press, 2007.

Howe, John. "Republican Thought and the Political Violence of the 1790s." *American Quarterly* 19, no. 2 (Summer 1967): 147–65.

Hunt, Gaillard. *The Life of James Madison*. New York: Russell & Russell, 1968.

Jackson, Andrew. *Narrative and Writings of Andrew Jackson; of Kentucky*. Miami, FL: Mnemosyne Publishing, 1969.

Jefferson, Thomas. *The Writings of Thomas Jefferson*, edited by Paul Leicester Ford. New York: G. P. Putnam's Sons, 1892–1899.

Kagan, Elena. "Presidential Administration." *Harvard Law Review* 114, no. 8 (June 2001): 2245–2385.

Kelley, Christopher. *Executing the Constitution: Putting the President Back into the Constitution*. Albany: State University of New York Press, 2006.

Ketcham, Ralph Louis, ed. *The Anti-Federalist Papers; And, the Constitutional Convention Debates*. New York: New American Library, 1986.

Kinkopf, Neil. "Index of Presidential Signing Statements, 2001–2007." American Constitution Society of Law and Policy. August 2007.

Knox, J. Wendell. *Conspiracy in American Politics, 1787–1815*. New York: Arno Press, 1972.

Kohn, Richard. *Eagle and Sword: The Federalists and the Creation of the Military Establishment in America, 1783–1802*. New York: Free Press, 1975.

———. "The Washington Administration's Decision to Crush the Whiskey Rebellion." *Journal of American History* 59, no. 3 (December 1972): 567–84.

Lawson, Gary, and Guy Seidman. *The Constitution of Empire: Territorial Expansion and American Legal History*. New Haven, CT: Yale University Press, 2004.

Lincoln, Abraham. *Abraham Lincoln: Speeches and Writings, 1832–1858: Speeches, Letters, and Miscellaneous Writings, the Lincoln-Douglas Debates*, edited by Don E. Fehrenbacher. New York: Library of America, 1989.

———. *Abraham Lincoln: Speeches and Writings, 1859–1865: Speeches, Letters, and Miscellaneous Writings, Presidential Messages and Proclamations*, edited by Don E. Fehrenbacher. New York: Literary Classics of the United States, 1989.

Locke, John. *Of Civil Government*. In Morgan, *Classics of Moral and Political Theory*.

———. *Second Treatise on Civil Government*. In Morgan, *Classics of Moral and Political Theory*.

Lund, Nelson. "Guardians of the Presidency: The Office of the Counsel to the President and the Office of Legal Counsel." In Clayton, *Government Lawyers*.

Lynch, Timothy. *Breaking the Vicious Cycle: Preserving Our Liberties while Fighting Terrorism*. Washington, DC: CATO Institute, June 26, 2002.

Machiavelli, Niccolò. *The Discourses*. In Morgan, *Classics of Moral and Political Theory*.

Madison, James. *The Papers of James Madison*. Chicago: University of Chicago Press, 1962.

———. *Writings*, edited by Jack N. Rakove. New York: Library of America, 1999.

Malone, Dumas. *Jefferson the President: The First Term, 1801–1805*. Boston: Little, Brown, 1970.

———. *Jefferson the President: The Second Term, 1805–1809*. Boston: Little, Brown, 1974.

Martin, Kate. "Legal Detainment?" Center for National Security Studies, 2004, in *SAIS Review* 29, no. 1 (Winter–Spring 2004).

Matheson, Scott M. Jr. *Presidential Constitutionalism in Perilous Times*. Cambridge, MA: Harvard University Press, 2009.

May, Christopher. "Presidential Defiance of 'Unconstitutional' Laws: Reviving the Royal Prerogative." *Hastings Constitutional Legislative Quarterly* 21, no. 4 (1994): 865–1011.

Mayer, John. "Outsourcing Torture: The Secret History of America's Extraordinary Rendition Program." *New Yorker*. February 14, 2005.

McDonald, Forrest. *Presidency of George Washington*. Lawrence: University Press of Kansas, 1974.

Meacham, Jon. *American Lion: Andrew Jackson in the White House*. New York: Random House, 2008.

Meese, Edwin. *With Reagan: The Inside Story*. Washington, DC: Regnery Gateway, 1992.

Mill, John. *Representative Government*. New York: Dutton, 1950.

Montesquieu. *Spirit of the Laws*. In Morgan, *Classics of Moral and Political Theory*.

Morgan, Michael, ed. *Classics of Moral and Political Theory*. Indianapolis, IN: Hackett Publishing Co., 1992.

Neustadt, Richard E. *Presidential Power and the Modern Presidents: The Politics of Leadership from Roosevelt to Reagan*. New York: Free Press, 1990.

Nicolay, John G., and John Hay. *Abraham Lincoln: A History*. New York: Century Co., 1890.

Paine, Thomas. *Common Sense*. Mineola, NY: Dover Thrift Editions, 1997.

Pearce, Roy Harvey. *Savagism and Civilization: A Study of the Indian and the American Mind*. Berkeley: University of California Press, 1988.

Pfiffner, James P. *Power Play: The Bush Presidency and the Constitution*. Washington, DC: Brookings Institution, 2008.

Phelps, Glenn. *George Washington and American Constitutionalism*. Lawrence: University Press of Kansas, 1993.

Pierson, William Whatley. "The Committee on the Conduct of the Civil War." *The American History Review* 23, no. 3 (April 1918): 550–76.

Plato. *The Republic*. In Morgan, *Classics of Moral and Political Theory*.

Polybius. *History of Rome*. In *The Oxford History of the Classical World*, edited by John Boardman, Jasper Griffin, and Oswyn Murray. Oxford, New York: Oxford University Press, 1986.

Prakash, Saikrishna B., and Michael D. Ramsey. "The Executive Power over Foreign Affairs." *Yale Law Journal* 111, no. 2 (November 2001): 299–300.

Randall, James Garfield. *Constitutional Problems under Lincoln*. New York, London: Appleton and Co., 1926.

Randolph, Edmund. "Second Day of Convention, Randolph's Notes and Speeches." In Farrand, *The Records of the Federal Convention of 1787*.

Remini, Robert. *Andrew Jackson and the Course of American Freedom*. Baltimore, MD: Johns Hopkins University Press, 1998.

———. *Andrew Jackson and His Indian Wars*. New York: Viking, 2001.

———. "The Constitution and the Presidencies: The Jackson Era." In *The Constitution and the American Presidency*, edited by Martin L. Fausold and Alan Shank, 34–56. Albany: State University of New York Press, 1991.

———. *The Life of Andrew Jackson*. New York: Harper & Row, 1988.

Richardson, James Daniel. *A Compilation of the Messages and Papers of the Presidents, 1789–1897*. Washington, DC: Government Printing Office, 1896–1899.

Risen, James. *State of War: The Secret History of the CIA and the Bush Administration*. New York: Free Press, 2006.

Rossiter, Clinton. *Constitutional Dictatorship: Crisis Government in the Modern Democracies*. Princeton, NJ: Princeton University Press, 1948.

Rousseau, Jean-Jacques. *The Social Contract*. In Morgan, *Classics of Moral and Political Theory*.

Savage, Charlie. *Takeover: The Return of the Imperial Presidency and the Subversion of American*. New York: Little, Brown, 2007.

Schelling, Thomas. "Hamilton and Emergency Power." *Journal of Strategy and Conflict* 18 (1960): 34–36.

Schlesinger, Arthur Jr. *The Age of Jackson*. Boston: Little, Brown, 1945.

Schmitt, Gary. "Jefferson and Executive Power: Revisionism and the Revolution of 1800." *Publius* 17, no. 2 (Spring 1987): 7–25.

Slaughter, Thomas. *The Whiskey Rebellion: Frontier Epilogue to the American Revolution*. New York: Oxford Press, 1986.

Smelser, Marshall. "The Jacobin Phrenzy: Federalism and the Menace of Liberty, Equality, and Fraternity." *The Review of Politics* 13, no. 4 (October 1951): 457–82.

Sofaer, Abraham. *War, Foreign Affairs and Constitutional Power: The Origins*. Cambridge, MA: Ballinger Publishing Co., 1976.

Storing, Herbert J., and Murray Dry, *The Complete Anti-Federalist*. Chicago: University of Chicago Press, 1981.

Syrett, Harold Coffin, ed. *The Papers of Alexander Hamilton*. New York: Columbia University Press, 1961.

Thach, Charles. *The Creation of the Presidency, 1775–1789: A Study in Constitutional History*. Baltimore, MD: Johns Hopkins University Press, 1922, 1969.

U.S. Department of Justice. Department of Justice Inspector General Issues Report on Treatment of Aliens Held on Immigration Charges in Connection with the Investigation of the September 11 Terrorist Attacks. June 2, 2003. www.justice.gov/oig/special/0306/press.pdf.

Watkins, Frederick Mundell. *The Failure of Constitutional Emergency Powers Under the German Republic*. Cambridge, MA: Harvard University Press, 1939.

Wilentz, Sean. *Andrew Jackson*. New York: Times Books, 2005.

Williams, T. Harry. "The Committee on the Conduct of the War." *The Journal of the American Military Institute* 3, no. 3 (Autumn 1939): 138–56.

Wills, Garry. *Bomb Power: The Modern Presidency and the National Security State*. New York: Penguin, 2009.

Woodward, Bob. *Bush at War*. New York: Simon and Shuster, 2002.

Yoo, Christopher, Steven G. Calabresi, and Anthony J. Colangelo. "The Unitary Executive in the Modern Era, 1945–2004." *Iowa Law Review* 90, no. 2 (2005): 601–731.

Yoo, John C. *Crisis and Command: The History of Executive Power from George Washington to George W. Bush*. New York: Kaplan, 2009.

———. Memorandum Re: Authority for Use of Military Force to Combat Terrorist Activities *Within the United States*. October 23, 2001. U.S. Department of Justice, Office of Legal Counsel.

———. Memorandum Re; Constitutionality of Amending Foreign Intelligence Surveillance Act to Change the "Purpose" Standard for Searches. September 25, 2001. U.S. Department of Justice.

Index

About the Author

Justin P. DePlato holds a PhD from the State University of New York at Buffalo in the field of political science. He currently teaches at the University of North Florida. He has published two books over his career, including this book focusing on the American presidency and *The Tell: Examining the Signaling Effects and Timing of Senators Cosponsoring Legislation.* He also enjoys writing short murder mysteries having published, *Meet Inspector L. Jack Hawthorne* and *The Swooping Crane.* DePlato resides in Jacksonville, Florida with his wife Angela and his three children, Bella, Juliana, and Harrison.

CPSIA information can be obtained at www.ICGtesting.com
Printed in the USA
BVOW08*2013030214

343436BV00009B/4/P